Tracks Across Africa

Tracks Across Africa

Another Ten Years

by

Craig Boddington

To General Bob Dietz —
from one old Marine
to another — Semper Fi!

Safari Press

The trademark Safari Press ® is registered with the U.S. Patent and Trademark Office and in other countries.

Boddington, Craig

Second edition

Safari Press

2008, Long Beach, California

ISBN 1-57157-287-2

Library of Congress Catalog Card Number: 2007929025

10 9 8 7 6 5 4 3 2 1

Printed in China

Readers wishing to receive the Safari Press catalog, featuring many fine books on big-game hunting, wingshooting, and sporting firearms, should write to Safari Press Inc., P.O. Box 3095, Long Beach, CA 90803, USA. Tel: (714) 894-9080 or visit our Web site at www.safaripress.com.

Dedication

To my partners Tim Danklef and Dave Fulson:
We disagree frequently and sometimes fiercely, but I'm
thankful for the weird and wonderful talents each of us
brings to the party. And I'm especially thankful to them
for rekindling my passion for Africa, just when
I thought I was almost done.

Table of Contents

Introduction

As the years pile up, it is frightening how much more quickly they seem to pass. I cannot believe that fully thirty years have passed since my first safari. I still have the photos, of course, and occasionally I even use one in a presentation or an article. But surely that incredibly young, slim, fresh-faced Marine lieutenant isn't me? It is equally hard to believe that twenty years have passed since I wrote my first "ten-year Africa book," *From Mount Kenya to the Cape*, or a decade since my second, *Where Lions Roar*. But so the sands of time have run.

Note, please, that I did not refer to the second book as a sequel to the first, and I do not consider this book a "triquel." The first book was hardly planned. In fact, I intended my first safari to be my one and only, to get Africa out of my system once and for all. Anyone who has hunted in Africa knows that was a foolish thought, but I didn't know it at the time. I soon learned better: All one African safari does—besides providing a lifetime of memories—is to make you yearn for another. The first volume seemed to come at a sensible milestone, but I will credit its existence mostly to my old friend and publisher Ludo Wurfbain.

That was a long time ago. I was still an editor trying to become a writer, and Ludo, having been successful at locating and marketing used books and reprinting some classic titles, was interested in publishing new titles. Through an accident of timing I had reached a milestone in African hunting that both of us, being young and foolish, thought might make a book. *Mount Kenya* became Ludo's first new title, and for quite some time I was his only living author.

I must admit that, having done it once, I viewed the second book as obvious when the second decade was reached. Equally, I confess that I eagerly began this book a few months—and safaris—before the third decade was completed. As sick as it might sound, writing a book is fun. Writing magazine articles is work. And I have no problem putting aside necessary work to have fun. I had fun writing the first two, and I had even more fun writing this one. All that said, there is little continuity between the three volumes, and what there might be is not intended. Each is simply an accounting, in more or less chronological order, of African hunts I have made during a decade of my life.

Now, all that said, as I worked on this particular memoir I did occasionally wish that a previous wonderful hunt had fallen into this volume rather than one of the others. More often, however, I wished that I hadn't written some things I wrote previously! As I will mention a couple of times in the course of this book, one of the great traps inherent in African hunting is to consider oneself an expert despite limited experience. Africa is a vast continent with a wide range of conditions as well as game, and here is a little-known fact: There are no "African experts." There are many people who have extensive experience and real expertise in a few specific areas. There are quite a few people, perhaps including me, who have limited broad-brush experience in quite a few areas. But there is no one who has even limited experience with the entirety of this huge continent. Even if there were such a person, his or her knowledge would be of limited value. Africa changes so fast that by the time one end of the continent was reached, the other end could have changed so much as to render impressions useless, if not downright wrong.

I thought I knew these things when I wrote the first two books, and, thinking I understood them, I believed myself cautious in my interpretations. I recognize now that I was not cautious enough. In my third decade of African hunting I have continued to learn, and now that I have a good background (if not an altogether open mind), I must admit that the learning curve remains steep. Now I fully recognize that I will never see it all, will never understand it all, and what I thought I understood might well have changed utterly since I last saw it. But, after all, that's part of the magic of Africa: She is too big to completely grasp, no matter how you try.

But my intent in writing this book was not to correct misinterpretations of the past or to update findings, and certainly not to regale you, my readers and friends, with tales of my derring-do. I've had good moments and bad. You can apply whatever superlatives you like to either, and I think you'll find that I have related them as equally and honestly as I am able. Obviously, this last is a caveat. I really try to be honest, but my memory is no less selective than yours!

I can say with complete honesty that neither of the previous two "ten-year Africa books" was planned, at least not until the milestone was reached and suddenly it seemed time to have some fun. Fun, by the way, has changed. Twenty years ago it was notebook, typewriter, and black-and-white prints. Ten years ago it was floppy disk and mostly color slides. In 2006 it was laptop—much of this book was actually written in camp in Africa, or on airplanes to and from. I noted, too, with some amusement, that there was a sharp delineation in photograph medium. Chapters one through nine were illustrated entirely with slides, excepting three lonely prints. At this writing I have no idea what photos will be selected for publication, but for chapter ten I submitted to the publisher seventeen slides and three digital images. How quickly things change: Chapters eleven through twenty-one were digital images only. I still have dozens of rolls of slide film that I now know I will probably never use!

So, as 2006 heralded the end of my third decade of African hunting, it was time to have some fun. Some books require a lot of research and border on work, but a book like this is pure fun, requiring only that I relive a lot of wonderful experiences and try to put them in logical sequence and context. The context I have chosen here, more so than in the previous two, is what I think I have learned about Africa and African hunting over the past thirty years. I now fully understand (*ouch!*) that I know a hell of a lot more than I did then . . . and I understand equally (double *ouch!*) that I don't know as much as I wish I did. I can only hope I'm making progress!

When I wrote *Where Lions Roar* a decade ago, I would have bet a large sum that our present volume would never exist. It wasn't that I was tired of African hunting—how could anyone ever be? Rather, I had done almost everything in Africa that I ever dreamed I could, and much more than I ever believed I could. Truly, in the eighties and early nineties I beggared myself over going to Africa. (And, no, a book like this doesn't pay for it, although I greatly appreciate your purchase!) It was like a sickness, an addiction, and I did far more than my means should have allowed. In the late nineties I managed to slow down. I made a couple of hunts that I really wanted to do, but for the first time since the late 1970s I skipped years here and there. This was as much because of military commitments as lack of desire, but at the halfway point of the decade I might logically have projected that this volume would be exceedingly skimpy!

As I will relate herein, things changed. Thanks largely to our television show, *Tracks Across Africa,* and thus thanks to my partners, Tim Danklef and Dave Fulson, the last few years have been, well, Africa-intensive. There were times when I remembered the adage, "Be careful what you wish for." But I did wish for it, and despite the whining I'm grateful for it. Perhaps the most important thing I've learned is that I still have so much to learn. At this point I do not project that a fourth "ten-year Africa book" will emerge a decade from now. That seems unlikely, but it's a long way in the future, and, heck, I might not even be here ten years from now. On the other hand, I wouldn't rule it out. I am sure now of one thing I wasn't sure of in 1986 or even in 1996: In 2016 there will still be a great deal of wonderful African hunting. Some of it will be better than it is today, and some will be worse. Our mosaic of hunting countries will have changed, as will the game available. Some things written herein will remain perfectly valid, and other things will have been invalidated by the march of time. I know better now than I did back then that I cannot predict the future. I can only report accurately and honestly what I have experienced, and this is what I have tried to do.

Craig Boddington
Dallas, Texas
Christmas Day, 2006

Sangha River

My third decade of African hunting began in the southwestern corner of the Central African Republic, along the Cameroon border near the Sangha River. Honestly, this was a hunt I wanted to make but hoped I didn't have to. It started in 1994 at a good French restaurant in Bangui, the capital of the C.A.R. Joe Bishop and I had just completed a successful hunt for Derby eland, and I was already booked for bongo two years later. A short, sturdy Frenchman joined us, and although he was out of practice on his English, his enthusiasm was infectious. It was some time before we learned that his name was Alain Lefol, a genuine legend. As a young man Lefol had represented France in the pentathlon, in his middle years he is considered one of France's best mountain climbers, and without question he is one of the best-known and most successful professional hunters in Central Africa.

We liked him, and although it would be three years before he and Joe had a suitable opening in their schedules, Bishop booked a bongo safari on the spot. I would go with him, of course, but I hoped to already have a bongo by then. This was not to be, however. In 1996 I had a great safari over on the other side of the C.A.R., near Sudan, but we ran out of rain. No rain, no bongo.

So as the plane descended to a red-mud strip in the green forest, I still wanted a bongo desperately, and I thought of this safari as a reprieve. Bishop, being Bishop, really didn't care. He had taken a fine bongo some years before and was going back only because he liked Alain Lefol. His attitude was far better than mine, and

The view across the Ubangi River from Bangui, Central African Republic. That's the Congo on the far side of the river, with fishermen trading back and forth pretty much at will.

far more generous. He would hunt with Alain while I would hunt with Alain's nephew, Jean-Christophe Lefol. But Joe made it clear that it was far more important for me to get a bongo than for him to do so. There would come a day when this would be tested, and it would be true.

The southwestern corner of the C.A.R. is true tall-tree climax forest rising from significant hills. Logging activity has opened a network of red-clay roads—treacherous when it rains, but providing more access than ever before. I suppose this is good in some ways. The forest roads are ideal for picking up tracks, and a safari can go deeper into the forest than was ever possible before the roads existed. Certainly bongo hunting is more productive today than was the case just twenty years ago. This is not because there are more bongo but because of the improved access, and also because, with elephant hunting now very limited throughout the forest zone, bongo is the great prize. Modern outfitters like Lefol concentrate on bongo because that is their primary draw in the region. Over time, of course, they've learned more about bongo and how to hunt them more effectively.

The same roads offer access to poachers, and as the human population burgeons, meat poaching is the true scourge of Africa's wildlife. But the forest roads were there and we would use them, at least as a starting point. On that first day they led us to Lefol's camp, an amazingly beautiful cluster of well-thatched huts sitting high on a hill among the great trees. It was June and the rainy season was well along, heavy showers every two or three days creating ideal conditions for hunting bongo. All game seems to move well after a rain, but forest game is a bit different. Not just the bongo but also the elephant, forest buffalo, and all the rest like to move when the forest is wet and quiet—and move very little when it's dry and the ground is noisy. We were getting plenty of rain, and were sure we would find tracks.

We did, but even then it isn't so easy. My previous experience had come in what is truly transition forest, similar to the great bongo hunting that southwestern Sudan used to offer. There we tracked without dogs,

A swampy area or bai *is a good place to look for sitatunga. There were fresh tracks in this* bai, *so we built a machan and waited endless hours, but we never saw a living creature.*

Big clearings like this aren't common in the forest, but they do occur and are always prime places to look for tracks.

and although it was thick beyond anything I had ever seen, it wasn't hopelessly so. Day and again we tracked bongo and heard them move ahead of us, and once, just once, I saw the briefest flash of red hide. This was frustrating, but I never considered it impossible. To this day I believe we would have taken a bongo had it kept raining. It did not; the rains passed us by the last ten days of the hunt, and with every day that passed we saw fewer and fewer fresh tracks—of anything. No rain, no bongo.

Now, a year and a month later and several hundred miles west, closer to the heart of the forest, we had rain. We also had an altogether different situation. The general denseness of the vegetation was beyond my imagination as well as my experience—the stuff was a wall of green. There are those who believe the use of dogs for hunting bongo is somehow less sporting than "pure" tracking, but I wonder how many of those hunters are of (or influenced by) a previous generation fortunate enough to have hunted bongo in transition or finger forest? The true forest starts in southwestern C.A.R., a blanket of green extending west into southern Cameroon, then another thousand miles west and a thousand miles south, across the bulge of West Africa and down through the Congos. It is daunting and it is not for everyone—a place where average visibility is just a few feet, and fifteen yards is long range.

This wall of green is home to the Pygmy hunters, who consider it paradise because it holds everything they might want. There aren't many Pygmies, so I suppose their impact on the forest is minimal. The majority live in small villages along the rivers, at least on a part-time basis, but they roam widely and freely throughout the forest zone, one of the last groups of true hunter-gatherer peoples on this planet. This month might find them hunting and camping in Gabon; next month they might be deep in the Congo. In the countries of the forest zone the Pygmies have a unique political status. Officially, they are "citizens of the forest," able to come and go as they please without regard for international borders and without passports or paperwork.

The Pygmies are distinctly short in stature, rarely more than five feet tall and often a few inches less. Their coloring seems to me a bit lighter than that of most Africans, and their front teeth are often filed to sharp points. This sounds like it would give them a fierce visage, but it does not because Pygmies are among the happiest, most carefree people I have ever been around. I'm not sure if it's innate or part of their culture, but they are blessed with good humor, always smiling and laughing. They are also among the world's greatest hunters. Their ability to track in the forest is legendary—and the legend is fact, not fiction.

To the Pygmies, anything that walks or crawls in the forest is food, and there is a humorous side to almost anything. One morning we were cruising down a forest road when one of our "famous fourteen" banged on the roof and said something to Jean-Christophe. He stopped and reached for the Benelli he kept behind the seat, and as he did I noticed an unrolled inner tube over on the shoulder of the road. It was a huge forest cobra, and the Pygmies wanted it for lunch. Thinking to also save the skin, Jean-Christophe carefully aimed the shotgun so as to "fringe" the huge snake. When we walked up to it I noticed only two or three pellet holes in the head, and I think I politely suggested that it might be a good idea to remove said head before stowing their lunch in the back of the truck.

This was a bad idea because beheading would ruin the skin. So we headed on down the road with fourteen Pygmies and a ten-foot cobra in the back of the truck. I doubt we'd gone two miles before the cobra came back to life. I heard a commotion behind me and turned to look just about the time the Pygmies made their exit. Imagine,

5

Like eland and kudu, bongo will reach up with their horns and break off branches while feeding. We found this fresh break while tracking, telling us we were getting close.

if you will, a black volcano erupting from the bed of the truck. We must have been doing forty miles per hour at the time, and before the Toyota finally came to a halt we had bruised and battered Pygmies—all laughing hysterically—scattered for two hundred yards. The cobra, though very much alive, was still groggy. I got a loop of him around my rifle barrel and pulled him out of the truck, then shot him in the back of the head with my .416. That seemed to quiet the snake down, but our trackers laughed for the rest of the day.

The Pygmies can follow the bongo, but getting a shot at one in that green hell is an altogether different story. This is where the dogs come in. In this area we used not a pack of dogs but just one small terrier. He hunted with us unleashed, ranging out just a few yards ahead of the trackers like a good flushing dog. It was explained to me that when a bongo was tracked up, the dog would distract it, hopefully long enough for the hunters to slip in, see the horns, and take the shot. There are no wild canines at all in the forest, so a bongo bull has no idea what this yapping thing at his feet is all about. Even so, results are not consistent. Some bongo will stop and try to kill the dog, but others will simply walk away, paying no attention at all.

Remember, I had already invested one expensive bongo safari in "pure" tracking, meaning without canine assistance. Rather than convincing me that dogs were the way to go, that safari had the opposite effect. I'd started without dogs, and I wanted to finish without dogs—at least until I actually saw the forest. Then I understood. If the dog would give me a better chance, not only to get a bongo but to actually see it and judge the horns before I shot, I was all for it. So we went forth with fully fourteen Pygmies and one little dog—and even then it wasn't so easy.

The year before, Jacques Lemaux had told me he believed a typical bongo hunt proceeded in distinct phases. First we would track fruitlessly. During this initial phase we would form a team with the trackers and I would learn how to be quiet enough and how to see better in the thick stuff. Then we would "make contact"—we would hear the bongo move ahead of us, and possibly even catch a flash of red hide. Then we would actually see a bongo, or enough of a bongo to call it a bongo. Finally we would get a shot.

That safari never progressed past the "making contact" phase. This one did. In fact, in the first half we got all the way to "seeing bongo"—

I was at the midpoint of my second 21-day bongo hunt when I took this beautiful bull, easily one of my very best trophies.

and, being a bit of a pessimist, I was convinced we'd never get to the final stage.

Even though we had good rains, it took a couple of days to find a fresh bull track, but eventually we turned up a beautiful bongo track sunk deep in the mud along the verge of a forest road. We followed it for just an hour or so and were crossing a rare clearing when the dog went mad in a thick patch just ahead of us. Jean-Christophe and I moved in, and were very close before we realized we were looking at the slender horns of a big female. In fact, we were too close! The cow saw us and charged, scattering me to the right and Jean-Christophe to the left. She passed close enough to touch and kept going into the clearing behind us. Our little dog caught her again there, and I even managed to take a few pictures.

Exactly what happened was never clear. She was very big, so it's possible my team misread the tracks from the start. It's equally possible that we started on a bull, but her tracks wandered over the top of his and that's where we finished. It is also possible that we never had her tracks at all, but the dog simply stumbled across her. One thing I do know: Without the dog, we would have made a horrible mistake in either of the first two scenarios, because we would never have seen the horns. Based on the tracks, we would have assumed it was a bull and would have fired into the first spot of red hide we saw.

In that initial period Joe and Alain also made considerable progress. I think it was no later than the second day of the hunt when they tracked up a youngish bull with twenty-eight-inch horns . . . and passed him up. Of course I gnashed my teeth at this, but Joe had a nice bongo and wanted a better one or nothing.

A couple more days passed without a fresh track, and I learned some things. After consultation with our Pygmies (in French, the common language throughout central Africa), Jean-Christophe elected to take a day-old spoor. They didn't expect to catch up, but Jean-Christophe explained that bongo bulls are quite territorial. This bull hadn't wandered out onto the road, but there was a good chance this old track would lead us to fresh spoor. We followed for a couple of hours, and it was nearly noon when we stopped for a break. By this time it seemed hopeless, and I was ready to give it up. Our Pygmies wouldn't hear of it, though, so we compromised. Another half-hour and we'd turn around. Ten minutes later our old track led us to a smoking fresh spoor, made well after daylight according to the Pygmies.

The second thing I learned that day was an object lesson in something I'd been told: Not all bongo stop for dogs. The track must have been very fresh, because we had him within the hour—except we had nothing but a few frantic barks and, when we approached, tracks that just kept going.

I don't know the percentage of bongo that will stop for one dog, but it must be low. A decade later I hunted over on the Cameroon side, where our Pygmies used a half-dozen small dogs. They told me that only one bongo in maybe two or even three could be stopped by the whole pack, so the percentage must be lower with just one dog. Certainly it seemed so to me. The following day we found very fresh tracks during a soft, gentle rain. This made for wonderfully quiet tracking conditions, provided we could catch the bongo before the rain wiped out the tracks.

We could, and we did. We were in heavy fern, no visibility at all, when our dog went crazy on the far side of a fallen log. Jean-Christophe

Alain Lefol's forest camp was a beautiful cluster of thatched huts sitting on a tall ridge. I am always amazed at a good African outfitter's ability to create such pleasant surroundings in the middle of nowhere.

and I got around it in time to see ferns waving gently from the passage of a large animal. It's interesting to note that on both of these occasions there were no running tracks. The bongo is supremely confident in his forest habitat, and in my experience he will rarely run. He doesn't have to; he can simply walk away from the few dangers he might encounter.

More days passed, and we were nearing the halfway point of the safari when we walked in to a small, hidden spring hoping to find a fresh track. Indeed we did, but this time it took our trackers a long while to sort out the proper spoor. Finally they did, and we took the track up out of the valley and along a ridge. The vegetation broke along the crest, creating an unusually open shelf. We were on this shelf, and had been tracking for just an hour, when a bongo bull appeared to our right, walking straight toward us. He must have been forty yards away, making this one of the most open places in the entire forest. I saw him so clearly—mahogany chest, white stripes, horns like baseball bats.

Obviously things were a bit confusing, but I got the rifle up and saw him through the cross hairs. And then Jean-Christophe inadvertently stepped in front of me. I got around him and almost had the rifle up again, but that was too much for this bongo. He turned to our right and stepped behind a bush, and that was the last we saw of him. The dog went in, barking, but the quarry never stopped.

In my entire hunting life I don't think I've ever been as angry, as disappointed, as frustrated, as petulant. I barely avoided a major tantrum, and simmered slowly for the rest of the day. All Jean-Christophe had been trying to do was exactly what he should have been doing—trying to see the horns, as his uncle had drilled into him. In the forest just a half-step can change the perspective entirely, so in retrospect I suppose my window was clearer than his. That's in retrospect. At the time, it seemed to me any idiot could have seen this was a huge bull, and I was equally shaken because I could easily have blown the man's head off.

At camp Alain got both sides of the story. To Jean-Christophe's credit, his story was exactly the same as mine: He had stepped in front of me, his reason being that he couldn't see the horns from where he was standing. Oh, well. I tend to cool off as quickly as I heat up, and certainly there was nothing to be done about it. As I said, I have a pessimistic streak. Between the previous year and this trip I had now hunted bongo for thirty days, and I figured I had just seen my last bongo for this safari.

Alain and Joe did a very generous thing, probably because, since I hadn't shot Jean-Christophe, they were now afraid I might shoot myself. They had discovered a hidden valley that held both water and a mineral lick, and it was loaded with bongo tracks. They had stumbled onto it too late in the day to try to follow—and now they gave it to us.

At first I wasn't sure it was much of a gift at all. Alain had given pretty good directions, but this secret place was far from any road and it proved extremely difficult to find. It was very late in the morning when, following old tracks, we finally stumbled into the mineral lick. There were tracks of all ages, and after a bit of casting around our team isolated fresh tracks of a bongo bull. Maybe a quarter-hour along the track we ran smack into a troop of chimpanzees. The dog went wild, as did the chimpanzees, and I was certain any bongo within miles would be long gone.

With some difficulty we got the dog back and proceeded. Just a few hundred yards later the dog went nuts again, but this time it was not a chimpanzee. Jean-Christophe knew immediately. "He's got him. Let's go!"

Ignoring vines and thorns, we tore through the underbrush toward the shrill barking. We made the last few yards on hands and knees, ending up looking into a low-ceilinged "room" with sapling walls. I could see the dog, darting and yapping. And then I could see the four legs of a much taller creature, a creature that was black and white and red. I had the shot, but we couldn't see the horns. Then the bongo broke contact, moving swiftly off to the right. As he exited we saw that his horns were long and thick, a wonderful animal—but it was too late to shoot.

I was too busy kicking myself to understand what was happening. "He's stopped again," hissed Jean-Christophe. "Now we know what he is, so we don't have to look again. Just shoot him!"

The dog had stopped him one more time maybe a hundred yards down the ridge. It was horribly thick, and we ignored rips in clothing and skin as we clawed our way toward the insistent barking. As we neared I couldn't see the dog, but I could see an ellipse of orange through a window in the leaves. That orange spot was bisected by a vertical white stripe—and that's all I could see. I had no sense of distance, but somehow I knew that

I was looking at the bongo's shoulder. I raised the heavy Rigby, centered that strange patch of orange, and squeezed the trigger. Perhaps I could see more than I realized, because now I saw the bull take the bullet hard, turn to run, and collapse completely out of view.

Jean-Christophe and I ran forward and found the bull down in a tiny clearing. The burnt-orange body and brilliant white stripes were amazing—but the horns were shocking. Heavy, perfectly matched, ending in polished ivory tips, this was a bongo worth waiting for. We took a few pictures, and then our crew set to work. First the bull was skillfully skinned, then the meat and most of the entrails were cut up and divided into loads. When we left, little more than a wet patch remained in the leaves to mark the passing of a great creature.

It started to rain just before we shrugged into our loads, a gentle rain at first that kept getting harder as the afternoon passed. The game trails became a boggy nightmare, and we were still several ridges from the road when dark caught us. We continued on, by flashlight in pouring rain, finally stumbling onto the forest road about midnight. That was just the beginning. We had parked at the bottom of a cul de sac, and got hopelessly stuck. Well, not quite hopelessly, because we had a winch. The next obstacles were great trees that had fallen across the road, their root systems weakened by the downpour. Jean-Christophe was prepared for almost anything, and his big chainsaw provided the answer.

It stopped raining shortly before we arrived in camp in a gray, soggy dawn. Joe and Alain were waiting, ready to launch search efforts if needed. We admired the beautiful bongo, and then I went to bed while Joe and Alain began their hunting day. In the Marines I'd often heard the phrase, "No good deed goes unpunished." Joe and Alain gave me the spot that yielded my bongo, and in return they never got one at all. In Alain's defense, they turned down a couple more bulls looking for something special. On future trips with Alain, both Joe and his wife, Sara, took fine bongo. But on this particular safari, totaling forty-two hunting days between Joe and me, we had one bongo between us, and nothing else at all. I still refer to it as "our" bongo—especially when Joe Bishop is within earshot.

Kenya and Kariba

In the late 1990s I would have bet a lot of money that this book would never exist. After I finally got my bongo, I had done pretty much everything in Africa that I'd ever set out to do or expected to do. I didn't appreciate the strength of the grip Africa had on me, though, and of course I couldn't envision the opportunities that would come along after the turn of the millennium. In my mind I would spend more time at home during the next few years, and spend more of my hunting budget climbing sheep mountains while I still could. But I couldn't seem to stay out of Africa.

For me, 1998 was largely a nonhunting year, mostly spent on active duty with the Marines. That spring I was part of a lengthy military mission to Kenya, part training and part humanitarian operations. We off-loaded our ships in Mombasa, then worked our way up the coast to the little town of Malindi, which served as our base. Our engineers improved roads and built a couple of schools and clinics, while our medical contingent held sick call in outlying villages and inoculated both people and livestock into the thousands. Once these operations were up and running, key members of the Kenya, Tanzania, and Uganda military joined us, and we staff weenies conducted training in peacekeeping operations, in which all three countries regularly participate under the United Nations flag.

It was a hectic period and also a bit nerve-racking. This was after the bombings of our embassies in Kenya and Tanzania but of course before "9-11." Coastal Kenya was known to be an Al Qaeda hotbed and also, for generations, a favorite spot for Somali gangs to raid. We had extensive security at all times, possibly overkill, but we had troops in there for more than three months without any serious problems. That deal was also a lot of fun. Rather than bringing in all the logistic support necessary for a peak of 1,500 troops, we leased the old Blue Marlin hotel in Malindi, visited in better days by Zane Grey and Ernest Hemingway. Rather than attempting to run a dining facility, we used a local caterer, whose menu often included buffalo, giraffe, and even zebra.

I hadn't visited Kenya in the two decades since hunting there had closed, and I was appalled at the obviously exponential growth in human population and also by the apparent near-complete loss of wildlife. There were a few hippo and crocs in the river, and the local papers occasionally reported incidents with problem elephant and buffalo, but in their ramblings through the countryside none of our troops saw any wildlife at all, save for baboons and monkeys. Since 1977 there have been occasional rumors of Kenya reopening hunting, and these persist to this day—but my opinion was then, and remains today, that Kenya no longer has enough wildlife outside her parks to support a safari industry.

The parks, on the other hand, remain magnificent. We did the best we could to arrange short tours to nearby Tsavo and as far as Masai Mara, and tried equally hard to make sure our troops had a few days off to take advantage of them. I was operations officer and nominally "2-I-C" (second in charge) for this shindig, so I couldn't get away as much as I would have liked, but I did manage to spend a couple of days in Tsavo, not far from where I'd hunted in 1977. Gone were the great elephant herds that had roamed the open plains, but there were some elephant, clearly a young herd on its way to recovery. There were lion, the classic maneless Tsavo lion, and I caught a quick glimpse of one of Tsavo's few surviving black rhino. But it was the buffalo that got me really excited.

We overnighted at a nice lodge set high on a ridge, with a lighted water hole right below. In late afternoon a few buffalo came to drink, but after dark a great herd came. A long staircase descended from the veranda, opening into a tunnel that ended in a bulletproof glass window a stone's throw from the water hole. We ran down the stairs when the herd approached out of the dark, and when we reached the window a

A young elephant on the Tsavo plains. Poachers ravaged these elephant in the late 1970s. Today they have recovered considerably, but what you will find is still a very young herd with a few older bulls.

great mass of buffalo milled before us, most just beyond the reach of the water hole's spotlights. These were descendants of buffalo I had hunted twenty years before and just a few miles east, but they hadn't been trophy hunted in bovine generations.

Harsh, dry Tsavo was never known for producing Kenya's best buffalo—but you wouldn't have known it from looking at this herd. I never saw the entire herd, a teeming mass of several hundred buffalo, but at a distance of mere feet I saw bulls measuring in the high forties, with the classic drop and sweeping hooks of East African Cape buffalo. I was enthralled, and stood there long after most of my companions returned to the lodge. I think it was there that I realized—and accepted—that I hadn't yet beaten the hold Africa had on me. . . .

It was a year later when the charter plane dropped Jim Morey and me at Russ Broom's camp overlooking Lake Kariba's flood plain in Zimbabwe's Zambezi Valley. Jim was looking for his first buffalo, and I was there to continue my African obsession. Initially we both hunted with Rory Muil, with the plan that after Jim took his buffalo I would stay with Rory while Russ took Jim east to Douma to look for a sable.

We followed a couple of bulls with negative results, and I think it was the third day when we found the spoor of a good herd crossing the two-track in front of us. They led us over a low ridge and then up a long valley, and in that dry year we saw the dust long before we saw or heard buffalo. The valley itself was choked with thick bush, and this was one of the few times I've stalked buffalo by their dust alone. We checked the wind and crossed the valley behind the herd, then climbed far enough up the next ridge so that we could see down into the valley. Then we simply kept pace with them, monitoring their progress by dust and bovine bellows without ever actually seeing buffalo.

Rory hoped the animals would reach an opening that would offer us a shot or at least allow us to see if there were any good bulls, and after several hundred yards it almost worked. The valley fanned out and opened up a bit, and the traveling dust cloud thinned to reveal black forms and swishing tails moving along slowly. Rory led us to a tall termite mound on the edge of the valley, a good vantage point with buffalo just below us. But they were still too packed for a shot, and they

I didn't have a lot of time off during my military mission to coastal Kenya, but there was a local snake park in Malindi that we visited. You'd never get me this close to a snake unless other Marines were watching!

The entire ecosystem of the Zambezi Valley was altered for all time by the creation of Lake Kariba, with some changes for the better and some for the worse.

veered away from us to leave the valley on the opposite side. In groups and singles they ascended a steep bank, then fed slowly into the bush beyond, about two hundred yards away—much too far for a shot but a perfect opportunity to see the herd. The cows came first and the bulls trailed them, probably eighty buffalo in all.

There were at least three mature bulls—no monsters but good, solid-bossed buffalo. Once the last buffalo had vanished into the mopane, Rory and Jim moved forward with one tracker, the rest of us trailing behind to reduce movement. The buffalo were feeding straight ahead on a level bench, and the hunters caught them immediately. From my "disadvantage point" all I could see were occasional black forms and the telltale swishing of long black tails, but just thirty yards ahead, Rory and Jim were in an ideal position at last. After a few minutes of duck-walking and crawling, Jim's .375 Dakota cracked and we heard the thump of a good hit. We ran forward in time to see Jim put in the finisher, and we all gathered around a nice mature buffalo with hard bosses, good shape, and maybe a thirty-seven-inch spread—to my thinking an ideal first buffalo for anyone.

The next morning Jim and Russ flew off to Douma, with Rory and me continuing in place. We looked at a few buffalo without

Professional hunter Rory Muil and I pose with a cow elephant taken as "PAC" (Problem Animal Control). It's impossible to say which elephant was to blame, but this cow was taken from a herd that had killed a villager just the day before.

seeing anything interesting, and then came a tragedy. A group of crop-raiding elephant cows killed a villager, and suddenly we had a "PAC" (Problem Animal Control) elephant available. It was impossible to determine which elephant had done the deed but easy enough to follow the correct herd. After just a few hours we caught them ascending a steep slope, apparently stopping to feed near the top.

We circled to get the wind perfect, and then Rory and I moved in for a shot. I think there were just six—no bulls and no young calves—but in the center of the group was a particularly big cow that we selected. I have shot few elephant, and despite admitted inexperience I did exactly what I do not recommend: I insisted on a brain shot. We got plenty close enough, maybe twenty paces, but we were on top of a little knoll and the elephant were feeding slightly below us. This put us at eye level or a bit above, an angle for a brain shot that is not found in any books. Even at that distance and with a scoped .416 Rigby, I couldn't visualize the shot properly, and I shot just below the brain.

This unpleasant fact was only determined somewhat later. At the moment it was instantly clear that I'd blown it, since neither the back legs nor the front legs collapsed. For us beginners, the easiest way in the world to lose an elephant is to attempt a brain shot and fail. The aftermath is one of the fastest things in the hunting world. All these elephant, known man-haters and at least one confirmed man-killer, screamed in outrage. The stricken animal turned instantly, and almost as instantly was covered by another cow. My only salvation was long practice in working a bolt (a double would have been even better). Without conscious thought I knew I'd messed up, and as the elephant turned I slam-fired a second solid into her shoulder.

Then Rory dragged me back, and immediately I understood why. Instead of stampeding away in panic, the other elephant, now silent, gathered and began scenting the air. As we retreated, they advanced to the spot the shot had come from and then began to hunt, leading with their trunks. We had no authority to take additional animals and didn't want to, so with the elephant slowly unraveling our scent we turned and ran, stopping only when we reached an open hillside.

I suppose the herd thought better of pursuit, because they never broke out of the trees. We waited a little while, then moved forward

When Rory Muil saw this buffalo, I think he said, "There's nothing wrong with that bull." Indeed! This bull has heavy bosses, a good shape, and a spread of 42 inches—a fine buffalo for anywhere in Africa.

and took the tracks. The elephant must have waited the same period, because we caught them again in minutes, one animal lagging back and then standing while her herd moved on. We were above her again as she faced us in a little valley, and this time Rory talked me through it and a finishing brain shot put her down.

Elephant hunting has not been my thing. They are magnificent animals, and although I understand they are now overpopulated in many areas and must be controlled, I have been perfectly happy to let someone else do the controlling. As I write these lines, that elephant and I crossed paths seven years ago and I have not shot another. But I do revere good ivory, and as I write I am on the eve of a specific quest for a big tusker in southern Tanzania. I hope I learned my lesson well: Absent much experience, the brain shot is too risky on an unwounded elephant. I'm trying to put it out of my mind, visualizing only the less fancy but far more certain heart and lung shots.

At that point in my career I had shot many buffalo, and there I do not claim inexperience. So I have no excuse and no explanation for what happened. We were driving through a patch of dry thornbush at midmorning when three buffalo bulls materialized just to our left. They disappeared quickly but didn't seem genuinely spooked, and although our glimpse was fleeting, at least one of them had appeared to be a dandy, a classic bull with heavy bosses, wide spread, and deep curl.

We left the truck quickly and circled around to get the wind right, certain the bulls had stayed in a big patch of thorn. We moved in slowly, bush by bush, and now could see black forms moving slowly toward us. There was an opening just in front of me, so I knelt and waited. I don't know if it was the same buffalo we'd seen, but a fine bull stepped clear, took a couple of steps toward me, and then turned to cross that gap. Rory whispered, "There's nothing wrong with that buffalo," and as he said it I held very carefully on the shoulder and fired.

The three bulls crashed away, and then we waited to hear a death bellow that didn't come. In time we took the tracks, me still expecting to find him dead. After less than two hundred yards we came to a dry sand river, the blood spoor leading us to thick *jess* on the far side. There was no concern yet; I've seen well-hit buffalo go farther. But there was a big problem. This narrow watercourse marked the boundary between

Jim Morey and Rory Muil with Jim's first buffalo. To my thinking this is an ideal first buffalo: fully mature, a good shape, and a normal spread of about 37 inches.

Russ's Tribal Trust Land (TTL) concession and Zimbabwe Parks and Wildlife's Chete Safari Area. We could not cross without permission and a National Parks game guard, and the game guard station was two hours away. Since we were still following a "dead" buffalo, I wonder if this interruption saved us!

Once the game scout was gathered up, less than an hour of light remained as we took the spoor across that dry river. On the far side the cover was pure *jess*, winter-gray and almost impenetrable. We were barely fifty yards into it, crawling on hands and knees, when the bull erupted just ahead of us. It was now hours since he had been wounded, and he was perhaps as surprised as we were. Fortunately, he crashed away in the other direction. Now, for the first time, we knew we were not seeking a dead buffalo, and the watery blood in his bed told us that he had been hit too far back. We followed a while longer, but dark comes early in the forbidding *jess*, so we had no choice but to back off until the morning.

That truly was one of the longest and worst nights of my life. I had (and still have) no idea how I'd hit the buffalo so poorly, but the evidence was clear and now I'd seen the *jess* through which we would have to follow him. I thought of a great buffalo bull suffering in the dark for my failure, and I thought about tracking him in the morning. I actively fear lion, dread following wounded leopard, and lack enough experience to have definitive feelings toward elephant. As I've written before, I respect buffalo more than fear them—but that night I was filled with fear. I slept only fitfully, once waking from a nightmare that began with me walking through the *jess* and ended with the buffalo's shining black nose and sharp horns emerging just beside me, much too close to stop. I sweated and tossed until nearly dawn, then got up and got ready to face the day.

Russ and Jim had returned from Douma with a huge sable. I can't recall their plan for the day, but Russ was kind enough to loan me his Rigby double .500. It provided the only comfort as I tried to put the dream out of my mind.

The spoor took us barely a mile in straight-line terms, but it wound endlessly through the thickest *jess*, and the long night was followed by one of the longest mornings of my life. We got on the tracks shortly after six and were still on them five hours later. The blood was consistent but never heavy, and the trackers held it extremely well. There were many thickets of the kind my dream was made of, brooding gray thorn where vision was limited and only luck could stop a charge. My palms sweated continuously, and I suppose Rory's did as well, but he never complained and never recriminated, and the trackers never wavered. We just kept at it slowly, one pace at a time, heavy rifles ready, hour after hour.

We were lucky. We caught the bull in one of the very few relatively open patches. He was moving just ahead of us, aware of our presence and circling to get the wind so his charge would be accurate. I shot him as he turned to come, dropping him with a high shoulder–spine shot, then shooting again, reloading, and shooting again as we moved forward. This I did well, but the first shot, which had been so easy, was fully eighteen inches left of where I was sure I had held. I wish I could tell you there was a lesson in this, but I'm not sure what it should be. Despite short range, despite a good rifle with a clear scope, I missed the mark. It wasn't the first time, and certainly not the last time, but we were all incredibly lucky no one got hurt as a result.

Kalahari

Dunes and streets. The red sands of the Kalahari stretch endlessly to the horizon in a succession of linear sand ridges or dunes, with shallow valleys or streets in between. Some dunes are unmarred stretches of smooth sand, but the Kalahari is a living desert of low brush, sparse grass, and occasionally the desert's signature trees: camelthorn acacia and dark, hardy shepherd's trees. It is spectacularly beautiful, and in winter not uninviting at all. In fact, when we stumbled out of our tents that first morning, it was shockingly cold and we were grateful for a brilliant sunrise peeking over the horizon.

This visit to the Kalahari was intended as a sort of side trip from the buffalo and elephant (for me) and buffalo and sable (for partner Jim Morey) hunts just concluded in Zimbabwe. It wasn't my idea at all, and, like most side trips, it was too rushed. Unlike some side trips, it was wonderful—and worthy of more time than we gave it.

At that time Jim was running Swarovski Optik's North American operations. It seems that an enterprising young professional hunter named Dirk de Bod owned The Gun Shop in Windhoek, and in that guise was Swarovski's Namibian distributor. Some of the Swarovski family members had hunted with Dirk and "suggested" to Jim that he needed to spend a few days with him next time he was in Africa. Or, as it was put to me: "Craig, after our buffalo hunt, do you mind if we run over to Namibia and spend a few days with this guy?"

No, I didn't mind. I wasn't sure it was a good idea, and I was pretty sure I had no reason to go. Today the concept of not caring whether or not I went back to Namibia seems laughable, but at that time I thought—quite wrongly—that I'd done what I could do in that country. On the other hand, taking a "side trip" of many hundreds of miles was hardly a new concept for me. Twenty years earlier I'd done several safaris in which I bounced back and forth between South Africa, then-Rhodesia, and then-South-West Africa. I'm not sure the connections and gun permits were really easier back then. Perhaps I was just young and foolish. Whatever, we could make it work—but, honest, it was just a favor to Jim and Swarovski, a favor well owed because they've been very good to me.

They did offer me one small carrot. Apparently this Dirk de Bod had a really good area far out in the middle of Namibia's Kalahari that I had never seen. And in this area he had (or claimed to have) truly spectacular gemsbok. I had never heard of Dirk de Bod, so I didn't know if this claim was real. On the other hand, I've long wanted a really good gemsbok and have known that to get one it is essential to journey to the depths of either the Kalahari or the Namib desert, country where there's lots of soft sand, no rocks, and the gemsbok get old without wearing down their horns.

This would not be my first try for a big gemsbok, and I didn't honestly expect it to be my last. "Big," in my lexicon, meant a bull over the magical 40-inch mark. We all know gemsbok females have much longer horns than bulls, and I have absolutely no problem with shooting long-horned cows. But that isn't what I wanted. I wanted a really big bull with massive bases and straight horns that reached forever, not the thinner but impossibly long, slightly curving horns of a big female.

Technically, I had actually reached this goal twice, especially given that I rarely reference trophy size and almost never enter trophies into records books. In 1981, in the Kimberley area of northwestern South Africa on the other side of the Kalahari, I'd taken a beautiful bull that measured an honest thirty-nine inches. Just a few years earlier, the last time I'd been in Namibia, I'd taken another spectacular bull of more or less thirty-nine inches. We humans like things neat and orderly, so both these bulls fell oh-so-slightly short of the forty-inch mark long established for a really good oryx (or Dall sheep, or buffalo, or sable).

Unfortunately, on a long, straight horn, no professional hunter can come up with a field judgment closer to the real thing than an inch or two. So I'd taken wonderful gemsbok bulls, but hadn't quite reached the proper and established "braggin' size." Maybe I would on this side trip, maybe I wouldn't—but at least I had something interesting to try for.

We caught an early flight from Harare to Johannesburg, and a quick connection put us in Windhoek at midday. So far, so good, and both Dirk de Bod and his partner, Pieter Stofberg, were there to meet us. Not all of our bags arrived with us, so we waited a couple hours for the next flight. The missing bags came in, thankfully, but it was nearly dark by the time we left the airport and headed southeast. We stopped and took the mandatory photo when we crossed the Tropic of Capricorn, but otherwise we simply drove, and it was a hell of a lot farther than I'd had any clue. Hard-surface roads turned to gravel, and eventually gravel turned to sand before we reached Hannes Steyn's farm deep in the Kalahari, close to the Botswana border. Midnight had long since come and gone and the night was clear, bright, and shockingly cold when we finally stumbled into a simple and absolutely beautiful tent camp in the lee of a brushy dune.

In the morning, coffee cups in hand, we ascended that dune and looked out across the Kalahari, immediately seeing a few gemsbok and springbok, both given away by white flashes in the morning sun. Caught in slanting light glancing off red sand, the fawn-gray gemsbok appeared oddly pink, a phenomenon that was repeated at sundown. We glassed for a half-hour from our vantage point above camp, then descended for breakfast. With the air finally starting to warm up, we checked our rifles, and then Dirk and I headed in one direction while Jim and Pieter Stofberg went in another.

We were clearly in a specialty area—plenty of gemsbok and quite a few springbok, but almost nothing else. At that time Hannes, Pieter, and Dirk were in a three-way partnership, with Hannes's family farm in the Kalahari as one of their concessions. It was low-fenced for sheep, and it was clear Hannes had taken care of his game. He had spectacular springbok, and during the next couple of years he and his partners literally rewrote the SCI record book for gemsbok. Over the next few days Jim and I helped!

It was long past dark when we crossed the Tropic of Capricorn en route from Windhoek to the Kalahari. That's me, Jim Morey, and Dirk de Bod "holding up the sign."

Even a brushy desert like the Kalahari is fairly open, so over the years many of the best gemsbok have been taken by chasing them with a vehicle. In classic dunes-and-streets country, that kind of hunting is not necessary. In fact, this area is ideal for stalking: From the top of any dune you can cover the entirety of the street below, and often the near slopes of the next dune can be reached without too much stretching of a rifle barrel. Dirk de Bod, I was pleased to learn, was an intelligent hunter but not a truck hunter. We used a vehicle to cover the ground we needed to cover, but we would ascend the tallest dunes on foot and use cover to glass the dunes and streets beyond. I liked Dirk long before we had ever fired a shot, and quickly rated him as one of the best professional hunters I had ever met.

Early on he showed me a magnificent cow gemsbok in a big herd. I had already stated that I wanted a big bull, so this was not a test for me, just a statement of fact: Dirk knew this old lady, distinctive by her amazing horns that swept back almost like those of a scimitar oryx. He knew she would exceed forty-five inches, and believed she would reach forty-six and change. I agreed, but this was merely a clinical discussion. Dirk accepted my desire for a big bull without judgment or prejudice, or even the slightest inference that I might regret the decision.

29

As I said, this was a side trip that deserved more time than we gave it. At that time Hannes had taken few gemsbok from his long-nurtured herd, and the potential was beyond limit. Our time was limited, but, after all, how many big gemsbok can you look at without getting confused? I think it was on the third day when we made our choice, a magnificent heavy-horned bull in a smallish herd of a couple dozen. Some of the cows with him had longer horns, but he held up well against them and Dirk was certain he was what we were looking for. I'd never seen a gemsbok of this quality, so I could only trust Dirk—as I was rapidly learning to do.

We stalked them on foot for a couple of hours, from one street across a dune and across the next street. We never bumped them hard, but every time we closed, the big bull was covered by cows or the cover was too thick. Dirk amazed me with his ability to hold that one bull in constant focus; he knew exactly which one we were looking for, but every time we relocated, I had to start all over again.

Finally we came around the toe of a sand ridge and caught the herd in an open street just a couple hundred yards away. We crawled a bit

Dirk's Kalahari camp was a lovely cluster of tents set in a sheltered little valley. We could climb the ridge above camp and glass for gemsbok and springbok, with the dunes and streets stretching away endlessly.

Wind action has created the Kalahari's unique structure of linear sand ridges (dunes) separated by more protected brushy valleys (streets). It's ideal country for stalking.

more, and then I got into a good sitting position. Dirk coached me as the bull worked his way through the herd, walking slowly out of cover, coming out from behind a cow, standing perfectly. Maybe he should have coached me on the shot as well. I had the bull dead to rights, and the big 8mm Remington Magnum was perfectly steady. As I squeezed the trigger, I felt as much as watched him walk out of the shot. I knew when the trigger broke that I'd hit him just a bit too far back. Dirk knew it, too, but his bedside manner is impeccable. He was unperturbed and totally confident: "We'll find him."

Indeed we did. It took a couple of hours of slow tracking and careful glassing, but we found him dead as Dirk had predicted. He lay with his great horns in the grass, and we whooped and hollered as we ran our hands along the length of them. I don't like to quote trophy measurements in print, because inches of horn shouldn't be one of the more important things about any hunt. But I'd set myself up for this one by requesting (demanding?) a bull of certain dimensions. Dirk de Bod found me exactly that, without any outward concern at all. In fact, he delivered quite a bonus. That gemsbok bull is a bit over forty-two inches on each horn, a magnificent trophy.

My gemsbok bull, set up for photos on top of a beautiful dune.

Jim Morey hit the jackpot with a huge springbok and a gemsbok cow over 45 inches on both horns. At the time this was one of the biggest gemsbok taken in many years, but since then several larger animals have come from this area.

A day or so later Jim Morey shot the magnificent cow we saw, and indeed her horns topped forty-six inches, one of the best gemsbok ever taken. That didn't bother me at all; I was delighted for him, and I'd got exactly what I wanted. Within the year my new friends took a bull exceeding forty-five inches in that area, plus a couple of cows even longer than Jim's monster. None of that bothers me, either. I like to hunt gemsbok, and I'm sure I will take more, but that beautiful bull killed among the dunes and streets is all the trophy gemsbok I will ever seek.

Jim shot a really fine springbok as well, and then, all too soon, it was time to leave. We had just a couple of days left, and Jim was hoping to take a Cape eland in brushier, better-watered country a few hours west, on the edge of the Kalahari. This country also held some number of greater kudu. As a writer, I'm often torn between "getting the story" and hunting, which I prefer to do. I'd done the latter, taking a wonderful gemsbok, so now greed entered the picture. If I could take a nice kudu, I'd have a much better story. Dirk did warn me that Kalahari kudu averaged a bit smaller than kudu in central and northern Namibia . . .

The soil was still very red and very sandy, classic Kalahari, but the brush was taller and there was much more of it, so clearly the desert here was transitioning into thornbush. This farmer had developed his game, and Pieter had no problem finding Jim a really impressive eland bull on our first morning. For our part, we found plenty of kudu, and they looked like perfectly normal, healthy southern greater kudu. However, all the bulls we looked at were seriously immature, and darkness fell with no kudu.

We needed to leave for Windhoek in early afternoon, which gave us just one more morning, hardly enough for a serious kudu hunt—but I had no intentions of being picky. Any mature bull would do.

We saw a few kudu early and then nothing. Dirk expanded the search pattern into a huge area of scattered thornbush, and in midmorning we found the tracks of several kudu fresh and clean in the red sand. We followed for a bit until kudu bulls started jumping everywhere. The one we chose was the largest among at least half a dozen, no monster but nice-looking and apparently mature.

The big 8mm caught him where his neck joined his shoulder and slammed him down, and we walked up to admire our prize. He had the odd, elongated hoofs common of Kalahari kudu. Other than that he was a very normal kudu bull . . . except that when we approached him, I wondered where the rest of him had gone. He was at least a third smaller than any southern greater kudu bull I have ever seen . . . and his horns were in perfect scale to his body. They finished two complete turns, and thus he should have been at least a forty-eight-inch bull. Instead, he was exactly the same size as our wonderful gemsbok, forty-two inches around the spiral!

If this was the biggest bull in the group, what of the rest? Dirk was horrified, and I thought it was hilarious that both of us could have been so fooled. We agreed we'd keep this one to ourselves, and until this moment I have.

Bale Mountains

The primary constant in Africa is change. Sometimes change is for the better, other times for the worse. Often it's neither, just change, and usually things don't turn out quite as bad as some would have us believe. Since at least Theodore Roosevelt's day it has been seemingly customary, almost mandatory, for anyone writing about Africa to spread gloom and doom, to predict the imminent end of the African safari as that reporter has known it. Ernest Hemingway indulged in this in the 1930s, Robert Ruark did in the fifties, and both Peter Capstick and I certainly did in the 1970s. I'm not sure why this is so, although I suspect a touch of ego is involved, as in "I hunted the real Africa, but you're too late." Perhaps I can be forgiven a wee bit, because Kenya closed shortly after my first safari and I was hardly alone in the belief that African hunting was doomed.

The truth is, and always was, that African hunting and the African safari are no more endangered than the vast bulk of Africa's wildlife. But there has been change, and there will be change. The 1970s and early eighties could well have been the low point. Hunting in Uganda fizzled out under Idi Amin. Hunting in far-flung countries like Angola, Mozambique, Chad, and Sudan was made untenable by civil wars that followed independence. Tanzania officially closed hunting in 1973, reopening in 1981. Kenya officially closed in 1977, apparently never to be hunted again. In that era only Botswana and Zambia took the place of the countries that were lost. But in 1980 no one could have predicted that new, dynamic safari industries in South Africa, as well as what is now Namibia and what was just becoming Zimbabwe, would not only supplant the lost safari countries but also make the African safari more available and more popular than ever before—although changed.

Today these southern countries field possibly 80 percent of the entire continent's hunting safaris. Add Tanzania, Botswana, and Zambia (all open at this writing), and I'm sure we are well over 90 percent. But we're missing some of Africa's most important trophies, found only in very specific areas. During most of my hunting career Central African Republic has been the standard destination for bongo and giant eland. She has not been without her challenges. In the north and east, organized poaching from Sudan and Chad has decimated many areas once rich with game. The C.A.R. has also had some political instabilities that have never exactly closed hunting but have made safaris unsafe now and again. Between 1992 and 1997 I made four safaris into the C.A.R. and enjoyed them all, finding the country wild and unspoiled, difficult and fascinating. Just twenty years ago neighboring Cameroon was a quiet backwater to the C.A.R., a bit less expensive to hunt but generally considered less desirable in both quantity and quality of game.

Today this situation has pretty much reversed. Cameroon, though incredibly corrupt, is more stable, and outfitters have been better able to secure and protect their hunting areas. There remain good areas and outfitters in the C.A.R., but today Cameroon has more good areas and outfitters, and produces more Derby eland and bongo.

Among all of Africa's hunting countries, however, the one that cannot be replaced is Ethiopia. The mountain nyala ranks high on anyone's list of Africa's greatest trophies, and unlike almost any other great prize you can think of, the mountain nyala exists only in Ethiopia's high country. Ethiopia is a bit different from the rest of the African continent. Until his overthrow by communists in the late 1970s, Emperor Haile Selassie could boast royal lineage far beyond any European monarch, all the way back to the Queen of Sheba. As a country Ethiopia was xenophobic, almost unknown to outsiders from Biblical times to 1900. So it was that *Tragelaphus buxtoni*, named after Ivor Buxton, became one of the last large mammals to be identified by western zoologists.

A few nyala were taken in the 1920s, mostly by British adventurers. This window was closed during the pre-World War II Italian invasion and occupation. After the war a couple of enterprising outfitters,

Colonel Negussie's camp, a neat collection of tents in a sheltered valley, proudly flies his Ethiopian flag. Oh, my, did it get cold at night!

American expatriate Ted Shatto and, a few years later, Hungarian Tomas Mattanovich, began offering Ethiopian safaris in the modern sense. The standard drill was to arrive in Addis Ababa and present yourself to the Emperor's court. Depending on affairs of state, it usually took several days of cooling one's heels to get an audience and get the permit issued.

During the revolutions—plural because a brutal Marxist regime ended the dynasty and then, in time and in turn, was overthrown—Ethiopia was closed altogether. But it was during the communist reign that a consistent hunting program was established and an Ethiopian hunting safari could be booked with firm dates and permits. Of course, Ethiopia was subject to periodic closure—due to revolution or seeming whim—and when she reopened, her hunting had not improved . . .

My buddy Joe Bishop hunted in Ethiopia in the mid-1980s with Colonel Negussie Eshete. A colonel of paratroops under Haile Selassie, Negussie did some jail time when the communists came to power, and started outfitting when the dust settled. Joe had been very happy with the good colonel, but not happy at all with his mountain nyala. Urged by his hunting partner, he'd made a too-quick decision to shoot, and

Joe Bishop on the edge of an almost impenetrable kaska *thicket. Called "heather," this stuff blankets the higher slopes on much of Ethiopia's mountains. At its climax stage, it is impossible to glass into, so you must catch nyala crossing more open areas.*

wanted to try again. Of course, he had to wait through a temporary closure, and then he had to get a date—so it was March 1993 before Joe and I hunted Ethiopia together, his second time and my first.

We had a great safari, but it seemed obvious to me that mountain nyala hunting was in trouble. Negussie's famous Mount Kakka area was being heavily poached, and habitat destruction was at least as severe. The lower slopes of the mountains were being denuded for firewood, leaving only isolated heather-covered peaks as islands of mountain nyala habitat. We saw plenty of mountain nyala and we both took bulls, though neither was the size we wanted. Negussie admitted that this area was deteriorating fast, and even then he told us he was trying to get an area adjacent to the Bale National Park, a place that had never been hunted and had lots of nyala, including big bulls. And then Ethiopia closed hunting yet again, ostensibly so they could do game counts and allocate areas.

It took five years, and perhaps there was some legitimacy in the closure. When hunting reopened, exclusive concessions were allocated for the first time, and firm quotas, minimum legal sizes, and a couple of strange wrinkles were added. Upon the reopening, Negussie got his new area, along with a quota of five mountain nyala per year. Once again it took us a year or so to get a date, but in March 2000 we knew that Negussie was a hundred percent successful on mountain nyala in the new area and had taken some very fine bulls.

In the planning phase of the new setup, mountain nyala had always been the top priority, and the new regulations required a hunt of at least twenty-one days to obtain a license (now $5,000 U.S., up front, no refunds). Bert Klineburger, Negussie's longtime friend and agent, assured us we'd have our mountain nyala in about a week, so we might as well go on to the Danakil area and hunt some other game. This sounded fine until we understood the latest fine print: In twenty-one days we could hunt just one area and only one of the "Class A" animals, a short list comprised of mountain nyala, buffalo, lion, and elephant (which was closed). In twenty-four days we could hunt two on the list and hunt two different areas. Three more days wouldn't have cost us all that much in the grand scheme of things, but we were just plain offended by this last-minute change in the rules. So we opted to hunt the mountains

Mountain nyala are most active during early morning and late afternoon, but once you're up the mountain you're there for the day. I filled a number of notebooks during the long midday hours!

only, understanding that the game there is very limited, so if we were successful we'd have little option but to go home early. This decision was probably the single most stupid mistake I have ever made in planning a hunt . . .

The Addis Hilton had been just fine. The newly opened Sheraton was downright spectacular, almost certainly the finest hotel on the African continent. Joe and I got over our jet lag in regal splendor, and at a reasonable hour the next day Negussie, Joe, and I took a commercial flight to Goba, gateway to the Bale National Park. Negussie's son, Danny, and professional hunter Sissai Shewemene met us at the airport on a sunny early afternoon, but it was getting dark and cold by the time we crossed the park, drove up a gentle valley, and pulled into Negussie's tent camp, replete with Ethiopian flag.

Mountain nyala hunting is considerably different from any other African safari I have experienced. The mountains are covered with tall, dense *kaska*, a heatherlike plant that provides an almost impenetrable haven for mountain nyala and the few other mountain species: Menelik bushbuck, reedbuck (both Chanler mountain and Abyssinian bohor), some wonderfully toothed warthog, and huge hyena. You will not glass up nyala—or anything else—in this stuff, but it is a glassing hunt because the nyala come out to feed in lower vegetation and occasionally cross openings. Depending on where you are, elevation can be moderate, perhaps seven or eight thousand feet, or extreme, up to twelve thousand. Elevation doesn't seem to make much difference in Ethiopia, partly because the thick vegetation—much like Nepal's terai forest—almost certainly yields tons of oxygen, and also (and probably more important) because, thank God, there are tough little Ethiopian ponies to help get you up there with the nyala!

Joe and I always play the "you-shoot-first" game. He is more patient than I am and usually wins, meaning that I usually shoot first. Given a whole bunch of luck, first can be very good—but on the other hand, the second shooter gets to take a look at the first shooter's animal and also at the reactions of the guides and trackers. When you go first, it's much more difficult to be certain that you really should shoot! Of course, I learned a long time ago that with Joe's luck it doesn't much matter whether I shoot first or not. Our bongo hunt in '97 was a glaring

Our horses tethered in a high saddle. Ethiopia offers one of few horseback hunts in Africa. These sturdy little ponies were a great blessing for covering ground, but, like all horseback hunting, sooner or later you must tie them up and do the rest on foot.

Joe Bishop took this exceptional Abyssinian bohor reedbuck. There is relatively little other game in Ethiopia's high mountain nyala country: a few Menelik bushbuck, klipspringer, reedbuck, and some huge warthogs and hyenas.

exception in that I got a huge bongo and he got nothing. Most of the time it doesn't matter who shoots first. Joe will get the larger trophy, and I learned to accept that a long time ago.

This time he won the game once again, and I would be first up for mountain nyala. This is an animal that Negussie hunts very intelligently, sending out spotters like the spokes of a wheel to occupy as many vantage points as possible while keeping his hunter or hunters in a central location, able to glass but also able to respond. We left camp long before dawn, eventually reaching a high ridge just after daylight. It wasn't long before we learned that this area was indeed different. We didn't see a lot of mountain nyala, but then you never do. We did see two or three bulls, relatively close and undisturbed, that were better than any mountain nyala either Joe or I had ever seen. And nobody was excited about them!

Joe won the game very early in the hunt. We were sitting in a rockpile glassing when tracker Dereby Bulcha signaled from a distant

43

ridge. Dereby is an old friend from our previous hunt and one of the best I have ever seen at spotting game. If he said he had a good bull, it was a good bull.

Sissai worked me up a tall ridge, circling to keep the wind right, and we were met by Dereby short of the crest. Sissai is fluent in English, but he and Dereby conferred briefly in Amharic, spoken nowhere else in the world. Pretty much in the dark, I followed them up over the top, and Sissai set up the sticks overlooking a shoulder-high (and thus fairly low) pocket of heather. I sort of understood that Dereby had watched a good bull go into this cover, and since it was late morning he was sure the bull was bedded and quite close. So Sissai and I waited, ready, while Dereby and another tracker made a loop well below the pocket, hoping to push the bull into the clear in front of us.

My guess is this might have worked but wasn't necessary. I felt a puff of breeze on the back of my neck, and Sissai instantly whispered to be ready. The bull was barely sixty yards away when he stood, but only his horns were visible above the heather. I followed with the rifle while we studied those great horns. The headgear was big and beautifully shaped, a fine mountain nyala for today, well into the thirties with a lovely lyre shape. But should I shoot, or wait and see what else this new area had to offer? Sissai felt I should shoot if I got the chance, and I agreed.

So I stood on the sticks while the bull, catching our full wind, bounded a few steps and then stopped. During the movement part of his back came up above the *kaska*, but when he stopped only his horns showed. Then he stopped again across the little bench in a place where the ground sloped upward maybe a hundred and fifty yards off. I could see only a hint of backline, but his neck was absolutely clear. I hate the neck shot, but I had the wonderfully accurate 8mm and I was very steady on stout sticks. I held central on the neck a bit behind the ear, then allowed an inch for the rise of the bullet's trajectory, and fired. He dropped perfectly to the shot, but it took us a long time to find him in that thick stuff, and even longer to get him to a clear spot where we could take pictures and bring our horses in to pack him.

Joe Bishop and professional hunter Sissai Shewemene set up for a mountain nyala drive. This one didn't work, but when a bull is glassed going into heather it can occasionally be pushed through a saddle or natural funnel.

Negussie, father and son, and Sissai were happy with him. I was happy with him, and Joe was delighted for me. Now, of course, he could get serious, and we all understood that my mountain nyala was just fine, but bigger bulls were around. We had a couple of slow days and a couple of drives that just didn't work, and at night and in the early mornings we darn near froze to death as temperatures plummeted well below freezing.

Even back in 1993 Negussie was getting older and having trouble with his eyes. This was not better in 2000, but with Danny and Sissai and great trackers to do the tough hunting, this was not a problem. As an outfitter, Colonel Negussie is second to none, and in Ethiopia the local people treat him like royalty, sharing information more freely and more truthfully than I have seen elsewhere in Africa. A local herdsman told us of a really big bull, so early one morning we worked our way in that direction.

He was on a high ridge just in front of us at daybreak, but it was too early and too soon: We were still on horseback, so we were caught flat-footed with no way to get around the wind. Although Sissai tried, the bull spooked and ran down into a deep, brushy canyon. We got only a glimpse, but it was enough. This was clearly a magnificent bull.

Sissai sent the trackers around a big ridge, hoping to bring him back to us. We climbed down through a patch of trees and set up on a lip overlooking a relatively open little valley, and had just reached the good vantage point when the bull appeared on the far ridge, not much more than two hundred yards away. Joe got on the sticks quickly but didn't quite get the shot off before the bull, no doubt pressed by our trackers, dropped off the lip and trotted across the valley in front of us, angling closer with every step. He was huge, heavy-bodied and heavy-horned, the kind of mountain nyala that everyone knew hadn't existed for at least a quarter-century. And he was ours. He stopped directly across from us at 150 yards—and then the rising sun peeked over the ridge behind him, full into Joe's riflescope. I understood almost immediately that he was seeing nothing but bright lights, so I took my hat and tried to shade the scope, but it was too late and there was nothing to be done. The moment was fleeting. In seconds the bull was trotting off again, and only in the last instant did Joe ever have him in the scope.

I was crushed. Sissai was beside himself. Joe was stoic and calm. On the other hand, Joe had never really seen the horns, and now it seemed most unlikely that he ever would.

Danny, Sissai, and the old colonel thought differently. The herdsman reported seeing this bull regularly, and Negussie thought he had seen him from a distance on a previous safari. It seems that mountain nyala are relatively territorial, at least when undisturbed. We had disturbed this guy, but the locals still expected that he might water at a spring down below where we had seen him, and in the morning we might catch him working his way back up.

We were there at the first blush of dawn, in a position that changed the angle a bit to preclude looking into the sun. My assumption was that we would see nothing. I have no idea what Sissai and Danny and Dereby and the rest of our crew really thought, and as it turned out, there wasn't time to think about it. Joe looked down at the base of the valley and said calmly, "Is that him?"

A huge nyala bull stood on a low rise well below us, and remained standing, looking up into the open hollow, until Joe's 7mm magnum

This is the kind of mountain nyala I had dreamed of. There were better bulls around, but I didn't know that yet, and I shot too quickly.

caught him full in the chest. We found him just a few yards down the slope, got him in the open, and Danny sent for the old man, who had remained in camp because of his eye trouble. It took him a couple of hours, but Colonel Negussie came up with dark glasses, a cowboy hat, and a huge grin as he agreed with his team: "They tell me this is a 'mountain nyala of before,' and they are right. Nothing like this has been seen for many years."

Perhaps not, in 2000. But since then a couple of larger mountain nyala have been taken. Perhaps more important, all of Ethiopia's small handful of hunting outfitters have secured, and are protecting, new hunting areas for mountain nyala. At this writing in 2006, mountain nyala hunting is actually better than it has been since Ivor Buxton hunted them in another age.

Can this last? With limited quotas and the habitat improvement and protection that the high license fees bring, yes, it can. A better question is, will it? I don't know. Ethiopia's hunting industry is tiny, and (except for those involved) of no consequence and no economic impact for a country so large. It is unknown whether mountain nyala hunting will continue, but despite its tiny scale, it is clear that this magnificent creature's best hope for survival is for regulated hunting to continue. I hope it does.

As for the rest of our safari, we dug around for reedbuck and warthog for a few days and then had little choice but to call it a total success and return to Addis Ababa. We were finished in just ten days, leaving the bulk of our three-week safari and paid-for days on the table. We did get one small bonus. Although Negussie phoned ahead, the Sheraton messed up our reservations. So, while we waited a couple days to get flights back home, they put us in the presidential suite. Africa was never, ever, like that!

I hope that by now I have given up on writing about Africa in gloom-and-doom terms. Anyone who does should quickly be reminded that: 1) Safaris in southern Africa are far more affordable than ever before, and 2) thanks entirely to the safari industry and the worldwide hunting market, there is more game in the southern African countries than any of us could have imagined just thirty years ago. In what remains of wild Africa, on the other hand, it is far more difficult to find positive examples. The mountain nyala as it stands today, in late 2006, is one of them. Hunting is more productive than it has ever been, and there are more 'mountain nyala of before' every year. This means they are increasing, but only where they are hunted and protected with equal care and bulls are allowed to reach full maturity. If common sense prevails, this magnificent animal has a chance. If hunting is closed, as is currently threatened, we could lose Africa's greatest trophy forever.

Limpopo to Ruaha

Honest, I didn't want to go. It was a great deal and a great hunt, but in my business you can grow old and tired much too quickly if you chase all the good deals. But I couldn't get out of it because they insisted I go. "It" was a September hunt in the western Selous, Peter Swanepoel and Doug Scandrol's country on the Great Ruaha. "They" were Remington's Art Wheaton and Nosler's Chub Eastman, along with my masters at the magazines I write for. The fact that I genuinely tried not to go seemed just as strange to me as to these worthies. After all, for at least the first twenty years of my career I would have danced jigs if any gun company invited me to Africa. This was the first time this had happened—and I didn't want to go. I'm sure everyone thought I'd gone mad.

I thought I had a pretty good case. It had been a busy year. Joe Bishop and I had hunted mountain nyala in Ethiopia in March, and in June Houstonian Riecke Baughman and I had done a quick, fun, and totally pressure-free hunt in South Africa with Johan Potgieter. We started in the open grasslands south of Johannesburg, typical Orange Free State terrain, and then went up north to the thick thornbush of the Limpopo drainage. I shot a nice Cape eland with the reintroduced .375 Weatherby and, even better (at least to me), took an extremely average kudu with a 1930-vintage left-hand-converted Springfield by Philadelphia riflesmith R. F. Sedgely, complete with original peep sight. I felt just like Papa Hemingway!

Both Riecke and I had taken everything we wanted and had a few days left over, so we finished that hunt with several days in Kruger

Professional hunters Rex Amm and Geoff Broom on the veranda of Rex's lodge in the ridges above Grahamstown. We glassed numerous beautiful bushbuck rams from this pleasant spot!

Park. Although I've often recommended starting or finishing a hunt in one of the great parks, it's actually something I had never done. This is proof positive of the lack of pressure we were under. So when the chance (or, perhaps better put, directive) to go on the Remington hunt came along, I'd already had my Africa fix for the year.

I'd spent quite a lot of time in Africa that year, although it wouldn't seem like much a few years later. My old friend Geoff Broom wanted my assistance in writing his memoir, so I'd started the trip with a week down at Geoff's beautiful home at Kenton-On-Sea, north of Port Elizabeth. We worked several hours every day, me grinding away on the laptop while Geoff spun his stories, and for breaks we walked along the rugged coastline.

We'd also taken a longer break to go inland to Rex Amm's place near Grahamstown. One of the things I hadn't done, but wanted badly to do, was to take one of those wonderful black Cape bushbuck, and Geoff figured Rex Amm was the guy to help. He had a lovely farm that truly was stiff with bushbuck. We only hunted one afternoon and saw several nice rams. Rex's lodge sat on a tall ridge overlooking a good-size lake, and we actually glassed bushbuck from the veranda. Late in the afternoon, using Rex's .243, I stalked a beautiful ram along the lakeshore, and later had him life-size mounted.

So, while I wasn't crazy enough to eschew going to Tanzania, I tried real hard to insist that this was a wonderful opportunity for someone who hadn't yet had a chance at Africa. Nothing doing. The primary hosts were Art Wheaton and Sean Dwyer, who had not been to Africa. Among other toys, they had the full suite of Remington Ultra Magnums: 7mm, .300, .338, and .375. Two, the 7mm and .375, were making their debut. They felt it would be better if someone with African experience raised the curtain. My old buddy Chub Eastman wasn't helping much—he wanted me to go. Maybe (though it would be inexplicable) nobody else at *Petersen's Hunting* or *Guns & Ammo* wanted to go, because my editors agreed: I was going.

Sigh (but not too loudly). I'd tried, and now I had to make the best of it. Remington sent me left-handed rifles in the .338 and .375 Remington Ultra Mags—a bit redundant and downright painful off the bench—but both rifles shot extremely well. I had almost gotten past my mental blocks to the point where I was looking forward to this trip when, en route, the roof fell in.

It started with just a little fog at our San Luis Obispo airport. We get a lot of what we call "tule fog," and I've seen it a lot worse. I wasn't worried because I had plenty of time to catch my connection at LAX. That extra time dwindled away, however, and I got to LAX just in time to have the gate for my Amsterdam flight slammed shut in my face. Now we had trouble. I called Barbara Wollbrink, the travel agent who had arranged this, er, mess (not that she caused the fog). Fortunately she is extremely competent and started to work her magic. At this point it was late morning, too late to make any European connections to Dar es Salaam. Twelve hours later I left on a red eye to Atlanta. The next morning I caught a South African Airways flight to Johannesburg. Looking like a reject from *Night of the Living Dead,* I checked into the transit hotel at the Jo'burg airport and six hours later flew north to Dar es Salaam. Surprisingly, I was only a day behind the rest of the crew, and there was actually someone there to meet me with an airplane standing by.

After the previous three days in airports and airplanes, I'd have preferred to go to a hotel and chill out. For at least a week. But I took comfort in the fact that the crew—Sean, Art, Chub, and Bob Maschmedt—would be out hunting, so at least I'd have a quiet camp to myself and could sleep the day away. Right. Art Wheaton and PH Cliff Walker were at the strip to meet me, and they were ready to go hunting. Brain-dead, I changed clothes at the strip, checked sights on the rifles, and prepared to go through the motions of hunting. It was going to be a very long day.

I don't remember much of it. I know at one point we were stopped in a little donga while Art and Cliff stalked a zebra. I was sitting on the ground, dozing, when for some altogether unknown reason I reached out and ran a long grass stem through my fingers. The sharp edge cut my right index finger almost to the bone. At least that woke me up! I think Art might have shot a zebra there—at least I have photos of it!

At the hottest part of the day we saw a buffalo herd moving at the limit of our vision, maybe three hundred yards away. This was what I'd been dreading. Now I had to walk. Thankfully we followed the herd for just a short distance before the wind swung around and the tracks ahead of us showed the animals were running. I'm sure we could have eventually closed with them, but I didn't yet understand how plentiful buffalo were in this area. Cliff suggested we wave off, something I couldn't politically suggest but was more than happy to agree with! We didn't see a whole lot more, and suddenly it was that golden time of late afternoon when the air is cooling and the shadows are long. I'd made it through the day, and all I had to do was get back to camp and crash.

We came out of some thick woods, and ahead of us stretched a broad dambo, bright green with new grass. Scattered in the green, like huge peppercorns on a vast pool table, was a great herd of Cape buffalo. This was the moment I'd dreaded all day long. I was in no shape to hunt buffalo, so in preparation for such an event I'd played "you shoot first" with Art all day long. I don't think he's really better at this game than I am, but he had all of his mental faculties and I did not. His story was that he'd never seen a buffalo shot, so he'd rather play second fiddle. I didn't believe that; I knew he was playing the host and expected me to

Geoff Broom with my beautiful, almost black Cape bushbuck, taken at Rex Amm's place while we were "working" on Geoff's autobiography, A Life on Safari.

play the grateful outdoor writer. Truly, I was grateful . . . but I was in no shape to shoot a buffalo.

Well, maybe I was after all. It was pretty clear that I was losing the argument, so I took the loss with grace, grabbed the .375, and ran after Cliff Walker. In the Selous Reserve legal shooting hours end at sunset, and we were scant minutes away. We jogged a couple hundred yards, reducing the distance by a third, then duckwalked the rest of the way, using a couple of big termite mounds for cover. We pulled in behind the last mound, breathed hard for a moment, and then Cliff peered around. The herd was extremely spread out, with a couple of the cows just fifty yards away. These we needed to ignore because a spectacular bull was just beyond them, feeding next to a small bush. At this point it was much too late to switch places with Art, and since I'd genuinely tried to get him to shoot first, I felt just fine. I'd hunted the Selous before, twice before to be precise, and I'd never seen a bull this good.

I crawled forward around the termite mound to clear some brush, remembering to look for mambas and such things along the way. There was

Art Wheaton with a really spectacular warthog. Much of the plains game in Selous is average in trophy quality, but every time I've been there I've seen some really good warthogs.

a little open furrow a third of the way up the mound, so I crawled into that and lay prone, wrapping my arm in a hasty sling. The shot was a bit beyond a hundred yards—perhaps beyond the sensible limit for buffalo—but this wasn't just any buffalo.

He took a couple of steps forward, then stood quartering just slightly to me. I put the cross hairs slightly forward on his shoulder, fired, and saw the bullet hit where it should have. No matter. The bull was off with the herd, with Cliff and me running hard to keep him in sight in the gathering dusk. He kept pace with his buddies for fifty yards, then slowed. I shot him again from behind, caught up when he stopped, and dropped him with a solid in the spine. He was really a fine buffalo about forty-two inches wide, a monster for the Selous and a great buffalo for anywhere. Honest, Art, I tried to give him to you! I fell asleep long before we reached Swanepoel & Scandrol's camp on the Great Ruaha River, managed to come alive long enough for dinner, and then was out for the count.

We were a most eclectic group. The professional hunters were Peter Swanepoel himself, American PH Marshall Smalling, and young Zimbabwean Cliff Walker. The hunters were Art Wheaton and Sean Dwyer, on their first safari and looking for a little bit of everything; veteran hunter Bob Maschmedt, who wanted a leopard most of all and cared about little else; and me and Chub Eastman. I had hunted in the Selous twice before, so I was happy to pretty much take things as they came and concentrate on buffalo. Likewise Chub, except that he had a small problem to overcome. A former Marine sniper and one of the mainstays in our industry, Chub hasn't yet accepted the limitations of middle age. Two weeks before the hunt he'd had to lay down his Harley to avoid being hit, and as a result one leg was in a cast from toe to crotch.

Maschmedt got his leopard right off the bat. Sean took a beautiful sable, and Art got some lion baits out that were never hit. I can't exactly explain that. The Selous is probably not the place for lion with the very best manes, but in my experience there are usually some lion around. We went the entire hunt without ever seeing fresh lion spoor in the block, and it certainly wasn't for lack of prey. At this particular time, September, the area was sort of OK for plains game. There were enough zebra, Lichtenstein hartebeest, and impala; quite a few reedbuck and warthog; and just a few

Art Wheaton's second buffalo was another exceptional bull, about 42 inches wide with a very good shape. This was late in the hunt, and we looked at an awful lot of buffalo before we found this one.

sable. Unlike other Selous blocks I've hunted, at this particular time there were almost no eland or kudu, and few Nyasa wildebeest. But, Lord, I have never, ever seen such a concentration of buffalo!

We could track buffalo if we wished, and for sure Cliff and his team knew how, but this was one of the very few places I have ever been where it usually wasn't necessary to track buffalo. All we needed was a bit of patience, and in the course of a hunting day we would run into two or three herds. Art's first buffalo was taken from a herd spotted from the truck at midmorning, just crossing a ridge at the limit of our vision. I hung back while Cliff and Art maneuvered on them for an hour or so. Eventually they caught a good bull crossing a short grass dambo, and Art shot him well and got him down with no problems.

There were so many buffalo around that this tactic worked well even for Chub—but first he had to prove himself. With Marshall at the wheel and Chub in the back, they came around an antheap and found themselves nose to grill with a lone buffalo bull. Without hesitation the bull lowered his head and charged. Sergeant Eastman, USMC, retained enough presence of mind to reach down, unzip his gun case, unlimber his .375 Ultra Mag, chamber a round, and drop the bull with a shot over the horns and down through the spine.

The bull's nose came to rest under the truck, and from that moment Eastman could do no wrong. This particular buffalo had a festering hip wound, and since it had been shot out of necessity, it wasn't put on his license. Come to think of it, neither were a couple more buffalo needed for rations at the game-guard station. The system they worked out was that Marshall would simply drive until a buffalo herd—or dust and birds indicating its presence—was spotted. After ensuring the wind was right, Marshall would ease the vehicle as close as he dared. Then, with great hilarity, the trackers would make a fireman's carry and literally manhandle Eastman within range of the herd. I went along a couple of times to watch the fun, and it was obvious that everyone was getting a kick out of it. Especially Chub.

Me, well, I sort of took things as they came, spending most of my time with Art and Cliff but occasionally going out with Chub and Marshall. My only specific goal was to take something with each of the four Ultra Mags. In the game-rich Selous this was not an especially tall order. Impala and warthog fell to Art Wheaton's 7mm RUM, and his warthog was a real monster, one of the best I've ever seen. I used his .300 RUM to take a fine zebra stallion. Even though the Selous is very far south, the zebra there have stark black and white skins, no shadow stripes, and are especially beautiful. Art used the .300 on his zebra and hartebeest, and also on a big Nyasa wildebeest. I didn't get a chance at a wildebeest, but I used the left-handed .338 RUM to take a hartebeest.

I also used the .338 to take a buffalo. I think this came out of a campfire discussion during which I opined that a 250-grain .338, because of its higher sectional density, would out-penetrate a 300-grain .375 and thus, at least under ideal conditions, would be perfectly acceptable for buffalo. A couple of days later we found ourselves glassing a herd feeding up an open dambo, and I had the .338 RUM in my hands. We closed to a bit over a hundred yards, hardly a close shot on a buffalo, and I got extra-steady in the fork of a tree. He stopped broadside a bit below me, and I could visualize the tricky high-shoulder/spine shot perfectly. I also figured there was plenty of open ground around him and no other buffalo especially close. If I blew it, surely I'd be able to get another Swift A-Frame into him—maybe two or three.

At the shot he dropped like a rock and never made the slightest wiggle. Cliff and I approached from behind and I paid the mandatory insurance, but that bull was as dead as any dead buffalo can be. I don't recommend dropping below .375 for buffalo hunting, but that's probably because you have to start somewhere, and also because .375 is the legal minimum in most areas. That experience proved to me once again that despite all campfire arguments, shot placement and bullet performance are more important than caliber.

We were all pulling for Art to get the lion he wanted so badly, but before you can get a lion you generally need to get one on a bait, and before that happens you must at least find tracks. This never happened, but as a consolation prize Art took a huge crocodile just a half-mile downriver from camp. Cliff knew this croc, a real bruiser that generally sunned on a little bank on the far side of the river. Cliff had a couple of blinds set up, depending on the croc's exact position. During the course of the hunt they made several stalks, but this croc seemed to have a sixth sense: Every time they approached, he slipped silently into the fast-flowing river.

One day, though, he made a mistake. Ignoring the blinds and the established routes, Cliff and Art crawled in behind some brush and Art made a spectacular shot from one side of the Ruaha to the other, anchoring the croc with a perfect spine shot with a little 140-grain Nosler Partition from the 7mm RUM. The recovery was even more interesting, with Cliff partly wading, partly rock-skipping, and partly swimming across the crocodile-laden river so he could get a rope on the prehistoric creature and we could pull it to our shore. At that point I had never taken a crocodile and had very little interest in this or any other reptile. Watching Art made me appreciate, for the first time, the difficulty in taking a crocodile: not only getting the shot but also the absolutely precise shot placement required to anchor the beast and prevent it from getting into the water and escaping. Several more years passed before I had a chance to take a crocodile for myself, but after I saw Art's, I knew I'd have to do that someday.

Lichtenstein hartebeest were the most common antelope in the area at this time. I used the .338 Remington Ultra Mag to take this bull.

Other than the lion he couldn't have, the animal Art wanted most was a really good buffalo, like the one I shot so easily on the first day. His first buffalo was a beauty, as perfectly shaped as any buff I've seen, but it wasn't a big boy. So we kept looking, and in this area at this time we turned down a lot of buffalo, which is at least half the fun. Finally Cliff found what we were looking for, a heavy-bossed bull that was clearly over forty inches wide. The herd was feeding up a narrow, open valley, and the wind was perfect. All we had to do was creep along the brushy fringe until we were opposite the bull and take the shot. But just as Cliff got Art lined up, the herd bunched and lay down, with the big bull hopelessly covered up by a press of cows.

It wasn't late in the morning, and the buffalo were in the wide-open, a hot sun gleaming on black hides. It seemed reasonable that they wouldn't stay there long, so we lay on a low termite mound for maybe a half-hour before the buffalo began to stir. When they got up, the bull presented himself nicely and Art hammered him with a 300-grain Swift. The herd vanished in a cloud of dust, but the bull was left behind, already down in the open when the dust settled.

Rarely have I seen a buffalo hunt progress so perfectly, and our last hunt on the last day was no exception. It was my turn, and we decided I'd take a final buffalo with Art's .375 RUM, the first example of a new dangerous-game version of the Model 700. This was one of the few mornings when we didn't run into buffalo, so about 10 A.M. we found where a big herd had crossed in front of us and decided to follow. The spoor was fresh enough that we expected to be on them in a half-hour or so. That came and went, as did another half-hour, and another. So much for an easy last day, but by now we were committed.

We caught them shortly after noon. The herd was huge, with clumps of buffalo feeding in an open valley and many more on a wooded ridge to the right. We never even saw the buffalo up on the ridge; it was just too thick there. Down in the valley were several young bulls but just one fully mature, hard-bossed bull. What the heck, it was the last day.

We crawled from one tree to another, finally pitching up maybe 130 yards from this bull. There were a lot of buffalo between him and us, so this was as close as we were going to get. I took a rest against a stout tree and waited for him to step out from behind another tree. While I waited, the whole herd lay down one by one, clump by clump—including our bull. The clumps of buffalo in the valley were clustered around a few shady trees, and we could see a few buffalo bedded up in the thick tree line to our right. The wind was just fine, but we were completely stuck.

Art was a few dozen yards behind with the trackers, a bad deal for him, but at least he was in good shade. Cliff and I were as far forward as we could get, unable to move and with just one sparsely leafed tree above us. The herd had walked far that morning, and now they were extremely comfortable. We lay and sweated for almost four hours before the first buffalo began to move.

Unfortunately, this wasn't our buffalo, or even any of the buffalo in the valley. At about four o'clock several buffalo in the tree line started to feed toward us. At first they were nearly a hundred yards away, no problem. But that distance was cut in half before the buffalo in the valley began to move, clump by clump. Now we had buffalo on our right at just twenty-five yards, and still our bull was bedded tight. Leading the group on the right was a young calf, momma buff right at her heels. Cliff was watching them, and I saw him slowly snake his double .577 into firing position.

I had long since eased into a cross-leg sitting position, rifle rested over my knees with a tight sling already adjusted. My bull was up now, but he was behind his shade tree. I snuck one last glance over my right shoulder. The little calf wasn't ten yards from Cliff, the big cow just a couple of yards farther off. Cliff was sitting up as well, his cannon held casually but the barrels tracking that cow. The right flank was well covered, but I was on my own with the bull—and I needed to do something fast because as soon as the calf winded us, there would be a huge explosion.

Leaving that problem to Cliff, I raised the rifle. The bull's head and neck were clear, his shoulder and chest still behind the tree. Then he stepped out and stood broadside. It was too far for fancy, but I'd better get it right. The vertical cross hair bisected the foreleg; the horizontal wire was just a bit lower than halfway up the body. The bull took the bullet hard, but immediately kicked into high gear and was lost in a surging mass of buffalo. I wish I'd seen what happened on the right, but now there was a sea of outbound buffalo over there as well.

The trackers came up fast, and we all ran after the disappearing herd, hoping to catch sight of my bull. We didn't, but we found him just over the ridge, standing in a grassy korongo. I shot him again, and once more, and he was down. The sun was just above the horizon by the time we got the Land Cruiser to him. The cool box was as welcome as the evening breeze, and I reckoned it a perfect way to end a good safari. I'm afraid I had a better last day than Art Wheaton, but after all, it was he who had insisted I come along. I'm glad he did!

Ennedi and Beyond

One of the few regrets in my hunting career is that I missed the great Sahara safaris of the postwar period. One of the best accounts is Roger Fawcett's "Sweet Sahara Safari," included in Peter Barrett's wonderful collection, *A Treasury of African Hunting.* The desert of what is now Chad was also the scene of one of Jack O'Connor's early African experiences, with Elgin Gates in the 1950s, a bit after I was born. In those days Ubangi-Shari was a huge colony encompassing both Chad and the C.A.R. A safari could begin in N'Djamena and travel up to the old French Foreign Legion outpost at Oum Chalouba, jumping-off point for hunting scimitar oryx and addax on the southern fringes of the great desert.

Once the desert antelopes were secured, the safari could travel on northwest to the Ennedi Mountains to hunt aoudad, or south to the Aouk or Aoukele River to hunt giant eland, lion, and big savanna elephant—or, time permitting, all the way south into the great forest for bongo and forest elephant. Or, in those carefree days of long safaris, all of the above! Most of the hunters who pursued the desert game are gone now, but I knew a few of them and all spoke wistfully of the sweet Sahara safari that is now part of history.

The beginning of the end came in 1977, when civil war brought to an abrupt end the last safari season in old Chad. The real end came a few years later. The Libyans invaded a weakened and divided Chad. Several more bitter years passed before the Chad forces, unconventionally equipped with TOW missiles on Land Cruisers, swept down off the central plateau and destroyed the Libyans' heavy armor. Burned-out Russian tanks, perfectly preserved in the dry desert air, still litter Chad, but the great herds of addax and oryx are gone. During the Libyan occupation they were machine-gunned from helicopter gunships, scooped up by convoys of following refrigerator trucks, and packed north to Libya. This was long known, with opinion on the true status of addax and oryx varying from seriously endangered to actually extinct in the wild. What was not known was the status of Chad's other wildlife, once extensive in both numbers and variety. But we with obsessive interest in Africa and her wildlife had long written Chad off the list of potential hunting countries.

Alain Lefol never did. As a young man fresh from France, he enjoyed one short season in Chad in 1977 and never forgot it. During the next twenty years he hunted in Zimbabwe, Tanzania, and the southern half of old Ubangi-Shari, the C.A.R., but he always hoped that someday he could again operate in Chad. Throughout multiple civil wars he kept in contact with both Chadean officials and French expatriates, and in 1998 he knew he had found viable pockets of game and believed he had cut through all the red tape. Not quite. The first couple of hunters cooled their heels in N'Djamena without permits ever being issued. Lefol didn't give up, nor did a handful of equally crazy clients who believed in him. In 1999 he fielded a couple of genuine safaris that took, among other things, very good aoudad and western greater kudu. The 2000 season was almost normal, with several safaris hunting in the Ennedi Mountains for aoudad, Dar-Sila for western greater kudu, or the Aoukele River country for korrigum and other game. On a longer safari, all three areas could be hunted. It seemed true that most of the herd animals once plentiful in Chad—Derby eland, western hartebeest, buffalo—were gone. But it was not true that there was no wildlife, or that the situation was hopeless.

The concept of being first in a new area or a newly reopened one sounds wonderfully and romantically adventurous. Unfortunately, there are also great risks—if not physical, then involving great danger of disappointment and financial consequences. I greatly admire my old friend Irvin Barnhart and the others who cooled their heels in N'Djamena the first time and yet had the perseverance and faith to try it again. Me, I figured out a long time ago that I couldn't afford to be first! So it was that by the time Chris Kinsey and I hunted there in early 2001, Chad was a well-established and

The scenery in northern Chad is fantastic. It's just on the edge of the Sahara, with incredible rock formations jutting up from the sand.

smooth operation—or at least as smooth as it was going to get. Chris, a bit younger than I, is at least as obsessed with Africa as I am, but running the family business limits him to one safari per year. The good news is that it's a good business and his safaris are generally darned ambitious. He has done as much in Africa as anyone I know, and much more than most. He's also a great guy and good hunter. We had a wonderful time, but Chad isn't for everyone—if, in fact, it is ever hunted again.

The flight from Paris to N'Djamena landed first in Brazzaville (you are correct in thinking that was not the direct route), where our gun cases were off-loaded. Being gunless on a buffalo hunt isn't a big deal; there's usually a tired old .375 around that will get the job done. Gunless in sheep country, which the Ennedi Mountains definitely are, is not a good deal. So we waited a couple of days, driving down to Lake Chad to shoot some ducks. Alain's short-barreled Benelli autoloaders, though fine for leopard and cobras, probably weren't perfect duck guns. But we shot a few ducks and laughed at each other while we waded around in the muck. And I was totally shocked when, on the second day and the next flight, our guns turned up just fine.

We flew in to a gravel strip just south of the Ennedi Mountains, and then ground our way through sand wadis until we reached Lefol's neat camp of good old Cabela's tents. Along the way we passed the spot where Elgin Gates and Jack O'Connor, and later James Mellon, camped, and Alain pointed out the ridge where Gates shot his aoudad. We would need to penetrate deeper into Ennedi, but Alain assured us that the aoudad were still there.

Indeed they were. Ennedi is a low range of sandstone cliffs and ridges. Without question it is one of the most beautiful areas I have ever seen, but how it supports life I haven't a clue. Sometimes years pass without rain, but a few pools and catchments remain along the bases of the hills—at least in some years. There is little vegetation up in the mountains, but lots of caves. The aoudad tend to go down into the wadis to graze during the night, then bed up on the ridges—often in the caves—during the heat of the day. These hardy animals are thinly dispersed in this inhospitable wasteland, but they are definitely still there. Historically, hunting aoudad was never considered easy and was never universally productive, so I wonder whether, in the heart of their

In their native habitat aoudad are much smaller in the body than those found in Texas. This is an average ram, but at this point in the hunt I was very happy to have him—and I still am.

domain where no human can long survive, there are almost as many as there ever have been. We saw aoudad every single day, a minimum of one ewe on a very slow day, and once I saw fourteen in several groups.

In Ennedi, by the way, aoudad is what you will see, and not much else. There are a few Sahara dorcas gazelle in the larger valleys, and still greater numbers farther south where the scimitar oryx used to roam. Chris took a lovely little Fennec fox that he wanted desperately for a museum collection, but there is little evidence of other wildlife today. Jack O'Connor reported that Elgin Gates took a pale and very large desert leopard when they hunted there together, so there might still be a few of those, but we saw no evidence of large predators.

We did see plenty of aoudad, though most sightings were hard-won. There is an easy way, but it takes a bit of luck. The aoudad will come down into the wadis to feed through the night, so in the early morning there is always the chance of catching them out in the open. I never saw one like that, but I believe Chris did, and on the previous safari my old buddy Bruce Keller took a real monster crossing an open wadi. Then there's the hard way: climbing up into the sandstone ridges early and walking and glassing until your eyes fall out. This is the way we saw most of our aoudad.

Chris hunted with Alain, while I hunted with Mairos, a young Zimbabwean, now deceased, whom Alain took under his wing and carried with him to Tanzania, the C.A.R., and eventually Chad. Mairos was good company and a fine hunter, with perhaps the unique distinction of starting as a tracker and ending up, much too young, as a fully licensed professional hunter in at least four countries. Together with local guides, we would head in different directions before dawn, hoping to catch aoudad crossing the valleys. When that didn't happen, we would look for tracks in the sandy valleys, then follow them up into the rocks until there were no more tracks. Then we would start glassing. When the sun became unbearably hot, we would follow the aoudad's lead and sit out the midday hours in a cave, working our way back in the afternoon.

Although we saw several aoudad, neither Chris nor I saw a ram the first few days, so Alain decided to pack up and head north, following a big wadi that led to the opposite side of the Ennedi Range not far from the Libyan frontier. We ground our way through soft sand for half a day and set up a camp of Cabela's tents in a rare grove of sere trees that offered a bit of shade. This was a remote country of big valleys and

An aoudad skeleton found in a cave. During the hot midday hours, aoudad seek shade, and almost all of the many caves have tracks and dung.

Hunting in the Ennedi Mountains is a true sheep hunt, not unlike hunting desert sheep. We saw aoudad every single day, indicating a surprisingly healthy population.

bigger ridges, and here we found lots of aoudad. On the first afternoon, in fact, Mairos and I came up over a little bench and spooked a beautiful ram. Breathing hard after a hot climb, I just plain missed the running shot. I was horrified, wondering if this would be my only chance.

Well, it wasn't my only chance, and it also wasn't my only miss. A day or two later, far up into the maze of ridges, we found the tracks of three or four rams. Again we jumped them, and again I missed a running shot. But this time they left tracks, and it was morning. By noon they would find shade and perhaps we could find them again.

We lost their tracks in the rocks several times but picked them up again in sand washes. The animals had slowed to a walk and seemed headed for a prominent rocky ridge, so we circled around to keep the wind right, hoping to locate them with binoculars. We actually did, catching them standing in a high saddle. Eventually they moved on through, and would almost certainly find shade nearby.

In any event, the rest was quite easy. We crossed the valley and then circled above the saddle so that this time we might avoid getting too close. The rams were on the far side just where they were supposed to be, in the shade of some jumbled boulders. We picked out what looked like the best one, and the 8mm Remington Magnum with its fast-opening 220-grain Sierra flattened him.

He was an average ram for Chad, but when we approached, I wondered what had happened to the rest of him! In that harsh climate the aoudad are much, much smaller in body, and usually smaller in horn, than the wonderful aoudad of Texas and New Mexico. But they are native-range aoudad and therefore special. And they aren't all smaller! In the same general area Chris and Alain found a large group in a cave, and Chris took the biggest ram with a brilliant shot. His was a monster, well over thirty inches and heavy, proof positive of Chad's great potential.

We headed back to base camp, packed up, and hunted dorcas gazelle on our way south. There were plenty, and both Chris and I took monsters. And now we embarked on the kind of African odyssey almost unheard of in these days of finite concessions. We drove south,

One of Alain Lefol's parking garages in the Ennedi Mountains. We could easily drive to the base of the mountains, but from there it's a pure sheep hunt, which means on foot in the rocks.

This is a really spectacular Sahara dorcas gazelle, taken in country that used to be home to addax and oryx. These, regrettably, are gone, but there are still large numbers of gazelle.

passing the ruins of Oum Chalouba, fueling and overnighting at a French military outpost, and then continuing on to the Sultanate of Dar-Sila, lost in another century.

The current Sultan traces his lineage back a thousand years and more, and his forebears in this remote corner of Africa successfully resisted French colonization. Today Dar-Sila remains an independent sultanate within Chad, and the Sultan himself—quiet, courteous, well educated—received us and welcomed us to hunt. We had come there for western greater kudu, the smallest and palest of the several kudu races and without question one of the most restricted of all the spiral-horned antelope. There are a few in isolated hill masses in the northern C.A.R., and just a couple of permits are available annually. Perhaps a few remain in western Sudan, across the border from Dar-Sila. Surprisingly, there are more than just a few in southeastern Chad, which describes the approximate location of Dar-Sila.

It was a long and brutal trip to get there, and the worst of the travel was yet to come, but the actual hunt was quite short. In the space of a couple of days Chris and I saw fully fourteen bulls, and we took our kudu on the same morning.

Dar-Sila actually looks quite a lot like much of Zimbabwe and northern South Africa, broad thornbush valleys stretching between chains of big, wooded ridges. There are quite a few warthog and some red-fronted gazelle, and the Sultan indicated that a few lion and leopard and even a few elephant roamed here and there, but there were definitely plenty of kudu, most of them living on the big ridges.

We enlisted the help of an entire village, our intent being to drive those big ridges and, we hoped, move kudu through natural funnels. Alain posted Mairos and me above a wonderful saddle. He and Chris moved along the outside of the "drive" while a number of villagers walked slowly up the far end of the ridge and along the crest and sides.

I caught the glint of the kudu's horns from at least a mile away, clear atop the highest point. It seemed totally impossible that this bull would come within range, but I certainly wanted him to! His horns made two complete turns, with straight points above the second turn, appearing to be in the low fifties, pretty much a size that doesn't exist among this smaller race. He was with several cows, and slowly they made their way down the ridge, often lost for minutes at a time and then reappearing. They had left the "drivers" far behind, so they weren't spooked; they were just moving along at their own pace.

I almost chanced a shot when they crossed an opening about three hundred yards across from me, but I held off and was very glad I did. The bull stopped under a tree in the saddle, less than two hundred yards directly below me. In a sitting position, resting over my pack, I shot him high on the shoulder, the downhill bullet exiting low in the chest but slamming him to the ground in the process. I ran down, certain of a new world record, and was totally perplexed: As with the aoudad, a whole bunch of the kudu was missing! He was paler in color than a southern bull, with fewer and more muted stripes, but the main difference was that, although fully mature and perfectly formed, he was little more than half the size . . . with horns in perfect scale to the body size. In the upper forties, he was a very big western greater kudu, and he might well be my favorite spiral-horn, but he sure fooled me as he came down that ridge!

A few hours later, on the ridge behind me, Chris took a wonderful bull of similar size, and that pretty much concluded our business in Dar-

Chris Kinsey with the beautiful little Fennec fox, taken for a museum exhibit.

This is a really good western greater kudu, but I have to admit he fooled me. This is the smallest and palest race of kudu, and the horns are perfectly proportioned to the body.

Sila. Oh, well, there was the court appearance that earned Chris the nickname I still call him by, Sir Chris of Chad.

It seems that the sultan enjoyed having visitors, and in fact he laid on a traditional parade for us, displaying some beautiful horses and camels. He also seemed to have developed a special liking for Chris Kinsey (and what's not to like?). So before the parade, here we were sipping tea and visiting with the sultan. When I tell the story, I exaggerate only slightly in describing the savage splendor of the sultan's court, with harem girls tittering behind hanging carpets. The sultan, having finished telling us of two great elephant bulls causing problems in a nearby village, and with parade time upon us, asked Chris, "So, my friend Mr. Chris, is there anything in my kingdom that you would like?"

I, of course, was thinking of the heavy-tusked elephant just described, but I had concerns that Sir Chris, then a confirmed bachelor (since reformed and married to a wonderful lady), might be casting his eyes toward the harem girls. No, not my friend Sir Chris. "Your highness," he asked politely, "I would love to ride a camel." And so it happened.

The next day, with the sultan's blessing and farewell, we headed south to the Aoukele River. The Aoukele flows into the Aouk, and these two rivers form the border between Chad and the C.A.R. The country is roadless and the border unmarked and unpoliced. Alain had penetrated much of this country on previous safaris, and he knew we would find red-fronted gazelle and korrigum, the giant topi also known as Senegal hartebeest. Chris and I definitely wanted these animals, but secretly I was hoping we might find evidence of western roan or perhaps even giant eland and buffalo.

What we found was an invasion by thousands of cattle and hundreds of nomadic herdsmen from Sudan . . . and very little wildlife. After decades of bush war, southern Sudan was very likely a wasteland. Regrettably, the Sudanese are fast turning much of central Africa into a wasteland as well. In the early nineties I had seen Sudanese poachers virtually eradicate eastern C.A.R.'s game as far as a hundred miles from the Sudanese border. Now I was seeing Sudanese cattle grazing southern Chad into a desert.

We established a spike camp on the Aoukele and struck out in separate teams—Mairos and me, Alain and Chris—for a couple of days. There were indeed some old tracks of roan, made during the rains two months

Red-fronted gazelle are fairly common in the thornbush of southeastern Chad. I was allowed two, and I took the one on the right first—and then, later the same morning, I had a chance at a real monster.

75

earlier, and Chris shot a fine oribi, but we would have to go farther to find the korrigum. So we decided to spike out from the spike camp, heading southeast together along the Aoukele until we found them.

The next couple of days were among the finest and most memorable I have ever spent in Africa. Up until this point we had seen flashes of just a couple of red-fronted gazelle, but as we progressed along the Aoukele we saw quite a few of them. This animal is described as the only gazelle that prefers thornbush to open ground, and indeed we found them in the riverine growth close by the watercourse. Chris and I both took exceptional specimens—and then we discovered the warthog.

The Aoukele country was once rich with a tremendous variety of wildlife, including all manner of herd animals in great abundance. This was clearly ancient history, and we were looking at just a few remnants. Buffalo, hartebeest, eland, and more were long gone. But in that part of Africa the people doing the poaching are almost entirely Muslim, and they had left the warthog strictly alone. Every time we found a pool we found warthog. I've seen other areas that had equal numbers, but never a place that had so many big warthog. Chris shot a monster. Then I shot a monster. Then Chris shot another monster. It was awesome.

This is Chris Kinsey's Senegal hartebeest or korrigum, so I have no idea why I'm holding a rifle and he isn't. We were at the limit of our supplies when we finally found them, and we each got one—but Chris's bull was the better trophy.

It takes a big gun to bag a trophy like this. Metal lasts a long time in the desert, and there still are quite a few Russian tanks from the Libyan invasion into Chad twenty years ago.

By nightfall we were far down the Aoukele. We briefly glimpsed one korrigum, but we saw no herds. We found a filthy pool along the river and built a fire there, cooking shish kebabs of gazelle interspersed with warthog, onion, and tomato, and we slept on mats under the stars.

In the morning we continued southeast, and at midmorning, at long last, we found a big herd of the big purple korrigum, once found in this region in tens of thousands but now reduced to just a few remnants. Chris took a fine bull, and we stayed after the herd and in the late afternoon I took one as well. Now we had a slight problem . . . we were almost out of water. With the hunt almost over, neither Chris nor I had any interest in partaking of the Aoukele . . . at least not if we had a choice.

So we called it a hunt, retracing our steps back to our spike-from-the-spike camp, then driving through the night to our spike camp and supplies. In that black, roadless bush GPS is a wonderful thing, costing us a sleepless night but saving us a very thirsty day! We arrived in camp well after daylight, drank our fill, and then collapsed in our now-luxurious Cabela's tents until late afternoon. The next day we packed up at our leisure and retraced our steps, first to Dar-Sila, then to that remote French outpost, and on by plane to N'Djamena.

I am often asked what is my favorite or most memorable African hunt. That's a tough one. My 1984 hunt in Zambia with Geoff and Russ Broom was fantastically successful. That one ranks high. So does my first hunt in Tanzania, in 1988 with Luke Samaras, hunting first with Michel Mantheakis in Masailand and then with Paddy Curtis in the Selous. But until 2001 I would have been most likely to reference my hunt in Kenya, that all-important first safari that started it all. There have been a number of great hunts since 2001, and of course all African hunts are wonderful. But in recent years Chad comes readily to mind when I'm asked such a question. The game we found is probably of interest to only a few long-gone Africa nuts, but the country was beautiful, the adventure was real, and today there are so few opportunities to hunt your way across literally five hundred miles of Africa.

Even that last opportunity may be gone today. Chad was never totally safe, and I do not want my reverence for a great safari misinterpreted as a blanket endorsement. Chad was not for everyone, and clearly that Sudanese invasion along the Aoukele was a time bomb. The next year it exploded. Asked by officials to help clear some of these people from a designated park, Alain Lefol was involved in an altercation that ended with shots fired and a spear piercing his arm and a machete in his leg. Although no body was ever produced as evidence, Lefol was charged with murder and spent six months in prison, steadfastly refusing to admit his guilt. He was eventually cleared, but part of the deal, apparently, was an attempt by certain folks, both French and Chadian, to take away his hunting areas. This didn't happen, and after all the dust cleared, Lefol conducted a few more safaris. At this writing, unfortunately, civil war grips this troubled country once more, so hunting is not possible. I hope it comes right, because sport hunting is the last and only chance for the remaining game in this, the last remnant of North African hunting.

Bishop Hills

The events of September 11, 2001, and the "global war on terror" that followed destroyed many peoples' lives, so please accept purely as a statement of fact, not as a whining complaint, that the aftermath of "9-11" changed my life dramatically—and permanently—or so it seems at this writing. Unlike many people, I think most of the changes in my life have been for the better over time, but as this volume progresses, you must be the judge of that.

After 9-11 there wasn't a great deal of hunting to be done. I volunteered for active duty early, but it was after the first of the year before something came up that the Marines needed me to do. The next year—2002 and on into 2003—was spent in uniform. This period in itself saw some interesting developments, some related to this narrative and some not. One mostly unrelated occurrence—certainly not a direct result of the long deployment—was that I found myself single again after I got home.

Also unrelated, but too widely reported to ignore, was the simple fact that when I got home my long military career was effectively over, although it took another year and a half to fizzle out. I was sent overseas to take command of a combined/joint task force, meaning troops from multiple nations and multiple U.S. forces. It was a one-star command that had considerable political implications, partly because I had both a Czech and a German battalion and partly because the mission included some sensitive training for specific personnel of various Persian Gulf states (some of which welcomed us and some of which barely tolerated us).

We started out at a beautiful lodge in the central plains west of Windhoek. It was a great introduction to Africa—but it could spoil you.

I had been board-selected for brigadier general the previous year, but because of backlogs the Senate hadn't yet confirmed me. Prior to departure, my immediate superior, Lt. Gen. Mike Hagee, an active-duty three-star, directed me to pin on stars when I got to Kuwait. Ultimately, I think the only thing that saved me from a court martial was that, knowing this was wrong, I didn't do it. Three days later, wearing the colonel's eagles I was entitled to, I reported to my boss in Bahrain, Lt. Gen. Earl Hailston. Hailston had asked for a one-star to fill my job and understood I would be confirmed momentarily, so he "fixed the problem." In front of at least a dozen of his staff members, he administered the oath of office and pinned stars on my collar. Many of you will say I should have refused—but few Marines would say that, and nobody who ever worked for Earl Hailston would suggest such a thing! Win, lose, or draw, I was stuck in the subterfuge.

The promised confirmation didn't happen, so I was hung out to dry, and I suppose Earl Hailston was as well. I was supposed to rotate home in September, but things were heating up, and besides, I liked the job and I liked working for Hailston. So I extended, hoping I would be confirmed before we got caught. Unfortunately, the reverse happened, and it was ugly for quite a while. Hailston was a great general and a great Marine, and he went to the wall (almost literally) insisting that he alone should bear responsibility. He remains a friend. But as the finger pointing progressed and the Marine Corps leadership gathered to protect the flag, I discovered that I had very few friends above the rank of colonel, and I became the scapegoat.

By now the other three-star, Mike Hagee, had become commandant of the Marine Corps, a position that has become as political as it is important. During the investigations, Hagee was somehow unable to recall conversations he and I had regarding the illegal frocking, including one that took place in my headquarters in Kuwait after I learned that the promised confirmation would not be forthcoming anytime soon. At the conclusion of that conversation General Hagee looked me in the eye and said, "Craig, no matter what happens, none of this will reflect on you."

On the strength of that promise, I fought it out for a long time, believing that in the end Marines would look after Marines. I was wrong. Officially, Hailston took most of the heat in the first investigation, but

Namibia's central plains are especially good for steenbok. We passed several good ones until I figured out Kimberlee (left) and Brittany weren't interested in the smaller antelope—and then, just at dark, I jumped in and shot this beautiful little ram.

he was allowed to retire with his three stars intact. Both General Hagee and I received "non-punitive letters of caution" from the secretary of the Navy. I have no idea what was said to Hagee, but the secretary was surprisingly jovial with me, and told me that he believed we would get past this and I would be confirmed. He was wrong.

The forces protecting the flag were far too strong, and in a short time I was investigated again, essentially for the same thing with a couple of new wrinkles. The second investigation cleared me completely, explicitly exonerating me of all charges and implicitly reversing the findings of the first investigation. My wrongdoing in the first investigation was that I "allowed myself to be improperly frocked." The second investigation changed this to "you were improperly frocked." ("Frocking" is an old custom that means, essentially, wearing the rank and assuming its responsibility but not drawing the pay that goes with it.)

I saw this change in semantics as a big difference, but none of it mattered. Early in the process the senior reserve two-star at the time, Arnold Punaro, told me in a private interview, "You will be the only person hurt by this." I didn't believe him, but he was right and I was wrong. I was investigated, harassed, and threatened for nearly two years. When I finally threw in the towel after over thirty-one years of service, I was completely content to be rid of the bastards forever, and I haven't looked back. But that's getting ahead of the story, as well as sidetracked.

Directly related to this story is the fact that while I was gone, my relationship with my older daughter, Brittany, changed dramatically—definitely for the better. Prior to 9-11 I had promised I'd take her to Africa as a high-school graduation present, and we planned the trip for the summer of 2002. When she was little, Brittany would look at my mounted lion and say, "Daddy, I want to shoot a lion." But when she was about eleven this changed, and it had been years since we had talked about what I do for a living. Some of her friends knew that I wrote, but I'm sure their parents thought I was a pornographer, since the subject I wrote about was never, ever mentioned. Still, I wanted her to see Africa, so we were going to do this, and on her terms. ("Daddy, you wouldn't, like, shoot an animal in front of me, would you?")

It would be difficult for me to afford a trip to Africa if I couldn't write about it, and after all, I do write about hunting. But I had it figured out. We'd go with Dirk de Bod and see a bit of Namibia, and at some point we'd send Brittany off shopping for a couple of days with Dirk's wife, Rina. Dirk and I would shoot the place flat during that period. I'd get a couple of stories, and Brittany would never know. After all, it wasn't likely she'd be reading *Petersen's Hunting* magazine, was it?

We put the trip off for a year because of my deployment, and while I was gone a major sea change occurred that has altered both of our lives. I'm not sure exactly what caused it, but when I got home we were talking on the phone and Brittany said, "So, Daddy, if we're really going to Africa this summer, don't you think we should go to the range so that I can work on my shooting?"

After picking the phone up off the floor, I agreed that would be a good idea. So we started our range work, initially with Brittany, but then somehow I found I'd been co-opted into taking not one but two seventeen-year-old girls to Africa. Her buddy Kimberlee Miller joined us for range sessions, first .22s, then .22 centerfires, then a .243, and finally a Kimber 7mm-08 I'd gotten for the purpose. At my insistence, but on their own responsibility, both girls did the California hunter-safety course and got hunting licenses, and in turn I took them both pig hunting. This was a prerequisite. If they found they liked it and could handle it, then we'd see what Africa offered up for them.

One more related incident happened while I was overseas. Joe Bishop had never been to Namibia, and he was looking for a "fun hunt" for his wife, Sara, and their two boys. I put him in touch with Dirk de Bod, of course, and they had a hunt planned for sometime in the summer of 2002. Joe also had an elephant hunt scheduled a couple of months earlier, in Botswana with Robin Hurt. I think it was sometime in May or early June when Joe called me from Botswana, catching me at my headquarters in Kuwait.

"Boddington," he said, "tell me again where 'Nambia' is." I told him it was several hundred miles southwest of where he was standing. "OK," he said, "we got the elephant, and Robin and I are going to 'Nambia' to buy ranches."

I was stunned, but thinking fast. I knew Dirk wouldn't steer him wrong, so I made sure he had Dirk's number and got Joe's promise to call Dirk before he did anything. Sometimes things work out. Dirk de Bod is as heavily booked as any professional hunter I know, but Joe caught him between safaris and they hit it off right away. Robin bought a ranch toward the highlands north of Windhoek, while Joe, in partnership with Dirk, bought a fantastic piece of property about an hour and a half east of the Windhoek airport, hilly country with a wide range of habitat.

When Brittany, Kimberlee, and I arrived in Windhoek in August 2003, both Dirk and Joe met us at the airport. Their ranch had been Engadin Farm, but I saw that Joe was driving a new Land Cruiser with a bold sable antelope logo on the door announcing "Bishop Hills." At that time they were just getting things going. The camp was barely started, and Joe's house was far from complete. The place had good numbers of natural game, primarily kudu, gemsbok, and hartebeest, and they were just beginning restocking efforts with eland, zebra (both kinds), wildebeest (both kinds), and the Namibian prizes, sable, roan, and waterbuck. I was anxious to see it, but Dirk had other plans—partly

We finished the safari with a few days in Etosha National Park, one of southern Africa's best-kept secrets. We hit it just right, seeing a lot of elephant and quite a few lion.

The Damara dik-dik was the trophy I wanted most from the trip, and this one is huge. I used a .22 Hornet barrel on my Thompson/Center single-shot, and it worked just perfectly.

to show me and the girls a bit more of the country and partly because their ranch wasn't quite ready for company.

So instead of all of us heading east to Bishop Hills, Joe went east and Dirk took us an hour west to a lovely game lodge in Namibia's central plains. He was right: The accommodations were a wonderful intro to Africa, and there was a lot of game. The first morning we checked the rifles, and I noted that my two jet-lagged beginners weren't in their best form. This might or might not be a very long safari, but I was worried. Dirk probably was as well, but he kept it to himself.

We just looked around the first day, making a desultory stalk on the common zebra that Brittany wanted, and letting the girls get a first-hand look at a variety of animals. Neither wanted wildebeest (good deal—they're expensive!), and neither wanted the smaller antelope. This area was exceptional for steenbok and not bad for common duiker, but after several of each offered themselves up, I got the message: The little guys were too cute to shoot. OK, Dad can hunt too. Just at dark we stalked a really good steenbok, and I shot him with the .22 Hornet barrel I'd brought for a T/C Contender carbine. This was only the second steenbok I'd ever taken, the first falling in Kenya so long ago.

The next morning we drove a couple hours south to a place Dirk knew of that was exceptionally good for springbok. This, too, worried me because I couldn't imagine anything harder to hit, but Dirk knew exactly what he was doing. At midmorning we fixed up a makeshift brush blind near a water hole, not a living creature anywhere in sight. A half-hour later Brittany shot her first African animal, a nice springbok. A bit later Kimberlee shot a real monster. Then Brittany shot a better ram. All shots were just fine. I started to breathe a whole lot easier, as did Dirk.

A bonus there was that the landowner had a number of semi-tame cheetah, not quite tame enough to pet but tame enough to climb into the cage with. We got some great photos, and headed home with the safari well underway.

Our "deal" was that the girls could each have a zebra, and Namibia has both types. Inexplicably to me, Brittany decided she liked the striping pattern of the common zebra better, while Kimberlee (to me, wisely) preferred the mountain zebra found only in Namibia. I was trying hard not to establish a pecking order between them, and really we didn't—things just sort of happened. We found the common zebra first, feeding up a long valley, and I got my first taste of what would become increasingly common: sitting back in the shade, waiting to hear the shot, while Brittany made a stalk.

When the shot came, I ran forward with the trackers to find Dirk and Brittany up on a sidehill glassing ahead. The shot, supported by sticks, had been about 175 yards. The distance didn't worry me too much; Brittany had practiced a lot off the sticks and that was probably her best position. But she was shooting her little 7mm-08, definitely light for zebra, and we didn't yet know how the 150-grain Swift Scirocco bullets I'd set her up with would work on larger game.

We tracked the herd for maybe three hundred yards, found no blood at all, and I thought my worst nightmare was just beginning. Dirk and the trackers thought otherwise. They went back to where the zebra had stood and started over, finding it stone-dead in a little depression barely fifty yards away. The little Scirocco bullet was balled up against the hide on the far side, and we didn't worry too much after that. A day or so later we found a herd of mountain zebra moving along the base of a low ridge. We circled and came in above them, crawling down through the rocks to within fairly close range. Kimberlee made a perfect shot, and now it was time to pack up and head for the hills—Bishop Hills.

When complete, Dirk's camp would be wonderful, but at this stage only cement foundations marked its location. There were good guest quarters near the farm manager's house, a big rondavel with separate rooms, so we were just fine—except that it was colder than hell! We all darn near froze, and I was glad we didn't start there. But, man, was it a beautiful farm—rugged hills and brushy valleys and lots of grass. Dirk had known of it and took Joe there, and Joe had bought it almost instantly. I could see why.

We hunted by a combination of waiting over water holes and stalking. The plan was to hunt only the native game: kudu, gemsbok, perhaps hartebeest, perhaps warthog. The "perhaps" part was a bit weird. While we sat at water holes several very good warthog came in, but neither girl was interested, classifying the animals as "ugly." Pretty much the same applied to hartebeest. However, the last afternoon we were there Brittany got a shot at a really good old hartebeest bull, dead rest at maybe 150 yards, and she missed him clean. It was the only shot she missed on that trip, and it took me a couple more hunts to figure out that girls are different—or at least this girl is. If she wants the animal, she'll center-punch it, regardless of the shot. If she doesn't really want it, she can't hit it!

Kudu and gemsbok were on the wanted list. (We concentrated on a different sort of trophy hunting: "So, Daddy, which animals have really pretty skins that can be made into purses and things?") It was purely luck of the draw, but Brittany took both her kudu and her gemsbok by stalking, while Kimberlee took both animals from blinds. All were darn good trophies and all well taken with fine shooting. Brittany's kudu came with a fast shot at nearly two hundred yards, one ridge to another off the sticks, and once again the little Scirocco bullet was balled up against the hide on the far side.

Off and on Dirk and I had been casting around for a good kudu for me but hadn't seen anything really good. On the last morning there the girls decided to sleep in while Dirk and I made one last try, agreeing that we'd head for the barn no later than noon. Shortly after daybreak we ran into a gemsbok bull too good to pass, so I shot him and we took him back to the ranch. After a look at our watches, we headed

While the girls were shopping, Dirk and I hunted for a big hartebeest literally within sight of the Windhoek airport control tower. This is a migration area, and in August there are hundreds of hartebeest in big herds. This one is a real dandy.

back out. An hour before our self-imposed deadline we glassed a really lovely kudu bull, made a stalk, and I made a really bad shot when he ran on me. Fortunately I was shooting the big 8mm Remington Magnum, and he didn't go far before stopping to offer another shot. This time we got him down, and returned to the farm just on schedule. The kudu was a really beautiful bull of 55 inches, but equally enjoyable to me was taking both kudu and gemsbok, the two primary Namibian species, on the same day.

Now the girls had a choice. We were going to spend a couple of nights and a day at Dirk's house in Windhoek, and they could either go shopping with Rina or go south of town and look for a hartebeest with Dirk and me. Since I already knew how they felt about hartebeest, I was pretty sure of the answer . . . but I was almost as certain that shopping would have won even if we'd offered up giant sable.

Darn near in sight of the Windhoek airport control tower is a broad, brushy plain that holds amazing numbers of hartebeest. None of that country is game-fenced, so there are plenty throughout the year, but in August hundreds and hundreds of the animals in herds migrate through. It's also a great place for really good warthog. Since I don't consider them ugly at all, I didn't hesitate for a minute when we saw a real monster pig right off the bat!

The country is big and broken, and it took us a while to find the big herds of hartebeest. When we did, there were oceans of them, but before we found them we drove straight into three cheetah hunting along a little watercourse. They trotted a little way ahead of us, and a big male stopped and looked back at less than a hundred yards. It was a golden opportunity, and I expected it would never come again. But I knew I couldn't take the cheetah home, and here on natural, unfenced land they were doing no harm at all. I didn't shoot, and while I knew that was the right decision, I wondered if I would ever see another.

It was late afternoon when we finally found an entire valley full of hartebeest, a couple hundred in one herd. This is tough stuff for me because they all have horns and at first glance all look alike, but Dirk picked out a huge bull right away. I didn't see much chance of closing for a shot and isolating that bull, but we shadowed them for a long time and finally caught that exact bull standing clear. He dropped to the shot and was every bit as big as Dirk had judged him.

Brittany and Kimberlee enjoyed their shopping safari, and fortunately used surprising restraint, and from there we headed north. At that time Dirk was still part-owner of a lovely tent camp in the highlands north of Windhoek, so we spent a day there—partly because he wanted us to see it and partly because it got us a distance north in one jump. The camp was truly magnificent, the lodge and tents built into a rocky kopje overlooking a big dam. It was scenic, totally overrun with baboons that terrified the girls, and in the mornings and evenings it was also ferociously cold! The highlands, above 7,000 feet in elevation, are incredibly beautiful, and the area is good for klipspringer, leopard, and the occasional really big kudu. It is also one of the best places in Namibia to hunt free-range mountain zebra. I guess it was my turn for a zebra, because the girls graciously allowed me to shoot a big stallion one warm afternoon while

Etosha lacks the variety of some of Africa's great parks, but it makes it up with volume of the common animals. Huge herds of springbok come to the water holes.

they took a canoe out into the lake and watched the baboons along the shoreline. At this point I think they had hunted enough; they were proud of themselves and I was proud of both of them.

The next stop was all mine, the personal highlight of my trip: a quick hunt for Damara dik-dik. The seemingly random distribution of African wildlife always amazes me. The Damara variety is clearly a dik-dik, almost indistinguishable from its East African cousins. It prefers the same dry thornbush habitat and yet is isolated from the several other varieties by thousands of miles of Africa. Go figure!

The Damara dik-dik is a beautiful little bluish antelope with straight, sharp horns, and in my experience is one of the largest-bodied of the tiny dik-diks (though not all references agree). He is widely distributed in northern Namibia but is found nowhere else in Africa. When I first hunted in what was then South-West Africa, north of Omaruru with Ben Nolte, we saw dik-dik almost every day, but back then they were completely protected. Today they are hunted under tightly controlled permits, with farms of the "standard" 10,000-hectare size within dik-dik range allocated no more than four permits each, usually just two.

Dirk took us to an isolated farm not far north of where I'd hunted with Ben Nolte so many years ago, a pretty place dominated by a huge monolith. We had an evening and a morning, and planned to finish the trip in Etosha National Park. I was a bit skeptical about allocating just one long day for such a great prize, but Dirk wasn't worried. Nor was he worried when, that first evening, we saw only a small female.

As usual, he was right. These dik-dik love the heavy bush at the base of hills, and when the sun starts to warm, they step out to catch some rays. We saw two or three from the vehicle, and then we climbed up onto a rocky hill and worked our way along, looking down into the brush below. We hadn't gone far when a pair appeared in a small clearing below. Dirk immediately recognized the male as a very good one. We got down and crept a bit closer, but either they had seen us or it was time for them to move—both slipped off into thick bush before we could shoot, the female one way, the male another.

I wasn't exactly horror-stricken, because we were now seeing plenty, but I was disappointed. Dirk wasn't concerned at all. "Get your rifle ready and don't move. They're very territorial, and he will come back."

He was right again. I got the .22 Hornet rested over a rock and lay still, and in a few minutes I saw just a hint of movement at the limit of our vision. Slowly, very slowly, he came forward one step at a time, a ten-pound antelope offering at least as much excitement as a huge kudu bull. The horns came into view, and one more step would expose the shoulder. He took it, I squeezed the trigger, and that concluded the hunting portion of our safari.

We finished up with two really great days in Etosha National Park, definitely one of best-kept secrets in Africa. We saw legions of springbok, gemsbok, and zebra, plenty of kudu, and a lot of elephant. The rhino, of which there are many, eluded us, but we did well on lion, seeing them on four different occasions. Etosha was a great finisher to the trip, as Kruger Park had been a couple of years earlier. However, if I had it to do over, I'd go to a great park like that at the start of a first safari, a great way to become familiar with the game and the country. But first or last, Etosha is a Namibian must! The trip had been a total success for all, the only problem being that I had created a monster. Brittany was genuinely appreciative but wanted to know, "Where can we go next, Dad?"

Limpopo

It was in 2003 that the pace of my African hunting suddenly and unexpectedly picked up. For the first time in my adult life I was free of Marine Corps responsibilities, and at the same time new opportunities that I'd never envisioned began coming along. As I wrote at the beginning, in 1997 I would have bet that this book would never be written, because I couldn't imagine there would be enough material. In late 2006 and early 2007, as I'm writing this, I realize that there is more material than needed for a normal-size book. This gives me the great luxury of simply skipping over a very few hunts that were less than memorable (as Mom and Dad taught, if you can't say anything good, don't say anything at all!). This is one I was sorely tempted to skip, but that would mean I'd have to neglect a couple of really good young guys who very much saved the day.

As many hunts do, this one started at the Safari Club convention, a wonderful place to shop for hunts but also a place where, well, exaggeration isn't unusual. You know the adage, "If it sounds too good to be true. . . ."

I was just starting an endorsement arrangement with SureFire, something neither side had done before, so we were feeling our way along. A few folks have criticized me for this role, but here's the way I saw it then and still do: I've used SureFire lights ever since I first saw them, and consider them the best illumination tools on the market. In several thousand magazine articles and now twenty books I don't think I've ever written more than a couple dozen words about flashlights. So it

The Limpopo Valley is definitely one of the very best places to look for really big southern greater kudu. We were hoping to find a 60-inch monster and we failed, but we saw many very fine bulls.

feels clean to me, while a paid endorsement for a gun, scope, or bullet—the stuff I write about all the time—seems off-limits, a bridge I choose not to cross (despite offers).

Anyway, my initial role with SureFire was limited, essentially trading my image in a few ads for a couple of hunts. So, my old friend and SureFire contact, Cameron Hopkins, came to me with a plan. It seems an American operating in northern South Africa had suggested he put together a small group of writers and then "guarantee" that if we'd all hunt hard, at least a couple of us would go home with "60-inch kudu."

As you probably know, I've spent a lot of time, money, and effort looking for such a kudu. I won't build up the suspense: This volume will conclude with no kudu in that class brought to bag . . . not then, not later. But I'm always on the lookout for such an opportunity, so of course I was interested. The location was right: Northern South Africa, essentially the Limpopo Valley and the rugged ground to the south, is definitely one of the places that produce extra-large kudu with some regularity. On the other hand, I knew going in that a couple of things were wrong here. First off, it broke my long-standing rule to avoid hunting with Americans. Note that this is my personal rule, and not necessarily a good one. However, with apologies to great departed American PHs like Charles Cottar, Cotton Gordon, and my old friend George Hoffman, and equal apologies to exceptionally competent American PHs like Jeff Rann, Doug Scandrol, and my good friend Joe Coogan, I'm a journalist. I go to Africa to learn and record as much as to hunt, and I've always figured I could learn more from someone who was born there. So I was a bit skeptical about an American-owned outfit, especially since its primary qualification appeared to be the financial ability to buy a game ranch. The larger concern, however, was that in my experience nobody, but nobody, can guarantee a sixty-inch kudu—unless, of course, they had already put a tape on it!

Honestly, at that time it had been years since I'd done much hunting in South Africa, and I didn't realize how common the "put and take" business had become. I just figured this guy had a few really big kudu and maybe one of us would run into one. In fairness, perhaps that was the case, but I doubt it. So, in mid-September, just a few weeks after

This is a really beautiful kudu bull, with wide turns and good conformation. He is exactly 55 inches around the curve, and that's a superb kudu. Unfortunately, he was misjudged badly, but that doesn't make him less beautiful.

*An unusual sight near the **Limpopo River**, the desiccated skeleton of a warthog in the hole, facing outward as he died. The previous year was dry, and in a drought the mature warthog are the first to go—which is why big warthog are scarce.*

LIMPOPO

Brittany's Namibian safari, I was on the SAA flight from Atlanta once again. I was skeptical, but, after all, it wasn't my *shauri*.

Our group was comprised of Cameron Hopkins and myself, Brian Sheets from the NRA, and Steve Comus from SCI. Brian was on his first safari and had a wonderful time (how can you not?), as did the rest of us. The primary issue lay in the promise. The area had very good kudu, but none of us took anything even approaching a 60-incher, and I'm fairly certain nobody saw one. All kudu taken were very, very nice bulls, but all were misjudged by a minimum of five inches. This in itself isn't unusual, since kudu are exceptionally difficult to judge precisely. But if you promise X but consistently deliver Y, it begs the question: How do you know you really had a 60-inch kudu since you apparently can't judge them anyway?

I looked over a lot of beautiful kudu, and the one I took was a lovely bull with deep spirals. We got onto him in heavy cover at close range, and the horns were lost in a bushy tree until he ran, offering no shot. We followed, casting in circles with the wind, and a truly marvelous piece of hunting got us on him again. Already assured that this was the bull we were looking for, I didn't waste a lot more time looking at the horns. He was walking through thick bush at about a hundred yards, and I dropped him with a 200-grain Sierra from my .300 H&H. He was, and is, truly a beautiful bull. But when we walked up to him, I was pretty sure I was looking at a fine bull with wide curls that would probably go 55 inches.

I hate tape measures, I really do, but I hate it even more when people think I'm stupid. Now, as I hold the horns of a fine kudu, I'm assured once more that this is the 60-incher I've dreamed of for so long. I don't like myself for it, but I know different. So there's really no solution other than to dig for the tape: 55 inches on the button, a beautiful kudu but a long way from a 60-incher. But I didn't make the guarantee, did I?

At the lodge there were photos of a handful of spectacular kudu that I didn't tape but I suspect made the grade. As the hunt ensued, obvious and escalating tension arose between the American and his South African partner. I could be wrong, and for that reason I'm avoiding names, but here's what I think happened: I think there were indeed at least two 60-inch kudu on this property when the commitment was made, and I

97

OK, I thought this business about calling klipspringer was a joke. But I went along with the joke, and in less than half an hour Jasper and Willem called in six klippies, three pairs, to this very spot.

think this was known because they'd been taped when bought at auction. I think they got shot long before we arrived, and my primary regret is the lack of honesty in the whole thing. On the other hand, if my guess is correct, none of us would have been there if we'd known we were looking for released kudu of known dimensions!

I did take what remains my very best waterbuck, almost but not quite thirty inches, and I also took a good bushbuck and a nice warthog still-hunting along the Limpopo, always a fun hunt. But because of the controversy, I would have left that entire hunt out of this opus were it not for some really interesting things that happened at the tail end.

As a side trip, Cameron had arranged to hunt leopard at the same time. The permit obtained for him was in mountainous country about three hours southeast. The rest of us hadn't anticipated this because, after all, Cam was sort of the host. However, serious money was on the line with a South African leopard tag, so he gave it several days and then came back—primarily out of concern for the rapidly deteriorating fates of his clients but also because he now understood that these clever South African ranch leopard would come in only at night, which was not the way he wanted to take a leopard.

OK, by now I understood that I was not going to get a 60-inch kudu. But I also understood that Cameron had actually had a huge tom leopard feeding, and I knew that this area consistently produces some of Africa's best leopard, however difficult and nocturnal they may be. I also knew that a valuable permit was being wasted. So I asked if I could go sit on the bait for the few days remaining, and of course I'd pay for the cat if successful.

So it was that I met Jasper Aitchison and Willem Enslin, two young South African hunters I liked very much and who impressed me very much. I wish I could have helped them more than I did.

On the leopard, well, it was real—very real. I saw the tracks, and it was one of those genuine northern South Africa–southern Zimbabwe cattle-killing monsters with a track like a young lion. Unfortunately, we were a day late. He had come and fed heavily the night Cameron had abandoned the hunt and again the next night. But now it was the third night and it was too late. I sat the three nights that I had, but he didn't return, and we found his tracks not on that bait but in another canyon a couple of miles away.

None of this was a problem. My leopard luck, or lack thereof, is legendary, so no hard feelings. It was worth a chance and it didn't work, but I came away believing that these two young professional hunters knew exactly what they were doing with big leopard. In that part of the world nobody bats a thousand, but these youngsters have taken a number of really big cats. They also showed me a very fine part of South Africa—big mountains without game fences—and they taught me a couple of new tricks.

We had only three nights and partial days, with mornings spent checking baits and a 3 P.M. appointment in the blind. Not much time, but their intent was to show me a couple of their specialties: mountain reedbuck and klipspringer. I had never actually hunted the former on purpose; the only one I'd ever shot was kind of incidental to hunting vaal rhebok. I had hunted klipspringer on purpose, but it had been a matter of checking small kopjes in Zimbabwe's lowveld until a klippie appeared and stood accommodatingly on a rock. This hunt was in big mountains, an altogether different deal.

The first day I failed altogether on mountain reedbuck (me, not the boys). We started on top, a blessing, and worked our way down—

and then back up—big grassy ridges that the men said were perfect for mountain reedbuck. We were glassing, but we were also listening for the animals to give themselves away with their shrill little alarm whistles. We saw quite a few, including a huge male, but he got over a ridge without offering a shot.

No problem. We followed, found him again on top (this time with binoculars), and made a brilliant stalk. I think we got within a couple hundred yards, close in this big, open country, but he was still a small target at that distance. I was sitting and reasonably steady, but a female masked the ram. When she moved, I was no longer steady, and he was moving again before I got the shot off. Sometimes failing to shoot when the opportunity arises counts just the same as a miss, and that was one of those times.

Willem and Jasper looked at their watches, as did I. We'd circled most of the way back to the truck and burned up the day—it was past noon, we were an hour from our leopard blind, and we needed to be there shortly after three. "OK," said Jasper, "we've got time to make a morning run on these reedbuck tomorrow. Let's leave them and go get a good klippie." Huh? Given a chance encounter, nothing takes more than a few seconds, but I knew that hunting a klipspringer on purpose was a serious effort.

I also figured that these big, grassy ridges weren't the right place to look. In that regard, at least, I was correct. "Klipspringer" literally means "cliff jumper." Klippies like rocky hills and rocky faces. We bumped our way down the mountain, dropping off the heights, then turned onto a tarmac road and skirted around the highest ridges. A few kilometers down the road we turned onto a little gravel track that led into heavy thornbush and came to a stop after just a couple hundred yards. I was perplexed, but I went along with the gag, grabbing my rifle. After we'd walked maybe a hundred yards down a gentle incline, at least part of the puzzle became clear. The bush gave way to flat boulders, and then the earth dropped away into a deep and completely hidden box canyon with cliffs on three sides and heavy brush below. Yes, this was perfect klipspringer habitat—but I wasn't about to miss even the remotest chance for that big leopard by scrambling down into the canyon.

We approached carefully and set up on a scary overhang, at least a hundred feet of sheer drop below. OK, good place to glass, but I wasn't

Jasper Aitchison called in this nice klipspringer using a plain old American varmint call. He does it all the time, but this is the first I had ever heard of hunting klipspringer in this fashion.

seeing any movement. "OK," I was told, "you sit here and be really ready. We're going to call them in."

I have no idea where these young guys had learned this. Since then I've mentioned it to a number of seasoned professional hunters who offer klipspringer. No one else had ever tried it (though some have now, with good results), and only a couple had heard of it. The call was a good old American dying-rabbit varmint model, undoubtedly similar to the sounds a klipspringer would make in distress. Still playing along with the gag, I got as ready as I could without going too close to the edge— I'm terrified of that kind of plunging dropoff!

At the first series of calls a pair of klipspringer appeared in the bottom, then bounded up toward us from rock to rock. They stopped at the edge of the brush just below us, and we got a good look at the male. He was shootable but not special, so we passed. By that time another pair was headed our way, first seen as tiny moving dots scampering up the bottom of the canyon at least five hundred yards away.

These two stayed in the canyon bottom, and long before they were in range we knew the ram carried very good horns. I got into a sitting

This is a nice southern mountain reedbuck, the first one that I've ever taken by hunting them on purpose—and, considering I had to catch an international flight that very evening, a darn good trophy.

position, awkward at that downhill angle, and when he stopped about a hundred yards out—mostly straight down—I shot right over him. He and his mate turned and went back, but he made a mistake and stopped on top of a boulder in heavy brush. Just enough of him was exposed for a much more difficult shot than the first opportunity, but this time I rolled him off the rock. At the shot another pair coming down the far canyon wall turned and dashed back to safety, bounding from rock to rock as only klippies do. That made six klipspringer in as many minutes, many more than I've ever seen from one spot.

I wanted a klipspringer because the mount of the only other one I'd shot had been totaled in an earthquake earlier in the year. I doubt I'll ever shoot another, but it was amazing to see them respond to the varmint call, and I'd like to see that again.

Of course the leopard didn't come that night. We hadn't really expected him to, but we had to try, didn't we? The next morning we had just a few hours to hunt before a frantic airport run to get me to my plane. We started out on top once again and walked a couple of ridges without seeing any reedbuck. We were circling back when we all, even me, heard a shrill whistle. A group of reedbuck bounded up out of a hidden swale, and a good ram paused above a bit of rimrock. This time I did it right, dropping into a sitting position and shooting just as he started to run. We packed him back to the truck, dropped him at the ranch, and I made my flight back to the States with time to spare. It's been several years and I haven't seen either Jasper or Willem since, though I'm sure our paths will cross. My guess is both of them will be in the business for a long time, and I hope they do well. They deserve to.

Mayo Oldiri

Most of us who fall under the spell of Africa continue to be bewitched by the great literature of Africana. This is good because Africa has spawned the world's best sporting literature, and reading about it is almost as good as being there. The pitfall lies in placing too much credence in what you read. As mentioned before, the only constant in Africa is change. Sometimes it's for the better, sometimes for the worse, and it's often very rapid. Anything written about Africa, including this volume, runs the risk of being dated before the ink is dry, and anything written a decade or two earlier may be very fine reading but must be taken with a grain of salt and much current research before any hard data on outfitters, areas, and game can be accepted as Gospel.

In the early years of my African experience Cameroon was a quiet backwater to what was once Ubangi-Shari, then Central African Empire, and now is Central African Republic. In both countries the elephant were ravaged by the late 1970s, but throughout my African hunting career the remaining game was similar: In the north it was giant eland, roan, and other "savanna" species; in the south it was bongo, giant forest hog, and other "forest" species (the quotes mean that there is some overlap both ways). There were numerous good outfitters in the C.A.R., and probably almost as many in Cameroon. But Cameroon was little known to Americans, with old Jacques Guin the only name readily recognized.

Right or wrong, it was an article of faith that the C.A.R. was the better destination of the two, better organized and offering more game.

Cameroon was less expensive, and I had long believed that her southern forests held a greater concentration of bongo, but I believed they averaged smaller, and still do. I had heard, read, and believed that Cameroon held relatively few Derby eland compared to the C.A.R. but had considerably more western roan.

Through the 1990s I made four (count 'em, four) safaris into the C.A.R., two into the northern savanna woodland and two into the southern forests. Nothing I saw convinced me that my beliefs were incorrect. In the south I struggled to get a bongo, but when I finally did, he was a monster. In the north I struggled to get a Derby eland, but plenty enough of them were around. I never even saw a shootable bull roan, although I came upon some number of those animals along the way. So it was the lure of a big western roan that finally took me to northern Cameroon.

In the common dialect of northern Cameroon, *mayo* means "river." Mayo Oldiri is the name of Spanish entrepreneur Antonio Riguera's hunting outfit. In the north his main camp is indeed on the Mayo Oldiri, just one of several northern (and several southern) hunting blocks that his outfit controls. I wish I could say that I discovered Antonio and his bright, efficient, and attractive daughter Raquel, who handles all the hunting business, but I did not. That discovery goes to Cameron Hopkins, who asked me out of the clear blue if I'd be interested in a February hunt in northern Cameroon. Indeed I was, with visions of western roan dancing before my beady little eyes.

We based out of an amazingly comfortable, well-appointed, and well-supplied camp on the Mayo Oldiri, but also hunted the adjacent Mayo Nduell block, once home to Jacques Guin himself. We saw western roan—oh, my, we did—but the big surprise was that we saw everything else as well. There remain wonderful hunting areas in the interior of the northern C.A.R., but the areas I hunted personally had been heavily poached, mostly by gangs of Sudanese meat seekers. By the same token, I certainly cannot speak for all the areas in northern Cameroon, nor can I assure you that by the time you read these lines the situation will even remotely resemble what I saw. But I can tell you that in February 2004 Mayo Oldiri and Mayo Nduell were shockingly wonderful, and these areas clearly had been well looked after for a number of seasons.

If anything, these areas were too good! On any given day we saw numerous western kob, western hartebeest, and sing-sing waterbuck. On any given day we would see a handful of Nigerian bohor reedbuck, a couple of harnessed bushbuck, and glimpses of duiker, both red-flanked and western bush duiker. Even roan would be sighted at some point on any hunting day. Without seeking them, we would run into at least one herd of West African savanna buffalo almost every day, and I saw Derby eland from the road on three or four occasions, again without seeking them. Lion are scarce, but we saw a few lionesses. They went about their business without paying us any attention. We saw elephant on several occasions, and they moved away calmly without panicky screaming or demonstrations. These areas had been free from poaching and overhunting for a very long time. This was not what I'd expected or had led myself to believe.

None of which is to say the hunting was easy. The "common game" was easy, but the great prizes remain just that, and this is Equatorial Africa, blistering hot even in midwinter, with few roads. Cameron and I were a good match because our intentions differed. His main goal, most sensibly, was a Derby eland. Mine was a western roan. His secondary goal was a roan, while mine was unclear. Cameroon has an odd and most frustrating licensing system that divides her game into classes in both forest and savanna. In the northern areas the primary "Class A" animals are roan, buffalo, and eland, with small or occasional quotas for korrigum, lion, and elephant. Most of the other antelope species are "Class B," with small game sort of falling into a catchall "Class C." Ground rules: On a hunting license, only two from Class A and four from Class B are allowed.

If you think about it, this is very good marketing: More than one safari is required to satisfy each hunter! For me it was frustrating. What I really wanted in my heart of hearts was first and foremost to take a western roan. Then I badly wanted one of those red, odd-horned buffalo. And then I also wanted another Derby eland. But the rules are the rules, and I had to choose. My decision was not to choose but rather to let hunting luck make the decision. We both took this course with the more common species: me because I had taken them all save western hartebeest in the C.A.R., Cameron because they were all new to him!

Professional hunter Steffan Ndonga and I with a nice sing-sing waterbuck, my first Cameroon trophy. We saw good waterbuck almost every day, and I really shot too quickly—we saw much better trophies before the hunt was over.

International flights to Cameroon come into the major port city of Douala, a world away from northern Cameroon. Charter flights are expensive, and commercial flights to the northern city of Garoua are irregular. We took the option of driving. After all, it doesn't look that far on the map. This, friends, is a course of action I do not recommend! We drove through the day, through most of the night, and through most of the next day, gratefully finding a wonderful camp of comfortable rondavels just ahead of dark. In contrast, on the way out we drove four hours to Garoua and took a two-hour commercial flight back to Douala!

The plan was for Cameron to hunt with Steffan Ndonga and for me to hunt with Zimbabwean Guav Johnson, but Guav was home recovering from one of the myriad tropical ailments and didn't come in until about the fourth day of our hunt. So we both spent the first few days hunting with Steffan, sort of taking things slow and seeing what the area had to offer. Truly, it offered almost too much. In those first couple of days Cameron shot a good western kob, we both shot nice hartebeest and waterbuck, and I shot a superb western bush duiker. By the time Guav Johnson arrived we were both nearly out of Schlitz on our Class B animals—and in some cases we had been a bit too hasty. I'm not sure we could have found better hartebeest, and for certain my duiker was spectacular, but in days to come we would both see truly exceptional waterbuck. Western kob were everywhere, as common as impala are in southern Africa. Really good ones were scarce, but they were out there if one took the time.

And then there was Cameron's roan. Remember, I was conditioned to hunting my tail off for roan and seeing none. On the first day we saw the best roan I had ever laid eyes on. Cameron was the shooter, and we followed the animal into the thick stuff without getting a shot. On the second day we saw a huge herd in a grassy valley, and another fantastic bull appeared to be among them. This time we got ahead of the herd and almost got a shot, but the bull hung up in high grass and didn't quite give us a good look. Steffan acknowledged it had been a very fine bull, and now I was intrigued. Just how big were these things? I have some experience with sable and can judge them fairly well, but I obviously had no idea how to judge roan.

It was probably a cruel prank, but I decided that Cameron must win (and thus actually lose) the "who-shoots-first" game on roan. After all, Steffan was his PH and I was just poaching on his hunt until Guav arrived. Moreover, roan was my primary goal and his secondary. I should wait. Or so I rationalized, should we chance upon another bull that looked as good as these two had. We did, just toward dark on the third day. We caught just a glimpse of a nice bull on the far side of a grassy valley, with just enough light for a stalk. Somehow, with little difficulty, I got Cameron to take the lead behind Steffan.

A hundred yards into the grass we found that the bull we'd seen was a thin-horned youngster—but another bull beyond him had thick, wonderfully curved horns. The men crept forward a bit and Steffan put up the sticks. The bull died in house-high grass, and it was almost dark when we found it. It was a magnificent creature, ancient with polished horns, the kind of roan we'd been seeing and the kind I would be very happy to take home. But Cameron had been my guinea pig, so I measured and studied the bull carefully. Just on 28 inches, he was a very fine roan, and now, for the first time, I sort of knew what I was looking for.

Guav arrived in camp in due course, soft-spoken with a wry sense of humor, a most remarkable young man. Working in Cameroon from

The animal I wanted most was a really good roan, and I definitely got what I wanted. We saw shootable roan every day, but when this bull stepped out, there was no question.

January through May and Zimbabwe from June until the rains come, he does more hunting days than any professional hunter I know—and he pays the price. Too skinny and plagued with multiple annual bouts of malaria, the kid was killing himself. I advised him to go home and stay home, but I didn't mean it. I wanted to hunt with him again, and did in the forest two years later. I gave him the same advice then—but I sort of hope I'm able to do a couple more Cameroon hunts with him!

His first question was the obvious: "What are we hunting?" I told him we were hunting roan, eland, and buffalo. His answer was equally obvious: We could hunt only two of the three. Not so fast, I told him. We could hunt all three until we took one. Then we could hunt the remaining two until we took one. He went off shaking his head, but that's exactly what we did.

We looked at quite a few roan, and I'm sure we saw a shootable bull every single day. But we were seeing enough that we were in no great hurry, so we looked them over carefully and agreed we might do a bit better. We tracked eland on several occasions, starting with Steffan and finishing with Guav. One day we almost got one. We started on the fresh tracks of a big herd and caught them flat-footed three times. A big bull was in there, but every time we got on them, cows covered him. The last

I had believed that giant eland were much less common in Cameroon than in the C.A.R., but that wasn't true in the Mayo Oldiri areas. Sign of eland, tracks and broken trees from feeding, was common, and we actually saw eland from the road several times.

time was just before sunset. We stood atop a big ridge, watching them run down through a brushy valley, then settle and start to feed far up on the next ridge. It was too late in the day to go after them, but the bull was in the clear, maybe six hundred yards away. He was truly a monster, dwarfing the cows in body size, and he had incredible horns above a coal-black neck ruff. So much for Cameroon eland being smaller!

The next day we hunted our way up to Mayo Nduell, intending to stay for a few days because Guav believed that area held somewhat more roan and perhaps a few more buffalo. On the way we encountered three different herds of buffalo and worked our way into all three. Now, the buffalo from the northern C.A.R. all the way across north of the forest zone were once classified as "northwestern buffalo." Today the buffalo of the northern C.A.R. and remnants in Chad are called "Central African savanna buffalo," while the buffalo in Cameroon and on to the west north of the forest zone are called "West African savanna buffalo." As you move west they get somewhat smaller, and the mix of black and red animals becomes ever more red. Even so, most herds will still have plenty of black individuals, and black seems very common among the mature bulls, if not predominant. These buffalo don't have impressive horns, but they are clearly different from southern buffalo—and I wanted a red buffalo. The only buffalo I'd ever shot in neighboring C.A.R., now considered "Central African savanna buffalo," had the smaller, separated, upright horns, but the body color had been black. This time, it was a red buffalo or nothing.

This is a bit like hunting bears for color phase, turning down a big black bear because you're looking for a brown or cinnamon rug. The record book doesn't care, so maybe this all makes sense and maybe it doesn't. But this area supported such foolishness because there were lots of buffalo, and on that particular day we were into them throughout the morning. A couple of herds were easy to slip into, and another led us a merry chase for several hours, but we walked away from all of them. Either the herd held no mature bulls or the mature bulls we saw were black. I still recall one great, burly, black bull that had really good horns for this breed of buffalo, and we actually discussed taking him.

I said no, and was pleased to see that Guav was just fine with that decision—many professional hunters would have torn their hair out, or torn me a new you-know-what on the spot. At the moment buffalo were everywhere, it wasn't terribly difficult to look them over, and we were still in the mode of hunting buffalo, roan, and Derby eland.

We got into the Mayo Nduell camp at the hottest part of the day, dropped our gear, had a quick lunch, and then lay and sweated for a couple of hours. In the "cool" of a still-sweltering late afternoon Guav decided to travel a little circle that should take us through some good country for roan and also along the edge of some of the area's best korrigum habitat. We actually saw a few of the big purple antelope, and I could have taken a good one quite easily, but that's yet another Class A animal, so I didn't even look. Things were complex enough already!

On the way into camp we'd glimpsed a nice herd of roan that held a bull worth a second look, and our initial thought was to see if we could find that herd again. We did not; in fact, after spotting the korrigum we saw almost nothing until just before sundown. We had just passed through some fairly thick trees and entered a burned area with a big clearing off to our left. On the edge of that clearing seven or eight roan

The buffalo in northern Cameroon are now called West African savanna buffalo. Wh... and I passed up quite a few black bulls before I found this one.

ll them, they are a mixture of red and black in any given herd. I wanted a red buffalo,

were feeding along. All were cows, but we figured a bull must be nearby. Guav cut the motor before they heard us, and we managed to get a bit closer and set up before the bull walked out.

He came from the left, striding into his harem, and this roan required no discussion and no hesitation. He dwarfed the cows, and his horns seemed almost sablelike, not only in length but also in the "C" curve they described. I'm not sure if a single word passed between us, but as soon as he was clear I shot him in the center of the shoulder with the big .375 Weatherby. He ran with the herd, went down, but was up again quickly. We ran with him, I shot again, and it was almost dark as we approached.

The references always describe the roan as the second largest antelope. Although I'd never shot one of either race, I've seen a few East African roan in Tanzania and a few southern roan on game ranches in Namibia. In Zambia I have shot a couple of what they now call Angolan roan. None of these impressed me as the "second largest antelope"—I would have given that honor to a big kudu bull. Maybe the references are talking about the western roan, because this was truly a giant of an antelope, as Cameron's bull had been, and his horns were monstrous. As darkness gathered in the burned-out grass I took some of the worst "trophy photos" I've ever shot, and it's a shame because this roan is truly one of my very best African trophies.

We were just passing the halfway point of the hunt, and now, for the first time, decisions were required. I could now have a Derby eland or a red buffalo, but not both. Once again I deferred the decision to the luck of the draw, but it seemed most likely that the buffalo would win— or, perhaps better put, an individual buffalo would lose. There were a lot more buffalo moving around than eland, and since eland remained Cameron's primary goal, Guav and I were steering clear of what was considered the best eland country.

I think we did track another herd of eland without making contact, and for sure we looked over a couple more herds of buffalo without finding the bull we wanted. Either could have been just a matter of time, but if we kept looking at buffalo, we were bound to shoot one relatively soon. In general this was surprisingly easy buffalo hunting. The local lexicon for the terrain in northern Cameroon (as in the northern C.A.R.) is "savanna," but this is really a misnomer intended

The most common antelope in this region is western kob, seemingly almost as plentiful as impala in much of southern Africa. That said, there weren't a lot of big ones. I saved one license until the very end looking for the best kob we could find, and this is a nice one.

to differentiate the north from the true forest to the south. Technically it's savanna woodland or Terminalia forest, much of it not very different from mopane woodland in Zimbabwe or Brachystegia woodland in Zambia, except that Terminalia is the dominant tree.

It is much, much, much thicker than true savanna, but it's nowhere near as thick as the southern forests or, for that matter, the *jess* of the Zambezi Valley, and there are numerous open, grassy valleys or dambos. Buffalo often can be seen from a considerable difference. Thanks to a combination of effective antipoaching and the relative scarcity of lion, the buffalo are relatively calm and easy to approach. This was much different from some of the heavily poached areas I've hunted in the C.A.R. where buffalo, once bumped, would run all day with the wind at their backs! Sometimes it took some circling and tracking, but we were able to look over most of the herds we saw. However, I sense that these buffalo gather in smaller herds than do southern buffalo. We saw a few groups of thirty and more, but herds of a dozen to twenty seemed more common, and we never saw gatherings of hundreds, as is common with southern buffalo in good areas.

This locally famous hippo lives in the river near Garoua, northern Cameroon. One of the locals actually swims out to her and brings her to the bank to be fed. You wouldn't catch me in that water!

Guav and Steffan did have a great deal of respect for these buffalo, considering them ill-tempered and dangerous. This may be a function of the large areas of tall grass, where any encounter would be too close. A couple of seasons earlier a PH had been killed when he chanced upon a buffalo while crossing a grassy valley. They showed me this spot, and Guav showed me another spot where the same might have happened to him except that he happened to have his rifle in his hands, ready. Honestly, I didn't see undue aggression in these buffalo, and in fact saw no significant difference between them and any other buffalo save for color, body size, and horn conformation. But I bow to the experts! We were very careful in the tall grass, but in general had little difficulty getting close enough to buffalo to look them over well.

When it happened it came quite easily . . . or would have if I'd done my job. I was shooting a left-hand Weatherby Mark V in synthetic stock, chambered to .375 Weatherby Magnum, a great rifle and a great cartridge for this country. The scope was a Leupold 1.5–5X, which has at least as much eye relief as any scope on the market. Even so, the mounts put the scope a bit far back. It had cut me once on the bench, but I didn't do anything about it because I truly believed I could stay away from the scope in field-shooting positions. I was wrong. It cut me a couple of times during the course of this safari, the last time implanting a fairly nasty gash between my eyebrow and the bridge of my nose when I shot the roan. Tired of bleeding, and with my buffalo goal now getting serious, I took the scope off and checked the iron sights. They were just fine, and of course up until then every opportunity at a buffalo had been quite close, so I did not reattach the scope.

We picked up the spoor of a good-size herd moving along a watercourse. The dung was still hot, so we expected to catch them in the grassy valley just ahead, but they had already moved up into the hills. Tracking was fast, and within a half-hour we caught a glimpse of buffalo moving ahead. We maneuvered a bit to the left, but the animals were moving faster than we were and we came in behind the herd and had to take the tracks once more. We never saw the herd again, but just a few hundred yards farther on we spotted the trail animal moving through a gully ahead of us. He was a good, mature bull and was mahogany red in color. We advanced quickly and caught him going up a burned ridge at about eighty yards. Obviously I'd have been better off with the scope in place, but it was too late for that. He stood almost broadside for a moment, quartering slightly away, and off the sticks I should have been able to make that shot, scope or no. But I didn't. I hit him a bit forward, then skipped the second shot across the top of his back as he ran over the crest.

We ran to the top and saw one buffalo walking away, and I figured we had a good chance to clean up the mess right there. Correctly, but unfortunately, Guav stopped me. There had been a herd and we didn't know where they were, so we couldn't be sure this was the right buffalo. So we let him walk, and we followed the blood right to his tracks. And then things slowed down considerably as we followed a definitely wounded buffalo.

He led us up and over a couple of ridges and across a wonderfully clear burned-over plateau. The blood was steady. We would find him or, given the reputation of these buffalo, he would find us. Beyond the plateau the ground dropped into a deep korongo choked with still-green grass, and the blood led straight into that grass. Guav and I looked at each other. This was surely where the bull would wait for us. We threw a few rocks and sticks down there . . . nothing.

This was my mess, so I wiped my palms and went straight in on the blood, Guav reluctantly agreeing to stay to one side where he was clear and could shoot. One step at a time, I followed fresh blood on the green stalks. Fifty yards took an eternity, and then the spoor took us out of the grass and up the far side. We paused on a little bench to get our heart rates back to normal, and our incredibly tall tracker pointed into thick brush on the ridge above us.

There was a hint of a horizontal red line behind some brush, and then that red line moved to the right. I took a step left, fired, and the red line lurched forward and was gone. We moved up carefully, and the bull was there, down and dead, a truly beautiful red buffalo with platinum blond highlights in his ears and black shading on his chest, like a bongo bull.

Cameron got his Derby eland a day or so later, and with about a third of the hunt remaining we were pretty much done. Guav and I dug around and found an extra-good western kob, which finished my license, and in the final days Cameron finished his with a good harnessed bushbuck. In the process of this digging around, of course, we saw more and probably better specimens of all the Class B animals we'd taken at the beginning, but at that time we hadn't known how good this area was. Now we do, and it's a place I intend to go back to . . . but that will be sometime in my fourth decade of African hunting!

Sapi

The safari that resulted in the *Boddington on Buffalo* DVD and ultimately gave me the impetus to write my book, *Buffalo!* a year later had a less-than-auspicious beginning. In fact, I was skeptical of the whole project from the very start. It started in a hotel room in Dallas one afternoon in 2001. That evening I was scheduled to speak to a Dallas Safari Club meeting, and although I've made hundreds of presentations I always have serious stage fright, which I try my best to conceal. What I really wanted was to be left alone so I could go over my notes and my slides. But Tim Danklef had requested—no, demanded—an "important" meeting.

I'd known Tim for many years through my old friend and mentor Geoff Broom. I'd been in his home with Geoff, and I liked him and trusted him, but I had no idea what he wanted to talk to me about. Tim had made several safaris with Geoff, and with several other good outfitters. Retired at a young age from the Anheuser-Busch marketing department, Tim was representing a few of his outfitter friends as "Timbuctoo Adventures," but I'd never booked a hunt through him and that's about all I knew. At the appointed hour the phone rang and Tim came up to my room, bringing with him Dave Fulson, whom I'd never met.

It seems that these guys, in addition to planning safaris and, in Dave's case, operating a guiding service in Texas and elsewhere, had been aggressively videoing African hunts for several seasons and had built up an extensive library of what I came to understand was "B-roll" footage—the spice that allows frequent and multiple cuts of live game and hunting and keeps the viewer captured. They had done a couple of pretty darned good DVDs and wanted me to team up with them to do a DVD that would be the end-all, final word on buffalo hunting. As laid out, it sounded interesting. I knew Tim, Dave seemed a good guy and a genuinely knowledgeable hunter, and the initial plan was to do the basics of the film with Geoff Broom.

Even so, I was a bit skeptical. I did a few hunting videos in the late 1980s. They weren't great, but they weren't bad. They taught me that I needn't fear the camera, but I got burned by three different partners. Despite promises, I never made a dime and wound up footing the bill for some hunts I didn't really want to make. I also learned that hunting without a camera is a whole lot more fun than hunting for the camera! In sum, by 1990 I had pretty much decided that print was my medium and I'd best stick with what I knew. At the time of my initial meeting with Tim and Dave, nothing had happened to alter that decision. However, as I'm sure you know by now, I'm such a junkie for Africa that I was unable to turn down a good buffalo hunt, even one for the camera.

Things changed fast. First "9-11" came and I went overseas for a year, putting our buffalo film on hold. Then Geoff Broom had shut down operations in Tanzania and bought a beautiful farm in the Douma area north of Harare, perched on the Zambezi Escarpment. I don't think the ink was dry on his mortgage before his farm was taken in Zimbabwe's infamous land reallocation. To make matters worse, about the time I got back from the Persian Gulf Geoff had an accident while elephant hunting in the valley. His client had taken a nice bull, and Geoff was hustling down a little embankment on his way to fetch the vehicle. A loose stone gave way and he went head over teakettle, badly shattering an ankle. This is a guy who has hunted dangerous game intensively for a half-century. Neither he nor any of his clients have ever been injured by an animal—but one little rock darn near ended his career. It did not, however: As I write these words Geoff Broom, at seventy-never-mind, is hunting elephant in the wild lands he loves. But when we needed to resurrect our plans for *Boddington on Buffalo,* his ability to hunt again was uncertain.

Tim set up the hunt for June 2004 with Andrew Dawson of Chifuti Safaris. Those who have seen the final result may be surprised at this, but I had never met Andrew until we pitched up in his camp. This in itself isn't all that strange. Zimbabwe has a lot of fine professional hunters, and there

I had never been in the Lower Zambezi and I didn't realize how wild and wonderful it is, much of it genuinely untouched Africa. The Chewore riverbed is an ideal place to look for buffalo tracks, and much of it cannot be reached by a vehicle.

are more that I don't know than those I have met. Too, Zimbabwe had been "off my beat" for a number of years while I'd been chasing strange things in other parts of Africa. In retrospect, while it isn't remarkable that I'd never met Dawson, it's surprising to me that I agreed to do this important project with a perfect stranger. A buffalo hunt is one thing, but once something is committed to film you have to live with it for a long time! I think I made a couple of alternative suggestions, brushed aside by Tim and Dave, and I guess we went forward based primarily on my faith in them.

In fairness, I'm sure Andrew had even more reservations than I did. He didn't know me, but I've been writing about his world for a long time. He knew of me, and in this business that's often a whole lot worse. I have no idea how Tim and Dave talked him into doing it!

I think it worked out wonderfully, as proven by the results on camera. Most men who carry a Zimbabwe professional hunter's license, having undergone the African continent's most rigorous apprenticeship and testing requirements, are extremely competent. "Daws" was no exception, and he was also a very nice guy. Generally soft-spoken (but firm when necessary), he's interesting in that he's a thinking hunter, always trying to figure things out from the game's perspective.

So on the appointed day we chartered into the Chikwenya airstrip on the border between Mana Pools National Park and Sapi Safari Area, close by the Zambezi River. We were quite a crew: Tim Danklef, Dave Fulson, my girlfriend Donna Grey, and me. Andrew and his wife, Heidi, were there to meet us, and after an hour of bouncing along the flood plain we pulled into Chifuti Safaris' main camp, a neat cluster of tents right on the river. That night we met Andrew's partner, Paul Smith, also for the first time. It's overstatement to say that we instantly became friends—they were as uncertain of me as I was of them—but for sure it didn't take very long!

Cameras aside, it was truly a very simple safari, with clear-cut and limited goals. In retrospect, this made it a wonderful safari. We had a full two weeks in which we hoped to take two decent buffalo bulls. All of us—Andrew, Paul, Tim, Dave, and me—are sticklers for taking fully mature, hard-bossed bulls. Beyond that, we all understood that the camera came first, and I made it clear that I wasn't interested in the biggest bull in the valley. Sure, that would have been nice, but our goal was to capture buffalo hunting the way we all loved it, not necessarily to search for an outlandishly exceptional bull. To that end we hoped to spend half the hunt concentrating on herds and the last half tracking bachelor bulls, the great old *dagga* boys for which the Zambezi Valley is famous.

We also wanted to do it right, with the right voice. I have done a great deal of African hunting, perhaps as much as any American who is not a professional hunter. But that's a key point: I am not a licensed professional hunter, or even a gifted amateur. I'm just a writer who likes to hunt, and I've managed to do a lot of it. One of my concerns with this new filming gig was to avoid setting myself up as the expert that I'm not, or as a hero that I'm not, or as an egotist that I hope I'm not. Interestingly, Andrew Dawson's concerns were similar, and perhaps even more worrisome: He would have to live among his peers with this film, so he was equally concerned that he not come off as a fool or, perhaps worse, a know-it-all. Had the chemistry not been right, these things could have happened to either of us, but we worked together well, with good points and counterpoints, and, for two guys with little camera experience, amazingly natural dialog.

IN THE HERDS

At Main Camp the sun sets over rugged hills across the river in Zambia. There is no human habitation in Sapi, or in Mana Pools to the west, or in Chewore North Safari Area to the east, or in Zambia's Lower Zambezi National Park across the river, making this one of the most unspoiled stretches of the Zambezi River. Hippo call through the night, and they can be glassed, along with sunning crocodiles, either on the opposite bank or on small islands throughout the day. In the evening herds of elephant come to drink along the far bank, and almost every night the roaring of lion drifts across the river—and sometimes sounds in the bush just beyond camp.

Tim and Dave have come to think of this area as their second home, and over time I would grow to love it just as much. But on this hunt we spent just the first night on the river, and the next day headed south to Fly Camp. It was June, and pools remained in the sand rivers and plenty of "pans" out in the bush still contained water. In a few weeks, as surface water evaporated, buffalo would concentrate on the river, but right now they were widely scattered, with more big herds in the southern part of the concession, toward the Zambezi Escarpment. This part of Sapi can be hunted from the river in a long, long day (we've done that, too), but to reach the old Security Road that bisects southern Sapi from east to west takes a hard three-hour grind from the river. A better answer is Fly Camp, just a handful of small tents on the west bank of the Chewore River.

We hunted our way there that first day, finding a bit of sign along the way but nothing fresh enough to follow. At first I was sorry to leave the river, and I'm sure Donna, who was enjoying her first days in Africa, was genuinely disappointed. But Fly Camp wasn't so bad. It was simple, with the dining room under the stars, but the tents looked right out onto the white sand of the Chewore riverbed, and lion roared there as well.

Over the next few days we got into several herds, and it was thoroughly wonderful. I had done a lot of buffalo hunting and over the years had been fortunate to run onto a number of very good bulls. I like buffalo hunting's tracking, walking, and, when you finally get into them, pure excitement. I even consider it something of a specialty of mine, one type of African hunting that I actually

The pools were drying up quickly, with the buffalo gravitating to the remaining water. This hidden spring up in the hills flows year-round and is always an ideal place to find buffalo or any other wildlife.

know a bit about. But I will never know enough, and I learned every day.

I did so partly because Andrew Dawson is truly a great professional hunter. I also learned from his two head trackers, Lumuc and Mukassa, who were as good as any trackers I have ever seen, not only following tracks where few could but also looking, thinking, and anticipating. And my learning curve was also boosted by this rare opportunity to concentrate on nothing but buffalo, in great buffalo country with no distractions.

We weren't always successful. Some herds crossed the Chewore, our eastern boundary, and eluded us. Others crossed into Mana Pools, our southern and western boundary. Others had no good bulls in them. Early one afternoon we found the fresh-from-morning tracks of a smallish herd, maybe thirty, and followed them into relatively open mopane woodland. We hit them in less than a half-hour, and they were bedded tight in little clumps that were too open for us to get closer and too thick to see the animals properly.

So we backed off and sat down, swatting mopane bees through the heat of the day. These horrible little insects don't sting, but they swarm your ears and eyes and drive you nuts. Everybody hates them, but they especially love Tim Danklef. Oddly, they didn't seem to like Donna much at all. So she sat back, relatively unbothered, and giggled at Tim and the rest of us as we swore and swatted.

Eventually the herd got up, and we maneuvered with them, occasionally getting just glimpses of a couple of promising bulls—not enough of a look to even be sure. With a half-hour remaining before sunset, Daws suggested we charge the herd to see what we could see. I hadn't done this in years, but it's a standard tactic in Zimbabwe's heavy cover, taught me by Geoff Broom and his son, Russ. In that last hour of daylight buffalo are generally at their calmest, feeding along and reluctant to split up with darkness approaching in lion country. When you run into them in that last golden hour, they typically will stampede for just a short distance, then pull up short and gather. Often the bulls will come to the rear of the herd and turn to challenge you, and though it's a terrible way to get a good shot, if you can keep up it's a great way to see the bulls in a herd.

So we ran with them, Daws and me with our heavy rifles, Tim and Dave with their cameras, and Donna keeping pace right behind. We almost ran afoul of a cow with calf, which is the greatest risk in this crazy technique, but after three or four long sprints we saw both bulls at close range. They were plenty wide and had good shape, but both had bosses that were clearly soft, at least a couple of years from full maturity.

If you see all the bulls and still have plenty of time left to hunt, then you've won. We won on that day, but there was another day that I'm not so sure about. That time we followed a good-size herd, more than a hundred, from the Chewore westward. We got out of the impossible riverine growth and caught them at midmorning in relatively open mopane. For a time things were textbook perfect, with the herd feeding along and us circling and cutting back into the herd to view different groups. We had clearly seen and discounted several bulls, but we only got glimpses of others that held promise. Then the herd started to lie down, black clumps supine in deepening shade.

We tried a couple of approaches, but the midday wind was becoming unstable. I had already relearned patience while swatting mopane bees, but now I learned patience mixed with wisdom. We took stock of the herd's location, marched back to the truck, and went back to camp. After

The first buffalo we took for Boddington on Buffalo *was a fine herd bull, probably about nine to ten years old and just starting to wear down his horn tips. We'd watched his herd pass for two hours, and he came out of left field and surprised us completely.*

a late brunch and a good nap, at half past three we were back with them, just as they started to get up. We circled and cut until five o'clock, seeing a couple of nice young bulls but still convinced we hadn't seen them all. So we charged, splitting the herd and running first with one group and then another. It was a magic hour, and darn good exercise, and a couple of times we pulled up short and eyeballed what seemed a good bull. But it was just the briefest glimpse, amid buffalo running everywhere and dust thick enough to choke you.

Weeks later, when I saw the video from that day, I began to wonder what in the hell we were thinking. Right there, perfectly caught by Dave's camera, is all the buffalo anyone could want, wheeling to face us like a Van Howd painting: deep curls, heavy boss, maybe forty-three inches. He's on the *Boddington on Buffalo* tape, an obvious shooter—but though the camera saw him, we didn't.

I think it was the next day when Lumuc and Mukassa led us to a hidden spring deep in the hills. It's a magic place where clean water bubbles out from under the roots of stately red mahogany trees. But that day we didn't see the trees for a while because the buffalo were already there. Mukassa knew this long before we got there. I saw some tracks when we left the truck, but we didn't follow them, figuring we would pick up fresher tracks at the spring. We hadn't gone far when Mukassa pointed up and smiled. Oxpeckers, small birds that live on buffalo parasites, were making directly for the spring.

Ages ago in Zambia, Russ Broom and I had followed buffalo herds thanks to circling cattle egrets, but this was the first time I had seen buffalo given away by oxpeckers, and I was skeptical. High overhead, they looked like any other small bird to me. By the end of the hunt I would never again question either Lumuc or Mukassa.

We heard the buffalo long before we arrived at the spring and approached carefully, eventually crawling in behind the cover of a big tree. The buffalo were just starting to leave the spring, and we'd already missed the front of the herd. Even so, we held our position for an hour and a half while at least two hundred of the black hulks passed in front of us, glistening with fresh mud and feeding slowly along. We figured there must be bulls in the rear of the herd, and we had a perfect spot with a narrow strip of open green grass right in front of us. We consciously passed up a big-bodied, heavy-bossed bull because the horn spread was narrow, and we grudgingly passed two spectacular young bulls, both well over forty inches but with bosses that were still very soft.

Now the flow of animals had slowed to a trickle, and every single one had passed either through that green strip or along a brushy fringe above it. I think it was Lumuc who grabbed Andrew's sleeve and pointed. To our right, off the path of the herd and coming directly toward us, was a very fine bull. He had deep curls, tips that were long and perfect, and there was nothing soft about his boss. Andrew grabbed me, I grabbed the Dakota .375, and, forgive me, I committed the cardinal sin of not making sure the camera was ready. Fortunately, the man behind the camera was Dave Fulson, and nobody is faster. He got the shot, as did I, taken frontally at no more than twenty-five yards.

The bull lurched forward a few steps, typical of a frontal shot, then turned to our left and wheeled in an arc across that narrow strip

Mukassa and Lumuc prepare a field lunch of sudza, *maize meal, and meat stew. It doesn't get much better!*

of green, never more than forty yards away. I shot three more times, seeing each impact, and Dave stayed with us both. Then the bull was gone in brush, and in seconds we heard his death bellow. I've been criticized for taking those extra shots, and Tim and Dave have been criticized by no less an authority than Robin Hurt for showing them. To me that's silly. The first shot felt good, but if backup shots are available and safe (meaning clear of other buffalo), I keep shooting. I'm not afraid of buffalo, but I take no chances with them. Before we walked up, I switched to the Rigby .470 and shot the bull a final time before we closed on him. That's sensible buffalo hunting, and I'm not in the least ashamed of it. For the record, the first shot, with a Swift A-Frame, was fatal. So were the third and fourth solids through the shoulders as the bull ran. Now, my second shot? Well, as near as we could tell, it never even hit the buffalo! That shot was at less than twenty yards, but the bull was moving through brush before he broke clear and I can only guess that the brush ate that bullet. That is partly why, when given a choice, I never bank on just one shot with buffalo.

Dagga Boys

That first buffalo was a classic herd bull, probably ten years old with completely hard bosses and yet long points and sharp tips. He was at his maximum horn growth—within a short time horn wear would exceed growth and the tips would start to wear down. This is the kind of bull that "scores" best by record-book standards, and hunting bulls in big herds is a wonderful experience. But to me the better trophies, and the buffalo we really should concentrate on taking, are older bulls that have been cast out from the herds and are living in bachelor groups with their peers. These old bulls love to wallow and are often covered in mud, giving them their name: *Dagga* is Shona for "mud," so a *dagga* boy is a mud bull, an old-timer heavy in body and horn but usually with worn horn tips.

Before starting to work on bachelor groups, we repaired to Main Camp for the real work of the trip, a couple of days of intensive on-camera interplay including seemingly endless discussions of tactics, guns and loads, trophy judgment, and so much more. It wasn't all that painful, really, and this was in large part why we were there, but I was glad when it was over and we could head back to Fly Camp!

More lessons awaited. None were particularly new, but absent the pressure of conflicting goals and with plenty of time to concentrate, the learning curve was steady. The primary lesson involved the significant differences between hunting bachelor bulls and mixed herds. Mind you, I had done both before, and on many occasions, but most of my buffalo hunting had been at least random, if not catch-as-catch-can, taking the tracks that presented themselves. I had taken good bulls from herds and good bulls from bachelor groups, but I'd never thought about the differences.

In some ways bachelor groups are easier to hunt. True *dagga* boys, as opposed to the bachelor groups containing bulls of all ages that you sometimes run into, are generally more sedentary than herds. They don't require as much grass or water, so their tracks often show they are watering repeatedly in small pools and traveling relatively short distances to feed and bedding cover. Once you get into them, there are far fewer eyes, ears, and noses to confound the matter, so chances of a shot are somewhat better—if you close with them.

That last is where *dagga* boys are often more difficult. Herds, needing big water and lots of grass, travel greater distances and leave more tracks. Older bulls are more secretive. You will find their tracks along sand rivers where small pools remain, and around unknown water holes deep in the bush. Good areas in the Zambezi Valley tend to hold lots of *dagga* boys, but finding their tracks isn't always easy. Then there are three more problems, all of equal significance.

First, the smaller the group, the more difficult the tracking. Following a herd is generally quite easy. Depending on the soil and grass, a group of four or five bulls usually isn't too difficult. Just one or two bachelor bulls are work for a master tracker, and in today's Africa these guys, an anachronism in our twenty-first century, are increasingly rare. Time is critical on most modern safaris, and of utmost importance on the seven-day buffalo hunts common today. If you follow buffalo and close with them, your time is well spent even if there isn't a shooter. But if you follow for a couple of hours and lose the tracks—always possible with *dagga* boys—that can mean a whole day lost.

Second, being sedentary and a bit reclusive, *dagga* boys often bed in the thickest, nastiest riverine growth close to water, cover where judging a bull and getting a shot can be almost impossible. We'd walked the Chewore's sandy bed through much of the afternoon, seeing old tracks and finding one old bull bedded in the lee of a boulder. We could have shot him, but his horns were narrow. We returned to camp with just an hour of daylight left, bypassed it, and took a drive along the Upper Chewore to see what we could find.

As we rounded a sharp bend, there in the riverbed ahead were six bulls. I suppose several were shooters, but our eyes were immediately drawn to a monster bull, his withers clearly standing above his fellows. He had the biggest bosses of any buffalo I have ever seen. This alone made him a trophy, but his horns carried the mass throughout and spread well beyond his ears. I would guess him at forty-two inches. The group, about a hundred and fifty yards away, was alarmed by the vehicle but not yet spooked. Shooting from a vehicle is illegal in areas administered by Zimbabwe's Parks and Wildlife. In any case I'm against the practice. As I've written before, buffalo hunting is all about the experience, and taking a bull so cheaply amounts to robbing yourself of most of the memories. But in this case a compromise was practical, and this bull was a great gift. All we had to do was step off the truck with the scoped .375, advance a few yards, and set up the sticks. The fact that we did not was more a matter of needing to hunt for the camera than purity of ethics.

Instead, we watched them steadily move into the riverine cover. They were still calm, so we could have followed them immediately and perhaps gotten a shot, but it was already dark in the thick cover, too late for the camera. So we left them and took their tracks the next morning. We bumped them four or five times, but they understood this game. We could see patches of black at twenty yards or less, but we never saw that bull. Hell, we never saw any of them close enough to shoot. They understood that their safety lay in the heavy green foliage, and they never left it. The next morning their tracks showed they had crossed the river into Chewore, and that was the last we saw of them.

The third problem is purely a numbers game. *Dagga* boys are, by any sensible definition, old bulls that are worthy trophies—but they don't all have big horns. Most will be average, a few will be huge, and many will have horns that are badly worn or broken. Luck is probably a more important factor than the law of averages, but most professional hunters are reluctant to follow just one or two old bulls, partly because of the difficulty in holding the spoor and partly because the odds of finding a big bull are relatively low.

If you can find three or more, the chances of both following and finding a shooter go up dramatically. But it still isn't a sure thing. Late one morning we found big tracks leaving the sandy bed of the Sapi River. At first Lumuc and Mukassa believed there were two. Then a third joined them, and when we found them bedded, there were actually four. We got very close before the first bull stood, barely ten yards away. He was a nice bull, heavy-bossed, with horns just at his ears, maybe thirty-seven, certainly thirty-six. One by one the others stood, then all ran up a little ridge and turned to face us. All four were cookie cutters of each other: good, fully mature bulls, shooters all, but indistinguishable in trophy size. It would have been a no-brainer for someone who hadn't taken many buffalo or was short on time. Neither condition applied, so we walked away.

The old Security Road, created for military purposes during Rhodesia's long bush war, parallels the Lower Zambezi about forty miles south. It crosses the Chewore and the Sapi and a dozen small tributaries in between, and in this June many of these crossings held small pools, several being used by buffalo. It was still early when we found the spoor of two *dagga* boys leaving one of these pools. The wind was favorable, and both sets of tracks were huge. Attempting to follow these two bulls broke the rules, but we had time.

Too, in Lumuc and Mukassa we had two great trackers, and, even better, they've worked together for years and are a great team. For the next three hours I was treated to some of the finest tracking I have ever seen, over hard-baked ground, through grass, across gravel tailings, through places where I could see no tracks at all. The going was very, very slow, and we actually covered relatively little ground as these buffalo led us back and forth as they fed slowly along. Two or three times the wind grew dicey, and without hesitation Mukassa took us away from the tracks of the two slow-moving buffalo. When the wind stabilized, we hooked back with total confidence and picked up the spoor once more. Several times I was sure—and not surprised—that we had lost the spoor, but Mukassa and Lumuc would fan out, casting forward, right, and left, and then retrace their steps until they found it. And they did so every time. It was one of my most memorable buffalo hunts before we ever saw the bulls, and when we found them it got even better.

We had descended a low ridge and just crossed a small erosion gully in the bottom when Lumuc stopped us, flat palm extended backward. With all noise and movement ceased, he pointed over the next low ridge. The signal was clear: The buffalo were right there. But there was nothing to see, just the crest of a tiny rise not twenty yards ahead and ten feet above us. Andrew bent close and Lumuc signaled once more, pointing to the sky and spiraling his finger downward over that low crest. He had seen two oxpeckers dropping down over that ridge, and he knew with certainty that the buffalo were there.

We crept to the top of the ridge, each step revealing more of the thick mopane beyond as we neared the crest. Nothing . . . still nothing . . . more nothing, and now we could see a small wooded valley with another low ridge fifty yards beyond. Then Mukassa pointed. I'd been looking too far. Fifteen yards ahead, on the near descending slope, was a stout mopane. Behind it was a black shape with horn tips extending from each side. Farther left and three yards farther on was another black shape.

Both bulls were bedded tight, momentarily unaware. Then the first bull rose behind his tree. The horn spread extending beyond his tree said he was a good bull, but there was no shot. The second bull stood, and he seemed similar but not quite so wide. Andrew said, "The right bull looks good."

There was nothing to be done about it at the moment, and I was fairly certain both bulls would bolt at any moment. The first bull did, trotting past his buddy down into the valley. Then he stopped, almost broadside, and swung his great head toward us. Andrew confirmed calmly, "The better bull is on the left now. Take him if you can."

The distance was still less than thirty yards. I raised the Rigby .470, settled the bead on the shoulder a third of the way up, and fired the right barrel. I couldn't see the impact over the recoil, but the bull ran hard to the left and I yanked the barrels down, swinging with him. The left barrel went off just before he passed behind a tree, and that bull was gone. I was barely reloaded when we heard his death bellow, but his buddy was still there, facing us. We took a few steps forward and stopped, and the second bull crashed away. My bull was just beyond the tree, down after less than twenty yards from two 500-grain Swift A-Frames side by side on his shoulder.

Andrew and I had both misjudged this bull. The horns were just outside his ears, so I'd figured him to be about 38 inches, with good bosses. This was no monster but a small cut above most of the bulls we'd seen. Andrew figured the same. We were both wrong, fooled by abnormal body size with ears to match. He was exactly, precisely 40 inches in spread, with worn tips but good shape, a perfect Zambezi Valley buffalo at the end of a perfect hunt.

Daylight Hyena and Accidental Grysbok

In the early days of my African hunting, quotas were more liberal and a lot more flexible. If you saw it, you could generally shoot it. This is changing over much of Africa, and is long gone in most of the Zambezi Valley. Quotas are tightly managed today, which is good, but it makes hunting ever more

A really fine Sharpe grysbok, encountered by chance while we were tracking buffalo. Most of the time it's better to stick to business, but it's always wise to capitalize on a rare opportunity when presented—and grysbok are much more difficult to come by than buffalo!

specialized. In the Sapi Safari Area that year, for instance, the quota was something like forty buffalo, but just a dozen kudu and a small handful each of waterbuck, zebra, and warthog. I had arranged for none of these, so that was just fine. The half-dozen leopard, crocs, and elephant bulls; the one Sapi lion; and the dozen or so hippo were long since spoken for.

The three most flexible species were impala, Sharpe grysbok, and spotted hyena. Impala are plentiful and the quota is large, supplying camp meat, rations for the game-scout station, and baits for the leopard hunters. The quota on both hyena and grysbok is finite (and much lower than buffalo), but both animals are so hard to come by that they are generally added to the "TR2" (hunting permit) of every buffalo hunter, just in case there is time. Hyena are plentiful and can be heard whooping and laughing every night, but they are hard to hunt because they are almost completely nocturnal. Baiting is the common technique, but it means getting up at 3 A.M., stalking a bait in total darkness, and hoping to catch a slow hyena just at gray dawn. Grysbok are also plentiful, but they are a tiny antelope and hard to spot in the underbrush. Normally you get just a quick glimpse, rarely enough to properly judge sex, let alone size.

Buffalo were our main objective, but of course I usually have other agendas as well. Two of them were to hunt hyena and to take a grysbok. In years gone by hyena were considered a pest, never a trophy animal. This was unfair to the hyena, which actually has a beautiful spotted skin as well as being very difficult to hunt, but that's the way it was. Twenty years earlier I had shot one on a failed lion bait in Zambia and had not saved the skin because the poor animal had a snare around its neck. I wanted to actually hunt one, and I can still say that I actually never have . . .

The first morning, en route to Fly Camp, we stopped at what is now known as Hyena Pan, so named because an obviously sick hyena was out in the water, belly deep and barely able to lift its head. At our game scout's request I shot it, and we discovered it had been badly hammered by either a lion or a leopard and infected wounds were all over its body. A few days later we passed by that place and were shocked to discover that a leopard had carried the stinking carcass far up a tree and devoured it, which makes one question why so many PHs are so finicky in selecting leopard bait!

A few days later we were cruising the bed of the Chewore River, headed back to Fly Camp at sundown. A hyena ran across our path and stopped, fully exposed, in some tall weeds just to our left. Tim Danklef knew I wanted a hyena, so he instantly said, "Shoot that thing." I started to comply, but Andrew reminded me that shooting from a vehicle is illegal. So I clambered down, was handed the rifle, and advanced a few yards to get a clear view of the still-stationary hyena. It was backlit by the sunset and appeared fluffy, and my thought was that it was a youngster. I hesitated and glanced at Andrew, who had his binocular up. He shook his head negatively, and I turned back to the truck. Tim was horrified. He insisted it was a big one, muttering that after all, a hyena is a hyena, and adding that we'd just bought ourselves a boatload of ridiculously early mornings.

Another hidden agenda was to introduce Donna to Africa. We'd been dating for a little while, and although she'd never hunted, she was fascinated by wildlife. When introduced by a mutual friend, she'd said that as a little girl, "Wild Kingdom" had been her favorite TV show. One of our first dates was a trip to the San Diego Wild Animal Park. Now in real Africa for the first time, she seemed to love every minute of it. She walked every step of the way on every buffalo tracking job and enjoyed watching the trackers work. The Zambezi Valley is harsh country, great for buffalo and elephant but hardly like the Serengeti for wildlife viewing. This seemed to bother her not at all. She reveled in what we did see, and over time we were fortunate to see not only plenty of buffalo and elephant but also had several sightings of lion and all the rest.

She had no idea whether she would be disgusted or fascinated by the shooting, but just in case, we'd spent some time on the range. One morning a necessary goal was to take an impala for the game scouts, and Donna became the designated shooter. She shot a fine impala ram perfectly, and over the next couple of years would become an accomplished huntress. But before she got a shot, we made two or three short stalks on impala that gave us the slip.

So, we were bombing along the main road, with Mana Pools on our left and the hunting area on our right, when a really big impala bounded out of the Park and into our area. Andrew stopped the truck, and we grabbed the .270 and the shooting sticks and began an approach. We got a brief glimpse of the impala still walking to our right, so we circled that way for maybe two hundred yards. Andrew pulled up short behind a stout tree, and in front of us was a small open meadow. No impala was there, but something was lying in that short grass. My first impression was lion, but it was a huge hyena, sound asleep. We might have done it differently if we'd thought about it, but Donna instantly handed me the rifle and Andrew set up the shooting sticks. Two seconds later the hyena stood and started off, and I shot him quartering away and dropped him.

He was a monster, the biggest hyena any of us had seen. Tim and Dave had stayed in the truck, missing a rare and totally unexpected filming opportunity, and the truck was well out of sight. Andrew, Mukassa, and Lumuc, trying to conceal grins, walked back to the truck, making gestures about horn size and telling Tim and Dave that we'd shot the new world-record impala. Andrew walked the truck in, much to their confusion since impala are more easily simply carried. And then we took pictures and video of an incredible hyena—and I still haven't hunted them!

Grysbok I have hunted—hard. I missed a very easy shot at one in Zambia in 1984. On other hunts in both Zambia and Zimbabwe I tried hard to find one but saw only quick flashes. In Mozambique in 1988 I actually shot a very good grysbok, but my elephant tusks got caught up in the ivory ban and were legally imported only after much delay. I never knew what happened to the grysbok skin and skull, but I never got them.

So I still wanted one, and here we saw several scamper into the brush without the slightest hope for a shot. Then one day, as we tracked buffalo, the trackers spotted a monster grysbok prancing through the woods directly toward us. Hell, I thought, given a chance like that, who cares about buffalo? I traded the double .470 for the scoped .375, made a quick stalk, and took the shot.

This had been a magic hunt, with all objectives and agendas (stated and hidden) accomplished, new friends made, and new partnerships melded. To that point I had spent relatively little time in the Zambezi Valley and none at all in Zimbabwe's Lower Zambezi below Kariba. I fell in love with its wildness and tough hunting, and I knew I would be back many more times.

Return to Bishop Hills

It was early March during a warm, green autumn in Namibia when professional hunters Dirk de Bod and Pete Kibble met us at the Windhoek airport. We were quite an entourage: hunters Dave Scovill, Jim Morey and his son Matt, and me; plus filmers Tyge Floyd and Dave Fulson. This would be the first "official" filming session for a new Outdoor Channel television show, *Tracks Across Africa*, marking yet another dramatic change in my life.

In addition to the DVDs they wanted to do, Tim Danklef and Dave Fulson had a sound concept for an all-African television show. They had years of good "B-roll" background footage and the capability to do the post-production. Truth to tell, they didn't need me at all, but they wanted me to host the show. Initially this was a huge problem with Primedia, the current owners of Petersen Publishing and thus the primary customer for my writing. Cameron Hopkins at SureFire stepped in, offering me almost a real job that included hosting the show with SureFire as the title sponsor. Despite some skepticism, we managed to sell The Outdoor Channel on the pilot show, and suddenly we were in the business of producing twenty-six original episodes. Although quite a bit of film was already in the can, serious filming began in Namibia in March, with the first show scheduled to air just after Christmas.

At that time Jim Morey headed up Swarovski North America. Dave Scovill was and is the editor of Wolfe Publishing's *Rifle* and *Handloader* magazines. You've already met Dirk de Bod, truly a great professional hunter, but you haven't met his sometime partner, Pete Kibble. I hadn't met Pete, either. Dirk and Pete are old friends who run totally separate operations, but when they have a bigger group than either can handle, they get together. At first they seem quite opposite. Dirk is much younger and very Afrikaans, while Pete, in his early sixties, is very old-school English. He's a Kenyan by birth, of hunting lineage, and he did his license and spent his first few years as a PH in East Africa under famous old hunters like Eric Rundgren and Fred Bartlett. In fact, much to Fred's dismay, Pete eventually married his daughter! The common grounds for Pete and Dirk are hunting ethics and love of the bush, and they operate well together.

The real star of this safari, however, wasn't any of us but rather young Matt Morey. His dad and I go back a long way, so I sort of watched Matt grow up, get his commission in the Army, and eventually ship off to Iraq. He had never been to Africa, and long before there was a TV show Jim and I had agreed that as soon as Matt got back safe and could take some leave, we'd get him there. That he turned out to be marvelous on camera was a pure bonus!

With the fanciest "tent camp" I've ever seen now completed, Dirk based his operations at Bishop Hills, which is where we started the safari. Pete's home base, a Kenya-style tent camp, was in some lower country just a couple hours away, so the plan was to pack up at mid-hunt and complete the safari in Pete's area. Mind you, this was a short hunt. Jim and I both had commitments at the tail end, so we had exactly eight hunting days. Dave and Matt had just two more. We arrived just after some good rains, so the country was green and lush, making cover-loving animals like kudu the very devil to spot. For my taste, it was also just a bit on the warm side, though it cooled off nicely at night.

As it turned out, despite less-than-ideal conditions, a very short time frame, hunting two-by-one, and trying to get everything on camera, we had the most amazing run of luck I have ever encountered. I should probably say "runs" because it applied almost equally to everyone. Everybody who wanted one shot a good hartebeest. Everyone who wanted one shot a good blue wildebeest. Everyone who wanted one shot a mountain zebra. Everyone who wanted one shot a good gemsbok. Everyone who wanted one shot a good kudu. And so forth, with some bonuses along the way, including black wildebeest, impala, and more. The only desired animal that was not taken was the klipspringer Jim Morey wanted desperately. In fairness to Dirk, Jim had several chances. In fairness to Jim, well, the klippie is a small target and there's lots of airspace around it . . .

Dirk's new camp was tents centered around a simple but well-appointed lodge. OK, technically I guess they were tents, but they had wooden door frames with glass windows and en-suite facilities with real running water. Dave Scovill and I bunked together, and I was glad for that chance. He and I had somehow gotten crossways a couple years earlier, and although we'd sort of mended fences before this hunt, we were both a bit nervous about sharing close quarters. Neither of us had reason to be. We hunted together some days and not others, we each had fantastic safaris, and we enjoyed each other's company.

Needless to say, Jim wanted to hunt with Matt as much as possible, but I sort of preempted him for a couple of days because we wanted some early camera time with Matt while Africa was new and fresh to him. That first morning, toward midday, he made a well-placed and very difficult shot at a good blue wildebeest way up on a brushy hillside. I didn't think it was a fluke. After all, Matt has shot all his life, the army has trained him well, and he swore he'd been practicing a lot with his .300 short magnum. But it was a really tough shot, centering a small window in thick brush, and he pulled it off perfectly.

I couldn't help but wonder if he could do that again. Turns out he could, just about anytime he wanted to! The next day he made a fine shot on a beautiful mountain zebra, and I guess it was a day or so later, hunting with his Dad, when he shot a beautiful kudu bull.

My hunt started a bit slow, sort of paddling along in everyone else's wake, but it picked up fast. I took a long poke at a hartebeest, which became the first animal to fall to a beautiful 7x57 that Dallas gunsmith Todd Ramirez had built for me. It's truly the nicest rifle I've ever owned, and one of my regrets with the TV gig is the grim reality that sponsors are important and I can't always use my own rifles.

At this early stage Ruger hadn't yet come on board as our rifle sponsor, so it was a bit of a free-for-all. The other rifle I had along was a Remington in .338, brought primarily because it was scoped with Swarovski's new integral mount system. I intended to use it for larger or

Matt Morey's first African animal was this blue wildebeest bull, cleanly taken with an exceptionally difficult shot as the animal moved through small windows in the brush.

tougher game, such as zebra and blue wildebeest, so I had it in my hands on about the third day when we looked at some wildebeest.

I was paired up with Dave Scovill that day, but I really don't recall why it was my shot. I think Dave had taken a wildebeest the day before, and in any case nobody needs to feel sorry for him. He had never hunted in Namibia and was having a ball and shooting something good every single day. Anyway, I was hunting with Dave on the first day I'd ever hunted with Pete Kibble. We spotted a group of blue wildebeest over a ridge and across a valley, on the upper slope of a second, taller ridge.

The wind was good and the animals were feeding along peacefully, so we left the truck and climbed the first ridge to get a better look. They were something over two hundred yards away, still feeding peacefully, but there were no good bulls in the group, so we turned to go, leaving them in peace. As we walked away the herd exploded, stampeding to the right. The wind hadn't changed and we were plenty far enough away, so I didn't understand the chaos. But Pete knew instantly what was happening. As we turned back, he put up the sticks and we saw a pale blur and a cloud of dust.

In seconds the cheetah had taken down a young wildebeest, and as the dust cleared we could see him—or her—standing on top of the carcass, just the head and shoulders clear above the brush. Remember, I'd turned down a chance at a cheetah a couple of years earlier. But this wasn't open ground. This was Joe Bishop's ranch, and just a couple of miles away he was trying desperately to breed up his sable and roan. He knew two cheetah were operating on his place, and the orders were clear: Get them out. I was on the sticks immediately, and then we saw the second cheetah in shorter grass to the right. I can't remember what Pete said, and I had no idea which was the larger of the two. It was clear, though, that the first cheetah, on the carcass, offered an almost impossible shot, and I thought I could hit this second one.

I could, and I did, but I underestimated the range and hit him a bit low. We heard the bullet smack home, a good solid *thunk*, and then he was gone, running to the right. The other cheetah was long gone. We

I shot this beautiful male cheetah the first day I ever hunted with former Kenya PH Pete Kibble. I knew I couldn't bring him home, but he has a place of honor at Bishop Hills.

Dinner is an almost elaborate occasion at Dirk's Bishop Hills camp, with excellent food served in a real dining room.

moved across the valley and found good blood spoor almost immediately. Dave had left his rifle in the truck, so he stayed behind me with a still camera while Tyge Floyd ran the video. I stayed close on the track with a tracker while Pete went left, a bit higher on the ridge. There was a ranch road up there, and if the cat kept going he would cross it, which is what I expected. Actually, at first I expected to find a dead cheetah within a few dozen yards. A low growl just ahead suggested this wasn't likely, so the obvious scenario was that he would move ahead of us and Pete, in a more open spot, would probably get a shot. After all, it was a cheetah, so what other options were there?

The cat came out of a small green bush that shouldn't have hidden a jackrabbit. He was snarling and spitting, and he absolutely scared the crap out of me. I danced back a couple steps to clear some brush, and I suppose that, had he been a leopard, he would have been on me in that instant. Or maybe not. I got the rifle up, saw spots through the lens, and fired, and everything kind of quieted down. Yet another finisher was required, and then we took a good look.

The cheetah is a smaller cat than the leopard, rangier but more slender in build. This was a big male, I suppose about as big as they

This is not a 60-incher, but it isn't far from it. With relatively shallow curls the height is extreme, making it one of the most impressive kudu I have ever seen. Jim Morey made a fine last-second shot just as it turned to leave, dropping it in its tracks. Dirk de Bod is on the far right.

get, and perhaps the most beautiful creature I've ever seen. I knew all along that I couldn't take him home, but we had him life-size mounted, and he has a place of honor in Joe and Sara Bishop's spectacular great room. At least I can visit him every time I'm in Namibia.

Our drama with Africa's cheetah wasn't quite over. A day or so later we drove over to Pete's place, and on the way we saw three cheetah napping by a water hole. From a ridge at Pete's place we saw four full-grown cheetah far out on the plain stalking a springbok. That made a total of nine cheetah in the eight days I hunted, less the one I shot. This animal has made a dramatic recovery in Namibia, and the Namibian hunting industry deserves to be rewarded by having U.S. Fish and Wildlife allow importation. But in our world of dirty politics, I hold out little hope.

Pete's country is a lot different from the Bishop Hills area. It lies essentially due east of the Windhoek airport, in lower and slightly drier country. In the main it's very flat and totals nearly a hundred square kilometers where several ranches have been joined, most of it unfenced.

There is one dominant mountain surrounded by vast plains that are game-fenced, this being essential because the area is home to black rhino and among the best herds of sable and roan in all of Namibia. Pete's camp, just being completed in that year, is not quite as fancy as Dirk's, more in the East African style with slightly less permanent tentage, bathrooms slightly less cosmopolitan (but still en-suite), and its own altogether different charm. His area is the easternmost natural range of the Hartmann mountain zebra, and there's a big ridge above camp where, on almost any given morning or afternoon, you can glass totally free-ranging zebra or kudu.

I think it was on our first evening at Pete's when I did one of the worst—or best—things I've done. Whichever it was, it haunts me. I got very lucky on the cheetah, and I'd taken a couple other animals. But what I really wanted most of all was to hold out for a huge kudu. We'd never seen a big one at Joe's, partly because of the heavy cover, but Dirk had also advised me to hold out until we got to Pete's. His area produces some of the biggest kudu in Namibia. So, here I was on the first afternoon there, hunting with Jim, who was being a bit, well, childish about the klipspringer he hadn't gotten and a blue wildebeest that we'd spent our last day at Joe's trying to find . . . unsuccessfully. Hell, I gave him first shot on a kudu.

It was nearly sunset when we saw the bull slipping along the edge of cover. The turns of his horns were a bit too narrow for him to push the magic sixty-inch figure, but he was one of the tallest and most magnificent kudu bulls I have ever seen. Jim followed him through several patches of dense hook thorn, almost didn't shoot, and then made one of the best shots of his life, dropping the bull with a neck shot just as he was leaving. My, what a beautiful kudu!

I did get a consolation prize that evening. There couldn't have been twenty minutes of light left after we got Jim's kudu videoed, photographed, and loaded, but even so, we ran into a small herd of wildebeest with a real monster among them. It was too late for any fancy stalking, so we simply walked right toward them until we were in good range, and I walloped the big bull with a frontal shot from the .338. He turned and ran with the group, and it was already pitch-dark when we stumbled over him just a few minutes later.

We got down to the last day, and I got down to business. This was the first half of a perfect Namibian double play, a gemsbok and a kudu on the same day. The gemsbok is a nice bull, dropped in its tracks with Dave Scovill's Kimber in .325 WSM.

We continued like that, with everyone taking pretty much everything they wanted. I kept looking for a really good kudu and we saw plenty, but we never saw another bull even close to Jim's beauty. On the last day I took yet another wonderful Namibian double: In the morning we stalked a herd of gemsbok and I shot a lovely bull with Dave Scovill's Kimber in .325 WSM. In late afternoon I shot a good kudu—not a monster, just a good, solid kudu bull—with the Ramirez 7x57.

It was a very easy shot, but it's worth relating because it involved a classic miscommunication between client and PH—fortunately without any tragedy. There's a high saddle between two ridges on Pete's place, and in this saddle sits a windmill that's visible for miles around. The tank is a favorite watering place for darn near everything, and on that warm afternoon we saw two kudu bulls slipping off into the cover. We got within fifty yards, and both bulls were pretty equal: good mature animals, one with longer tips and the other with a wider spread. I liked the one with longer tips, so maybe I didn't pay attention. But Dirk said, "Shoot the second one," meaning the one that was farther away. I shot the second one, meaning (to me) the bull following that first one.

Who was right and who was wrong? In this case it didn't matter because the trophies were pretty equal (or at least I choose to think they were!). But after the shot you should have heard the conversation:

"You must have caught brush," said Dirk, trying to be politically correct.

"No," I said, "I shot him low on the shoulder, through the heart. He'll be dead just over there."

"No, there was no reaction. You must have caught brush."

Dirk's tracker and lifelong mentor, David, whispered to his boss. He had been watching the same bull I shot. We walked to where the animals had stood, and David pointed up into the brush. A beautiful kudu bull lay stone-dead, shot through the heart with that little 140-grain Hornady from the 7x57.

On the way to the airport the next morning we hunted for a couple of hours and Jim shot a fine blue wildebeest. Before we reached the airport Dirk's brother-in-law and Joe's ranch manager, Tynus, called and reported that he'd found Jim's other wildebeest. So we finished with only that pesky klipspringer hanging out—and, among the four of us, more than twenty fine trophies captured on camera. It was an auspicious start to *Tracks Across Africa,* but it wouldn't always be that easy.

Drought Year in Sapi

Zimbabwe's Lower Zambezi had experienced its lowest rainfall in more than a decade. Good rains fell early, a strong harbinger. But then they petered out and stopped altogether. Our pilot, Giles, dropped the plane down as we topped the wall of the escarpment, and we could see the effect. It was late May, but already it looked like August. The vegetation was sere, with baked red soil showing where there should have been grass. The sand rivers had long since stopped flowing; we saw no pools in the Sapi and only a few puddles in the Upper Chewore. From the air, Sapi Safari Area looked like a wasteland.

Sapi is a relatively small concession, an irregular rectangle sandwiched between Mana Pools National Park and the two Chewore Safari Areas, North and South. Smaller than either of the Chewore areas, it is managed by Zimbabwe Parks and Wildlife essentially as a buffer zone for park animals. Quotas are much smaller there than in either Chewore: forty buffalo, five or six leopard, five or six elephant, just one lion.

In normal years the lion, jealously guarded by Mana Pools director Norman Monk, come and go. So do Mana Pools' big herds of buffalo, and the park's big tuskers wander in as well. Unlike most other Zambezi Valley safari areas, Sapi is not assigned as a package to one operator. Quota is expensive and must be bid on almost a la carte, but the quality of trophies there makes it worth the effort. In recent seasons my friends at Chifuti Safaris, Andrew Dawson and Paul Smith, had concentrated on Sapi and had achieved superb results: great buffalo, big lion (on the one and only permit), some heavy ivory, and, most spectacular of all,

Any pool that still held water was almost certain to have elephant around.

100 percent opportunity at good male leopard on bait in daylight. The drought year of 2005 would test their mettle.

We knew this would be a much different year. We didn't yet know the effect, but we made some predictions. Some were correct, and some were simply wishful thinking. Clearly, game would be already be concentrated around the sparse standing water, and the herd animals—primarily buffalo— would retreat to Mother Zambezi much earlier in the year. In a perfect world these things could be good for buffalo hunting, but the world is not perfect. Most of the sparse rainfall missed Sapi altogether. There was more water and better grass to the east across the Chewore, and to the west in Mana Pools. It would be a tough season, and yet it was a season that saw the taking of some of Chifuti's best trophies.

Weather is a wild card in most hunting efforts, and Africa is no different. After a really wet rainy season the grass can remain long well into the hunting months, making some species much more difficult to hunt. In a drought year, well, the game will be wherever there is water, and if that leaves out your hunting area, you're in for tough sledding. Like most hunting, seasons are set and plans are made with no knowledge of what the weather gods will offer. In 2005 we had a long and full season planned in Sapi with Chifuti Safaris. I would start in May with Hornady's Wayne Holt, filming a buffalo segment for the first season of *Petersen's*

Hunting Adventures TV show. Then Tim Danklef and Dave Fulson would come in and we'd film a leopard hunt for our proposed DVD, *Boddington on Leopard*. Then, after a short break, we'd gather in Sapi once more to film, we hoped, several segments for our own *Tracks Across Africa* television show. There was no hope for rain. Eventually, as grass and water were exhausted elsewhere, game would fall back to the river and things would get better. In the meantime, we'd have to make do with what we had. The pressure on Andrew and Paul was incredible, and we all did plenty of our own nail-biting—but it was fascinating to watch the progression of this unusual drought year.

TOUGH HUNT FOR A BIG BUFFALO

When Wayne Holt, cameraman Jed Henry, and I flew in, it wasn't yet clear, either to us or to PH Paul Smith, just how difficult things could be. Sapi has a shorter season than most valley areas, opening on 1 May and closing in September. Paul already knew Sapi held far fewer buffalo than normal, but there was some water in the Upper Chewore, a series of pans in the central area near what we call the Four Ways, and a couple of good pools south of the Sapi River on our side of the park boundary. All of these areas held buffalo, and, as always, there were a few *dagga* boys along the river line. We weren't worried.

Early on we got into a couple of big herds in the southern part of the area, but we worked them for hours without sighting any shootable bulls. I think it was the third day, along the boundary road, when we hit the fresh tracks of two *dagga* boys crossing out of the park, headed to one of the water holes we knew of. They might have watered and headed right back to the park, so we checked north and south but found no tracks. The obvious assumption was that after watering, they had drifted on into the concession.

Good assumption, but not the correct one. We followed the spoor directly to the first pool and bumped head-on into the bulls returning along their own tracks. Paul's tracker, Wanda, saw them first, stopped us in a bit of cover, and set up the shooting sticks. The bulls continued to advance, and we had them both at less than twenty yards. They were true *dagga* boys, mud-caked older bulls with hard bosses and worn tips.

Paul Smith and Wayne Holt with Wayne's marvelous buffalo. We all knew he was good, but his body size fooled us and we misjudged him considerably. This bull is over 45 inches wide, a fantastic buffalo anywhere in Africa.

One was narrow and easily dismissed, but the closer bull, which stood broadside, was a classic of his kind: good bosses, nice shape, a spread of maybe 37 inches but probably 36. In other words, he was a nice, average Cape buffalo bull. We passed on the first encounter, then followed when they spooked and took another look before they crossed the boundary into sanctuary. I could see the wheels spinning in Paul's head. We could complete the TV show right there and then and accomplish Wayne Holt's dream of taking a Cape buffalo at the same time. But lots of days remained, and this was Sapi in May. Surely we could do better.

Days passed with few sightings of buffalo and no opportunities. It was unseasonably warm as well as dry, and we tracked in the heat every day. Time and again buffalo eluded us, moving across one boundary into the park or the other boundary into Chewore. As the days progressed, Paul remained confident. I was getting worried, but it wasn't my hunt so I kept my concern to myself. At least I think I did. Wayne was clearly showing the strain, but he kept at it day after day.

There was little time for anything else but buffalo, and indeed little opportunity. Along the way Wayne took a fine Sharpe grysbok. This, we quickly learned, was one great advantage to a drought year. Grysbok are actually quite plentiful, but they're so small that you rarely see them—or, if you see them, it's just a glimpse of a small reddish blur darting into cover. This year, with the cover down, grysbok were seen frequently and many were taken.

On another day we found a hippo bull in one of the few pans that had enough water to cover that huge body. I didn't have a buffalo bull on license this year, but I did have a hippo and was hoping to take him on land rather than water, with a camera rolling. I borrowed Wayne's big Ruger in .458 Lott, and we removed the scope for the close shot—and likely charge—that we expected. I took one shot with the iron sights, and they seemed close enough. In fact, they were not. The zero was a bit low for the way I shoot iron sights, and this business of quickly trading rifles and not properly checking the sights was a mistake.

Come to think of it, as we advanced toward the hippo, sleeping belly-deep in mud, it occurred to me that this whole thing was a huge mistake. A hippo in deep water is a marksman's game. An extremely precise brain shot is absolutely required, but there is very little actual danger to the shooter. A hippo on land or in a small pool is altogether different. There, without enough water for sanctuary, the animals are often aggressive and a charge is extremely likely. I abhor the concept of inciting charges for a camera, but here we were advancing on a hippo in a small pool.

When he came up, I tried for the brain shot, but flubbed it and hit the beast a bit low, below the brain. At this point he could have charged, and my failure to check the sights properly could have become serious. He did not charge; he exited the pool on the far side, and I adjusted the hold and stopped him there.

We spent most of Wayne's hunt in the central and southern parts of the area because we knew there were more buffalo down there, but it seemed that the primary rut, normally May and June, was either early or late because of the drought. None of the herds we followed seemed to hold mature bulls, and as our hunting days waned, we felt we had followed most of the herds we knew about. With time growing short, we fell back on the Zambezi, where we knew there were *dagga* bulls and a couple of small herds drinking. This was a fallback position because buffalo typically leave the river and adjacent flood plain well before daylight. Tracks are fairly easy to find, and the hope is to catch them moving through open mopane. But the belt of mopane woodland south of the flood plain is narrow, and

In May there are usually lots of hippo in pans out in the bush, but not that year—there just wasn't enough water. From the tracks, this must have been one of the last hippo in the valley away from the Zambezi.

then you get into a huge expanse of thick *jess*, where it's almost impossible to sort the bulls and getting a clear shot is very unlikely.

Very early on the morning of the ninth day we found smoking-fresh tracks of a smallish herd leaving the river line, in a place where we knew the mopane extended for a couple of miles. We caught them scattered out and feeding in the last little valley before the thick *jess*. I stayed with the trackers and game scout while Paul, Wayne, and Jed made their approach. We had visual on a nice bull on the hillside beyond the herd, but they'd have to thread their way between several other buffalo to get close enough for a shot. It didn't happen. They were pinned down—Paul lying flat on his back in the open, Wayne and Jed hunkered behind a bush—when a curious cow came too close. She was perhaps ten feet from Paul when, amazingly, he somehow levitated from supine to standing, his .500 Krieghoff ready.

The cow stampeded in the other direction and buffalo exploded all around them. About this time a bull we hadn't seen appeared on a little rise above me, just his head and horns showing, and those horns looked wide, heavy, and wonderful. I pointed and waved, thinking that Paul couldn't see him. There was no shot, and the bull crashed away. When we gathered I asked, and Paul said he'd seen this bull clearly. Even on this next-to-last day, he judged him as too soft in the boss.

We took the tracks of the herd for a short distance, but they were still running hard when they hit the wall of drought-gray *jess*. We left them and turned back to the truck, and I could see bitter disappointment all over Wayne's face. Probably on mine as well.

The truck was only a few kilometers away, and I think we were back there at 8:30, with plenty of the morning remaining. Less than a mile farther east along the river road, Wanda called out and Paul stopped the truck. There, plain in the fine dust of the road, were the huge tracks of two buffalo bulls. Paul knew these bulls from their outsize tracks and said that both were monsters. They had been tracked before and glimpsed, with no shot, and although it was likely they were already in thick *jess*, we had little else going for us on this morning.

The ground was stony and baked hard. Tracking was slow and laborious, but trackers Wanda and Coffee did a magnificent job. Time and again they lost the spoor, circled back, and regained it. I have no idea what Paul was thinking, but I had little hope and I'm sure Wayne had none at all. It was nearly noon and hot, and we were moving through mopane interspersed with patches of *jess*. The spoor had led us through some thick, noisy stuff and was taking us along the lip of a brushy ravine when, behind us and to the right, a buffalo exploded out of the creek bed.

I was behind Jed, at the end of the line, so I got a clear glimpse of this bull as he scrambled from his bed in cool, shaded sand and charged up the steep, opposite bank. He was wide and heavy and beautifully shaped, but no human being could have shot him quickly enough. He gained the bank and the thick, dark growth beyond, and I could see him standing, just a blacker silhouette in black thorn. There was no shot, and would be none.

Then the second bull, bedded just to the right and out of sight, rose and rushed forward into view, not ten yards from where we stood. There was a partial cut on our side of the bank, and it looked like this bull, at least as big as the first, would rush up it and run right over us. Wayne had his rifle up but hesitated for an instant, and the bull turned to our left and rushed down the narrow streambed.

Senator Astle had bad luck on his buffalo, but had some pretty good luck along the way. His hyena was encountered in broad daylight running down a road, most unusual for these wary and mostly nocturnal animals.

I thought the moment had passed and he was gone, but he reappeared for an instant as he came up the far bank. Wayne took the quartering shot with his .458 Lott and the bull clearly faltered, then was stopped by Paul's double .500 and another shot from Wayne's big Ruger. The bull died right there, across the gully not forty yards from us, facing away as he'd been stopped in midflight.

We approached carefully, and the closer we got, the bigger this bull looked. Paul said 42 inches. I said bigger, at least 43. We were both very wrong. We all knew that the tracks were outsize, but we didn't yet appreciate that this was a giant of a buffalo in body size as well, and the horns were in proportion. He was almost 46 inches in width, with a huge boss and thick horns that carried the mass all the way to the tips. He was a dream buffalo, and hard-won on one of the toughest buffalo hunts I've ever been on.

BODDINGTON ON LEOPARD

My good friend John Astle came in with Tim Danklef and Dave Fulson as Paul's next client. John is also a retired Marine colonel,

My leopard hunt started out with great promise, with multiple cats feeding on various baits—except they were all females or young males. This is a very big female and she had us fooled for a while until she squatted to do her business.

and is Maryland's senior state senator. Donna was supposed to come in with them, but although her vacation papers had long since been put in, her employer threw a last-minute fit and she missed this one. Perhaps it's just as well, because it became a long, tough saga.

I would hunt with Andrew Dawson, who was just finishing a leopard hunt with Boris Baird. Typically, Andrew and Paul like to concentrate their Sapi leopard hunting in May and June. With plenty of water around, the prey species are widely scattered, so it's more difficult for the cats to make natural kills and thus easier to get them on bait. Also, the cover is thicker, so it's simpler to place bait amid lots of good security cover, enticing the cat to come in earlier. In this drought year neither of these conditions existed, and by now Andrew knew this very well.

He and Boris had had a tough hunt and had not been successful. Late in the hunt, far to the south along the security road, they had finally baited in a very nice tom, a morning feeder. They had video of him in wonderful morning light, but Boris wanted a seven-foot tom or nothing, and Andrew couldn't make that call. So they passed and with time running out had located the tracks of a couple of good toms. One was feeding on the last night, but he failed to come in.

Now it was my turn, but for the first half of the hunt we ignored these "known" leopard. This was not a mistake, but rather followed Andrew's standard leopard hunting tactics, which are normally magnificently successful. Andrew generally prefers to start his leopard hunts from Main Camp on the river—not because Main Camp is more comfortable or more scenic but because there is more prey. Thus, there are also more leopard near the river than in the south of the area. Also, within a hunting radius from the river camp are known hunting grounds of several big toms.

The story of this leopard hunt has been told in too many places and ways to linger on it here, but it turned into the most nerve-wracking, pressurized hunt of my career, and probably of Andrew Dawson's as well. This pressure was self-inflicted (in my case, not Dawson's). Based on Andrew's unmatched track record for leopard, we had calmly announced in the buffalo film that "Boddington on Leopard" was "coming in fall 2005." As the days passed, it slowly dawned on us that in this drought year we might not get a chance. Tim was grim, Dave was near panic, I was as nervous as a whore in church, and Dawson was taking the brunt.

There were leopard around, plenty of them. We had multiple sightings of females on bait, and saw fresh tracks of big toms here and there, but we couldn't get a male to feed, either on favorite trees or promising new sites. At the same time, Paul and Senator Astle were having another tough buffalo hunt. They had long since repaired to Fly Camp, where there was still more buffalo sign around, and with half the hunt gone we joined them up there.

The obvious goal was to see if we could get Boris Baird's unclaimed leopard back on bait. He looked perfectly fine to me, and a few weeks later he looked just fine to Marc Watts, who shot him happily. But, to the credit of both Andrew and Boris, he was not a seven-foot leopard. Like most good-size Zambezi Valley toms, he was a couple inches short of that magical mark.

Andrew never puts all of his leopard eggs in one basket, so we also explored for new sites, and rebaited for the big tom they had tried for at the end of Baird's hunt. The one quota that is generous in Sapi is impala, which is thus the preferred bait. In this drought year, however, it was often very difficult to find impala when we needed one, especially in the south of the area, but we managed, and I have to admit that my two-week hunt was very hard on the local impala population!

Toward the end, with pressure building like a huge thunderhead, things started to fall into place. We got the Baird leopard back on bait,

It was very late in the hunt and pressure was building fast when we finally got this big tom leopard on bait. Tim, Dave, and I were beside ourselves, but Andrew never wavered and never quit. As he says, "Things will come right." They did.

and he was still a morning feeder, though now he was an early morning feeder. On the morning of the ninth day, as we crept toward the blind in total darkness, we could hear bones crunching as the leopard fed. Andrew plans his approaches and organizes his blind for such an eventuality, and we managed to slip into the blind without disturbing the cat. The bait was not silhouetted. Andrew plans his baits with security cover as the first and foremost consideration, concealed approach second, blind site third, and actual tree dead-last. This is sound methodology, but this bait was in deep shadow. I think shooting would have been possible at ten before six. At 5:40 it was almost possible to visualize the cat moving as he fed greedily . . . and at 5:45 he was out of the tree and gone.

The day before, we had hung an impala deep in the bush, not far from a spring and near the confluence of several major game trails (a big tom's tracks were clear along one of them). Later that morning we found that a big male had hit that bait. So we put up the second of Andrew's prefab blinds, sited on a ridge ninety yards from the bait. We already knew, or thought we knew, that the Baird leopard was a morning feeder, so that evening we sat the new bait, but at full darkness nothing had come.

This bait was more than a mile from the nearest road, so it was late by the time we got back to the truck and ground our way another hour or so to camp. We were up again before three and headed to our morning feeder, so given both extreme pressure and sleep deprivation, perhaps we can be forgiven an incredible error. Once again the leopard was on the bait when we arrived, and once again he slipped away before shooting light, this time even earlier. We sat until a bit after seven, then slipped away. It was still too early to check baits, so we went back to camp, had breakfast, and then made our rounds. The Baird leopard had come back after we left, evidenced by fresh pink on the impala's haunch. Lord, why hadn't we given it another hour? The other leopard had fed during the night as well, so our course remained clear: Sit the bait deep in the bush that evening and, if that didn't work, try the Baird leopard again in the morning. I went to my tent and lay down. Unknown to me, on this afternoon the strain broke Tim and Dave, and they pestered poor Andrew with the dire consequences that would befall us all if we failed. As if he could do anything about it.

The leopard came in that night a couple of minutes after six. When a leopard comes onto a bait, the pressure that descends on the shooter's shoulders is like a massive weight, turning arms to lead and numbing fingers. The light was going fast, and Andrew asked me how much time I thought we had. I told him maybe five minutes, maybe a bit more, so he asked me to wait while we made certain it was the male (we'd seen tracks of a big female on the same game trail).

So I passed up the shot with the leopard standing clear and proud on the branch, and that was the right thing to do. Then he advanced to the crook in the limb where the bait was hung, and instead of reaching over the crook like any sensible leopard, he reached under the branch, obscuring the entire shoulder area. As the leopard moved Andrew saw it was the male, so he told me to shoot as soon as the cat was feeding. In a hushed but panicky tone I told him the vitals were covered. He saw it, and then we were all as panicked as I was. Sooner or later the cat would move and offer a shot, but we were running out of light very quickly.

No, I couldn't shoot him in the head—it was like he was bobbing for apples—and likewise the neck, not that I'd have tried either shot on a leopard in failing light at ninety yards. I think Dave came up with the idea, and when I was set, Tim grunted like a leopard. The tail stopped swinging as the cat visibly stiffened, and then he stood up. I adjusted the rifle upward, along the back line of the foreleg up into the chest, and the .30-06 flashed in the growing dark. We heard the wet thump as the leopard hit the ground. Good. Then grunting diminishing into the brush. Not good.

It was full dark by the time we reached the tree, and midnight-black by the time our trackers, having heard the shot, hiked in from the truck with pangas and more SureFires. These were long moments, and longer still were the ones as we took the heavy blood spoor in tight formation, flashlights searching ahead. The leopard lay still on brown leaves barely thirty yards into the forbidding brush, and we all, for different reasons, breathed heavy sighs of relief.

A Huge Crocodile

It was on the day I got my leopard that John Astle wounded and lost his buffalo. He hit it a bit high, and they followed an ever-diminishing spoor until nearly dark before they lost it completely. He won't be the first or the last to lose a buffalo hit in that fashion, but it's always a tragedy. John took it amazingly well, but it was a real damper on such a day. Of course, none of us knew that even greater humiliation awaited him.

We fell back on Main Camp along the Zambezi, where the next day our good Senator perfectly shot a really big hippo bull and where we both hoped to take a crocodile. I had never killed a croc, and it wasn't something I was particularly dying to do, although Art Wheaton's big croc on the Great Ruaha had piqued my interest. Tim and Dave, however, are both nuts about crocodile hunting, and they sort of talked me into it because they insisted it would make really good footage for the television show. OK, why not?

We spent a day in camp finishing up some talking stuff for the leopard film while John shot his hippo, and then, as I recall, we divided the river into two sectors so we could both hunt crocodiles without interfering with each other. We each had a leg of hippo for bait, and of course the option to stalk one of the reptiles as well.

The real bonus of the season was this huge crocodile, at 15 feet, 4 inches a tremendous lizard. Getting him took the most difficult stalk I've ever made, and one of the most difficult shots in my hunting career.

Andrew, Tim, and I were approaching an island near the middle of the river when we spotted a rectangular lump right on the point. It was a crocodile, of course, and looked like a big one, but a careful look revealed several crocodiles sunning. This would clearly be a great place to put a bait, but there was a little inlet to the right of the beasts, and then the raised bank of the main island. This provided a perfect situation for a stalk, so we decided to give it a try. We beached the boat on the far side of the island and crept up to an antheap that would allow us to see that point.

There were seven or eight crocodiles we could see and almost certainly more that we couldn't see, but one of the visible ones appeared much larger than the others. I make no pretense of being able to judge crocodiles, so I just went with the flow. After two hours of painstaking (and, in thorns, painful) crawling, we pitched up at the base of a stout tree maybe sixty-five yards from the big croc. Two other crocodiles that looked plenty big enough to me were directly across the inlet from us, barely forty yards away and apparently sound asleep.

After a close look, Andrew was undecided. The croc was clearly huge, but we couldn't see all of his tail, and some crocs are missing a couple of feet of tail from encounters with hippo or bigger crocodiles. So we dithered a bit, then decided to go for him, and I was trying to figure out the placement for this incredibly difficult shot. The croc was quartering slightly away, and for the brain shot at this angle I needed to hit him pretty much under the base of the horn, that odd bony projection on top of the skull. OK, I had it, and I had just pushed the safety catch forward when the crocodile started to move, slipping silently into the water. I thought Tim was going to kill himself.

The other crocodiles, including the two directly opposite, remained in place. We concluded we hadn't spooked the big boy and that what we had seen was just normal movement. So we stayed in place, hoping he would come back. He swam out to the point, and we could see his head in the water for quite a long time; then, like a big submarine, he swam around the point, finally hauling up on the opposite side among several other crocodiles. He wasn't that much farther away, but he was much less visible, just the head showing clearly between patches of reeds.

OK, another pressure shot. If I ever do this again, I'll use a lighter rifle with a lot bigger scope. I was shooting my old .375 with its Leupold 1.5–5X.

It's a wonderfully reliable old friend, but at 5X the intersection of the cross hairs covered up everything I needed to hit. I took the best rest I could against the tree and then moved the cross hairs up, down, left, right, and back again until I was reasonably certain they were centered on something I couldn't see, a point two inches below the horn and maybe an inch forward.

At the shot the 270-grain Hornady took much of the crocodile's brain skyward. The beast itself reared up, then thrashed while I kept shooting. The other crocs scrambled for the river, two leaping over the stricken animal like a covey rise of big green lizards. When things settled down, we went back to the boat and motored around the island to collect our prize. He was lying half submerged in shallow water as we approached, and I did the worst thing I've ever done to any professional hunter. I looked at Andrew and said, with childlike honesty, "He doesn't look very big."

Like I said, I can't judge crocodiles. He was a real monster, well over fifteen feet, the biggest Chifuti has ever taken and something like the third largest off the Zambezi. It turns out that Paul knew about this crocodile. Paul and Andrew don't compete with each other, so I don't know exactly what happened, but somehow they crossed signals on who could hunt where. We left the croc to get a bigger boat, and while we were gone Paul and John approached that island to look for that specific crocodile. They found him, all right, exactly where we'd left him in Lumuc's capable hands.

It got worse, at least for John. We got the big Pelican boat and managed to manhandle a ton of reptile on board. Meantime, down the channel, Paul and John were stalking another big croc, and the passing of our boat (carrying what might otherwise have been John's croc) spooked the one they were after. At least we left a hippo leg staked out on the point, and the next day John shot another good one out of a frenzied group of feeding crocs. For some reason he's still speaking to me, and we jointly hope we can finish up his buffalo business by the time this book sees the light of day.

Buffalo More or Less

Marc Watts came in to hunt with Andrew following my hunt. He had the incredible luck that seems to follow him around, taking one of the largest one-safari bags that Chifuti has ever seen: croc, hippo, sable, kudu, waterbuck, warthog, buffalo, and more. The "more" included the Baird leopard, which is now properly the Watts leopard. His hunt was not without difficulty. They had to work extra-hard for buffalo, and in fact Marc wounded and lost his first buffalo. He really does shoot well, so that proves it can happen to anyone. We had a couple of days of overlap, so I hunted with him his first couple of days and was there when he shot his big waterbuck. This is typical of Watts's luck: This waterbuck is the biggest they've ever taken, and they'd been trying to get him for two years. He hung out right on the border between Sapi and the no-shooting Chikwenya photo safari area, which is part of Mana Pools. Every time they looked for him, he would stand placidly on the safe side of the boundary. But on Marc Watts's very first morning, the superb animal ran across the road in front of the truck at least five hundred yards inside Sapi. Marc shot him, then shot him again, stopping him right on the boundary. The horns were about 31 inches, with bases like baseball bats, one of the biggest waterbuck I've ever seen.

On Marc's second or third day we tracked up a herd of buffalo but didn't see a decent bull. A cow buffalo was available on license, so I took Marc's double Rigby in .500-416, and as we moved in, our herd ran smack into another group of buffalo. Again Watts's luck held: I'd been there three weeks, and this was the most buffalo I'd seen! The second group spooked the first, and a mass of buffalo ran toward us. Dawson quickly picked out a cow without calf and told me to shoot the third buffalo. I was pretty proud of myself, even though the range was very close: I hit the cow in the shoulder, on the run, with both barrels. We found her standing a short distance away, and I finished the job.

That concluded my first sojourn in Sapi in 2005. About a month later I was back, primarily for several buffalo hunts conducted for our *Tracks* TV show. The NRA's Mark Keefe and Cabela's Jim Gianladis were there and had already taken their buffalo. SureFire's Cameron Hopkins's buffalo hunt was in progress, and Gander Mountain's Mark Baker and Mark Bussard were inbound. I wasn't hunting buffalo, but my daughter, Brittany, was with me, and a good buffalo was her objective.

By now the water in the southern part of the area was virtually gone except for a couple of springs up in the hills and a couple of stagnant pools in the Chewore. A lot of buffalo had retreated to the river line,

Marc Watts of Sable Trails Productions took one of the largest bags in Chifuti Safari history, including several exceptional trophies. This waterbuck had been seen for years, but usually in Mana Pools. The Marc Watts Luck: On the first day the animal was standing nicely well within the Sapi Safari Area.

and at the start of the hunt our group had gotten into buffalo easily and done well. Mark and Jim had taken very fine bulls with little trouble. Cameron, not understanding the impact of the drought, had passed up a couple of bulls he probably shouldn't have passed, and Tim, Dave, and Andrew (in that approximate order) were upset with him.

Perhaps they had good reason, because we hit a wall. The buffalo near the river vanished, and the ones up-country weren't any easier to find than they had been in May. The wall, however, had chinks in it, which is another way of saying that some people are luckier than others. Cameron went nearly a week without seeing a buffalo. Brittany tracked her heart out and her feet into blistered ribbons for nine days without seeing even a marginal bull.

Mark Baker and Mark Bussard had a business problem develop that they couldn't do anything about, so they cut their hunt from ten days to five. Then they missed an inbound connection, and by the time they arrived only

The only trophy Brittany brought home for ten days of supreme effort was this impala, nicely taken with her Ruger in .405 Winchester. At the same time some of our other hunters took nice buffalo on their first day. That's the way it goes sometimes.

three of their hunting days were available. In 2004 I would have promised anyone a shot at a buffalo bull in two days, provided they weren't too picky. In 2006 it would have been the same. In 2005 most buffalo were shot after the seventh day of a ten-day hunt. Mark Baker and Buzz Bussard shot their bulls on the first day of their three-day hunt. Buzz's bull was a good, solid buffalo, though no monster and, under normal circumstances, not a first-day bull. As conditions existed, the animal was a miracle.

If that's true, then I lack words to describe Mark Baker's bull. He was a single *dagga* boy with outsize tracks, traveling alone. In fact, he was the surviving buddy of Wayne Holt's buffalo. He had been tracked several times since May and had managed to slip off into the *jess*. This time, though, he made a mistake, and he was 43 inches wide, with deep hooks and big bosses. If this bull and Wayne Holt's bull stood together in the open, I'm not sure which of them I'd shoot. Wayne's was wider, but Mark Baker's bull was more classic.

Which left Cameron and Brittany. Late in the hunt Cameron got another chance and, in desperate haste, fired before Andrew gave him the go-ahead. He wounded the bull, and Andrew, caught by surprise, was unable to back him up. They followed into horribly thick stuff, and Andrew stopped the bull in a full-out charge at a matter of a few feet. In camp that night Andrew was still white, both from anger and from a very close call.

I guess that in some ways Brittany's buffalo was even worse. On her last morning, as if we'd ordered it up, we caught a huge herd just filtering up from the flood plain. We made a quick stalk, and it was still gray dawn when a nice bull was spotted slipping along on Brittany's side of the herd. She was on sticks, dead steady, and the shot looked good. It was not good. Nor were Andrew's backup shots. When things go bad, often they just get worse. Andrew carries his William Evans .470 every day of his working life, and he shoots it like a machine. His first barrel missed, and his second barrel hit the buffalo somewhere. As for Brittany's shot, sometime later we reviewed the footage and could see a stick break with the bullet's passing. I think the bullet was deflected, but whatever happened, we had yet another wounded buffalo on our hands.

The blood was good for a long distance. Then it began to peter out, and eventually the bull went back into the herd. Lumuc, Mukassa, Andrew, and I ran with the herd for miles, inspecting one group and then another. We never saw a bull that looked like it was hit. Eventually the herd bombshelled in multiple directions, and that was the end of that. Brittany took it well, but we were all sick. It was little comfort to any of us that both Tim Danklef and I had wounded and lost our own first buffalo, or that Dave Fulson had lost the only really big bull he ever had a chance at, or that even Andrew Dawson (who ultimately blamed himself) has wounded and lost buffalo. Brittany earned that buffalo, but sometimes it just doesn't work, no matter how much you want it to.

All Over South Africa

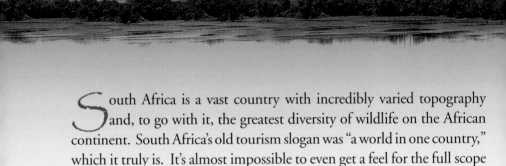

South Africa is a vast country with incredibly varied topography and, to go with it, the greatest diversity of wildlife on the African continent. South Africa's old tourism slogan was "a world in one country," which it truly is. It's almost impossible to even get a feel for the full scope and breadth of this country in one trip, but in June 2005 I tried pretty hard. That was partly by design, and partly, well, I'm not sure I'll ever know the full story.

There were some tense moments when brothers Tim Danklef and Dave Fulson and I were pretty certain we were getting a royal runaround. It's entirely possible we were, and it's equally possible that a young outfitter was trying to do the very best job he could for his clients. It really doesn't matter, because in the end most objectives were accomplished, and we all learned a great deal along the way.

We had just finished my leopard hunt in the Zambezi Valley, a classic hunt over bait for a daylight leopard. This, plus our on-camera discussions plus a great deal of wonderful "B-roll" footage that Tim and Dave had been assembling for years, would be the backbone of our *Boddington on Leopard* DVD. One aspect we all felt was missing was a leopard hunt with dogs. A century ago, in Kenya, this was a common way to take a leopard, and in recent years it has once again become an important technique in some parts of southern Africa. None of us had done such a hunt, and we had no footage. South African outfitter Abie Steyn, a third-generation houndsman, came to our rescue. The plan, or at least what we understood to be the plan, was that after we finished in Zimbabwe we would spend a few days with Abie and Dave would take a leopard over dogs while Tim did the camera work. I would just be along for the ride.

Abie's primary hunting area is along the extreme southern boundary of Kruger Park, in Mpumalanga Province, which is where we thought we were headed. We flew into Johannesburg and pitched up at Louis Bekker's Afton Guest House, where Abie's Dad, Tinney Steyn, met us with his truck full of hounds and told us our charter pilot would pick us up the next morning. We were a bit confused when we found ourselves heading not east but northwest, eventually landing in the middle of South Africa's Kalahari near the Botswana border. There to meet us was Styger Joubert of Tsoma Safaris, who took us to his excellent little lodge. Shortly thereafter Tinney Steyn showed up with the same truck full of dogs, having driven straight through the long night.

Styger was as confused as we were. He doesn't use dogs. Uniquely, he tracks his leopard in the Kalahari sands, and he had taken two huge cats within the previous two weeks. Adding to the dilemma was the fact that although his leopard grow big, they're thin on the ground and he customarily takes only two per year. So we weren't sure why we were there, and Styger wasn't sure why we were there, but we were there. So we devoted a couple of days to looking for tracks, and although we pursued no leopard, we learned a great deal about the almost-lost art of leopard hunting by pure tracking, which is possible only in extreme sandy soil like the Kalahari. Since that time I have taken a leopard with dogs, and if I can take just one more leopard, I'd like to take it by tracking with Styger Joubert.

I learned one more thing from Styger, and that knowledge made this weird side trip worthwhile. Most of his region is unfenced, but he has a large, brushy fenced area, and there he does a lot of South Africa's infamous "hunts" for captive-reared lion. This is a practice I have vehemently opposed. I no longer do . . . provided the operator is honest about what he's selling and the hunter (perhaps "shooter" is a better term) fully understands what he is buying. Styger Joubert does it right, as perhaps many others do. But some do not. His contract shows in three places that the hunter understands he is taking a captive-reared lion. The lion is released into his area, several thousand brushy acres, well before the hunt. The hunt is conducted on foot, by tracking. These lion have no fear of man and are probably more dangerous than

A nice lion on Styger Joubert's place. This is in a big, brushy enclosure where, well within both letter and intent of the law, Styger conducts hunts for captive-reared lion. While I don't wish to do such a hunt, Styger changed my opinion about this practice.

wild lion, but I have been opposed to this practice because at every SCI convention I see South African operators selling these hunts as though they were for wild lion, and it sickens me.

I still have no desire to participate in such a hunt, but I'm in a different place than many hunters today because I had the opportunity to take wild lion in the 1970s and 1980s before lion hunting became so limited and so outrageously expensive. Styger convinced me that there are some operators who are honest and forthright about it, and he made two more extremely valid points. First, as many as 7,000 lion are in captivity in South Africa, primarily because this industry exists. There is a strong move to outlaw altogether the hunting of captive-reared lion in South Africa. If that comes to pass, what will happen to those 7,000 lion? Second, the very existence of this kind of hunting takes a great deal of pressure away from Africa's beleaguered population of wild lion. So I'm now a believer. I don't want to do it, but if others do I have no issues, provided they know what they're buying and don't try to kid themselves.

We had a great time with Styger and his pretty wife, Melinda, but in just a few days, also for mysterious reasons, we were back in an airplane and flying all the way across South Africa to the thick thornbush of Mpumalanga Province along the southern boundary of Kruger Park.

Once again we flew while poor Tinney drove with his truck full of dogs, and Abie was there to meet us. We were prepared to hate him, but we liked him very much. I can only surmise that he had a camp-capacity issue and was trying to do the best he could. Or, since Styger had just taken two leopard quite easily, he thought he could slip in a third. Probably both. Whatever, we now commenced a serious leopard hunt with Abie Steyn.

Typically, he baits for leopard on private land not far from the Kruger boundary, in country where hunting cats at night with the aid of a light is the norm. He and his dad have dogs that are used for bushpig and for problem cats that come out of the Park, but the sport hunting of unwounded leopard with dogs is expressly forbidden in that province. Dave Fulson's leopard would be a test case, observed by a local game warden, and Abie had permission in writing from the game department to conduct this hunt with dogs.

Abie Steyn's safari camp is located near a superb private game park offering wonderful opportunities for photography as well as good hunting nearby. It was a real treat to get this close to a black rhino.

So far so good. Abie's brother-in-law, professional hunter Eric Strydom, was conducting a standard leopard hunt over bait with American Allan Skruby, and Abie had plenty of other baits out for us. The plan was to check baits until we found a good track, then call in the game warden as well as the dogs, and off we would go. We had a couple of females feeding but no males, and I think it was the second morning when Abie got a call. We were to present ourselves at the game-department office in Nelspruit, some forty miles away, as quickly as possible.

A man sat us down and pronounced that "someone" on the Game Board was nervous about publicity surrounding the dog hunt, and he was rescinding permission. We were angry. After all, we were there, and not without cost. Nobody cared. The last thing this jerk said was, "Remember, you cannot hunt leopard with dogs. If we get a problem animal while you're here, we'll call you. If you have a wounded animal, you may use any method of recovery. But you cannot continue this hunt with dogs. Do you understand?"

We didn't like it, but we understood. Around ten o'clock that night, from a blind just a few miles from Abie's camp, Allan Skruby wounded a huge leopard. Eric called Abie from his bed, and together they took a look at the situation. There was plenty of blood and they believed it had been a good hit, but the leopard had gone into nasty riverine cover. Worse, they were very close to the Kruger boundary, and if the cat went under the fence, there would be no recovery. They wisely decided to bring in the dogs at first light, and we were invited along to film. Sometimes God works in strange ways.

With the sun coming up behind us, Abie and Eric organized things like a military operation. Eric and Allan would take the right side of the riverine. Abie and the dog handler would take the left, and we could come along with him if we wished. Tinney, with a shotgun, would block to our rear, between us and the impassable Kruger Park boundary. We still believed this was all for a dead leopard, but it was good footage. It would get better.

I carried my old .375. Tim took my leopard rifle, a single-shot Dakota .30-06. Dave, who had been done out of his leopard hunt, carried only his camera. We started into the riverine with the dogs working ahead,

The Skruby leopard, finished in a full-out charge on camera. Left to right, PH Abie Steyn, Allan Skruby, me, Tim Danklef, and PH Eric Strydom. This is one of the really big leopard South Africa is known to produce.

and I doubt we'd gone fifty yards before the dogs gave voice up ahead. We followed quickly, and if there had been any doubt about what was going on, it was dispelled when we all jumped over a puddle of fresh, wet blood. This cat was still very much alive, and the dogs were working him up the streambed just ahead of us.

Now the chase was on, and it was the weirdest thing I've ever seen, more like kids running to a fire than grown men headed for a potential mauling. Abie stayed right with the dog handler, running hard. Tim and I ran right behind, jockeying for position as we tried to get in front of each other. Dave stayed right on our tail with the camera.

Much of the true Limpopo Valley is very flat with quite thick thornbush, making for limited vantage points. Werner de Beer uses water tanks to gain some elevation for glassing.

It didn't last more than a couple hundred yards, and then the hounds' baying stabilized. The fight was on. We cut out around a patch of thick green foliage and found, just ahead and to our right, an island of yellow grass maybe twenty yards across. The leopard was in there somewhere, snarling, and the dogs were in there as well, barking furiously. Dust rose and hung above the grass, and through the dust we could make out vague but furious movement.

We came closer, and Abie peered around a single bare tree. The leopard was right there, and they made eye contact for just an instant. It was as if the leopard instantly understood the true source of his troubles. He charged, ignoring the dogs, focusing on Abie Steyn and roaring like thunder.

I have no idea how Abie got his Krieghoff .470 up so fast, but he did, and his shot seemed to center the leopard. Five hundred grains of bullet, five thousand foot-pounds of energy, at less than five yards, and all this did was cause the cat to swerve slightly. At this point Tim had won the footrace, so Abie, Tim, and I were in echelon, and it was Tim's turn next. The cat was right at his feet when he fired his one shot almost from the hip, probably shooting over it. A step back, I was not in real danger and had a split-second more as the cat came clear. I swung with him and saw the cross hairs overtake him as the rifle went off. He was in midair when I shot, and he vanished into a thick patch of cover.

I have no idea what I saw or thought I saw, but I announced with certainty that the cat was down as the pack dogpiled on top of him. He was, not just down but stone-dead. Abie's shot was just a touch off-center, but it should have flattened him. My shot was pure luck, through the spine at the top of the shoulder, but it worked. Allan had hit him a bit low, and we were lucky to recover him before he reached the park. But we did recover him. Allan got a wonderful leopard, one of the biggest I've seen. Dave, always steady with the camera, didn't get a leopard, but he sure got some great footage.

We had a few days left, so we paddled around looking for this and that and got some great footage of both black and white rhino. Regardless of what had happened, Abie became a good friend, and I'd certainly hunt with him again. At this writing dog hunting still has not been approved in Mpumalanga province, and perhaps it never will be—but I think it should be. Obviously, recovering a wounded animal is far different from

I sat several nights hoping for a brown hyena and learned in the process that these animals may be among Africa's most wary creatures. One night a huge civet cat came in, and I couldn't resist! Although completely nocturnal, civet are quite common and make a beautiful mount.

starting out to hunt a leopard, but in that nasty riverine bush where Allan Skruby's leopard awaited, I am almost certain that without the dogs, somebody would have gotten chewed on.

In a few short days we'd traveled across South Africa from east to west and back again, from the Kalahari sands to dense thornbush. Tim and Dave's mission was complete, so they went home to start the laborious process they do so well, capturing and editing raw footage. I had two more stops to make that would take me from north to south in "the world in one country." I've long admitted to being an African junkie, and I always try to cram as much into a trip as I possibly can. This is partly because the most difficult and onerous part of any African hunt is the long plane ride. Once there, you might as well make the most of it. But it's also because I have a very hard time saying no!

My old friend Debra Bradbury, publisher of *Blackpowder Hunting* magazine, had done an advertising trade for a short hunt in northern South Africa with professional hunter Werner de Beer. We did some further horse trading, and after I saw Tim and Dave off, I found myself headed north from Jo'burg with Werner and Debra. Over the years, I'd spent quite a lot of time in the Limpopo Valley, so there weren't any antelope species I was desperate to hunt. Debra had likewise done several South African hunts, so she was in the same boat.

The area is particularly good for huge kudu, always of interest, and also has some of the largest southern impala. I did take an exceptional kudu, not the sixty-inch monster I've always sought (and am still) but a good one. We both took very nice impala, and there was plenty of other common game such as warthog, wildebeest, and zebra. But the main attraction was, well, a bit different. Werner had told us that his farm was really good for brown hyena, and we had a very good chance to get them on bait. The brown hyena is more solitary than his spotted cousin and, if anything, more secretive and more nocturnal. He is also considerably more attractive, with long, dark fur with white and tan highlights. He is not common and is protected in many areas, but permits can be obtained in some South African provinces and occasionally in Namibia.

Werner did indeed have brown hyena. I'm not in the least capable of determining a brown hyena track from that of a spotted hyena, but it wasn't necessary for me to take his word. Debra brought a trail camera, and the first night we set it up over bait it took a very good photo of a sure-enough (and apparently huge) brown hyena. Debra had first pick, and she set to it with a will. She sat in a blind for some absurd stretch like six nights straight—all night—but she never saw the brown hyena. The worst of it is the hyena was there on several occasions. In the morning we would find his tracks down one cutline or another, probably just out of reach of moonlight. It's even possible that he snuck in for a bite before moonrise, but this wasn't definitive because other night predators were around as well, primarily civet cats and honey badgers. One night she broke down and shot a big honey badger, which I think became her prized trophy from the trip.

A day or two after Debra began her vigil, a second brown hyena, clearly a different one because the tracks were slightly smaller, hit another bait. So my own vigil began. I guess I'm not as tough as Debra, because I found it just plain colder than hell! I sat five nights out of seven, taking a couple of breaks in between, and that was about all I could stand. I was in an elevated platform with a comfortable chair and three blankets. I started with long underwear, a sweater, and a hooded windproof jacket. As the evening chill set in I'd put on a watch cap and gloves, wrap a wool scarf around my neck, and pull up my hood. I sat on one blanket as a cushion as well as for insulation, put another over my legs and feet, and draped the third over my shoulders like a shawl. And I was still cold!

Sleeping was not a problem; it was just too cold to try. Moonrise was a problem. At the start the moon was coming up about sundown, perfect, but as the days wore on it came up later and later, and that long period of black dark before moonrise could have been an issue. But as far as we could tell, my brown hyena never reappeared. Perhaps it was my fault. Early one evening I shot a honey badger, a cool little trophy that I had never taken. A few days later, in the absolute dead of night, I shot a huge civet cat.

So maybe I spooked off the hyena, and perhaps Debra did as well. But I don't think so. I still haven't taken one, but I've tried for them on a couple of other occasions, and now I know a bit more about them. My old friend Dirk de Bod believes they are far more difficult to bait than leopard, and he approaches baiting for hyena with even greater care. More about that later in this book!

So at the end of our hunt with Werner, the score stood at hyena, two; hunters, zero, but we took some excellent consolation prizes along the way. The next and final stop on this South African odyssey was the Eastern Cape, easily my favorite part of South Africa. Werner dropped us at the airport in Johannesburg, where we caught a flight to Port Elizabeth. Situated along the rugged Indian Ocean coastline, it's one of the prettiest little cities I've ever seen. Outfitter Larry McGillewie was on hand to meet and greet, and he ran us up to his headquarters at Hellespoort, a large property near Grahamstown.

This time I had serious objectives. You might even call them scores to settle. It had been several years since I'd been in the Eastern Cape, but I'd left some unfinished business there. I'd tried several times to take a Cape grysbok but had failed miserably. In fact, although I'd seen numerous females, I'd never seen a male at all. This was the primary objective.

The bontebok is a much more brightly colored cousin to the blesbok. He is usually not difficult to bring to bag, but remains relatively uncommon and can only be taken from registered herds and imported by special CITES permit.

I also wanted to take a bontebok, the more colorful and much less common cousin of the blesbok, a specialty of the Eastern Cape. I had taken one once before, but the bontebok is a CITES I animal, meaning a U.S. Fish & Wildlife CITES import permit is required. I'd had one, but there was some foul-up and my bontebok arrived in the States days after the expiration of my import permit. I got the permit reissued, but my bontebok trophy had already been destroyed. Rules have changed, and if you let that happen today, you're probably going to pay a hefty fine as well! So I wanted to take another bontebok and this time get it home.

Debra also wanted a Cape grysbok (I had first dibs this time). She had no interest in bontebok but wanted a black wildebeest, another Eastern Cape specialty. We only had something like six hunting days, so I figured we would be plenty busy. But this was the first time I'd hunted with Larry McGillewie, and I didn't know him very well. He's unusually calm and soft-spoken, yet very direct. And he has an uncanny ability to pack more into a short time frame than any professional hunter I've ever known: "OK, we'll hunt around Hellespoort for a day or so. Monday evening we'll go get the Cape grysbok. It shouldn't be a problem. I have permits left for blue duiker, and you simply must hunt them the way we do. So Tuesday we'll go over to Adrian Ford's place and hunt blue duiker. I have an oribi for you as well, and Debra can take a good bushbuck. Wednesday we'll get the bontebok, and Thursday we should be able to get the black wildebeest. And then we'll see . . . !"

Whew! We did it all, too, and more. Monday evening we went over to Rex Amm's place. Rex is the guy with whom I took my first Cape bushbuck a few years earlier, but what I didn't know then is that he's considered the king of Cape grysbok. Larry knew of a few good rams here and there, but he also knew that Rex had the best properties. The Cape grysbok is larger in both body and horn than the Sharpe variety, a very pretty pygmy antelope with a reddish coat spiked with just a sprinkling of white hairs, almost a frosted effect. A very few dedicated local hunters manage to take them in daylight hours—and criticize the majority who hunt them at night. By luck, skill, or a tremendous expenditure of time, it is possible to get the Cape grysbok in daylight. However, they are extremely nocturnal and the vast majority of the relatively few taken annually are taken at night. This is said neither to explain nor to beg forgiveness; it's just the way it is.

Even at night it isn't a sure thing. I'd tried before with good guys in good places. I'd seen a lot of the pretty little antelope, but I'd never caught a glimpse of horns between those big ears. Undoubtedly some of the many I'd seen were males, but seeing the horns before they bolt is tricky. I was almost amused at the concept that "Monday night is for your grysbok." But so it was. We hadn't been on the property very long before we saw three or four females, and then a fine male, horns obvious, stood just at the limit of our vision. I shot him, and he turned out to be a monster. A cold, dark hour (and many grysbok) later, Debra shot hers. It was still early on a perfect night, clear, calm, and very cold, so we looked around a bit more. We each shot one of the pretty little genet cats, and Debra shot a silver jackal, a.k.a. Cape fox.

Tuesday we drove over to Adrian Ford's farm just south of Port Alfred. He and his wife, Elizabeth, have what I consider the prettiest piece of ground I have ever seen on this planet. They have several miles of rugged

Both male and female blue duiker grow similar horns. The horns of the males are a bit thicker, but in brush it is almost impossible to judge them. I was very lucky: This is a really big male and a wonderful trophy.

The Eastern Cape is perhaps the best bushbuck country I've ever seen. Debra Bradbury waits for a ram to step clear while Larry McGillewie and his best friend, Baku, assist.

coastline, with sand dunes giving way to lush coastal bush that rises quickly to grassy ridges, with thornbush valleys in between. Unlike much of South Africa, relatively little of the Eastern Cape is game-fenced, in part because many of the native species don't require it. Adrian has the densest bushbuck population I've encountered and a lot of common duiker, and he and his neighbor share a good herd of bontebok that wander back and forth. But his specialties are the tiny blue duiker that love the dense coastal thickets, and the oribi that prefer the open, grassy ridges above.

The blue duiker are actually quite numerous but very difficult to spot. Adrian Ford hunts them with a pack of small terriers trained expressly to hunt this animal. I had taken this smallest of all forest duiker up in the C.A.R., so I wasn't all that excited about it. McGillewie insisted that I needed to see how it was done in South Africa, and indeed he was right. It isn't a pell-mell chase like most dog hunts. The terriers go into the bush with handlers close by, and push the thickets fairly gently. Sometimes the duiker come charging past, but more often they slip through quietly well ahead of the dogs.

Adrian posted us at likely crossing places that offered a wee bit of visibility, and Debra shot one on the very first drive. I thought this might be a bit too easy, but we did a half-dozen more drives without seeing another duiker, although we heard a few scampering through the bush. It was nearly noon and I was on a little trail bisecting a thicket, standing in shadow with the shotgun ready. The drive had barely started when I saw just a hint of movement in thick stuff twenty yards down the trail. I focused on the spot but saw nothing. Then a tiny blue duiker stepped into view. He saw me and reversed before I got the shotgun all the way to my shoulder, but he was too late. Unlike many of the forest duiker, both male and female blues have similar horns and it is almost impossible to properly sex them. I got lucky. Mine was a very big male, far better than I had taken in the forests a thousand miles to the north.

We ran into Port Alfred and had lunch at a really good seaside restaurant, then returned to see if we could find an oribi, one of the larger members of the diverse group we call pygmy antelope. The oribi is a beautiful yellow antelope with sharp black horns, a creature of open grasslands found discontinuously from southern Africa all the way to Chad. In South Africa he is found only in a narrow belt of coastal plain roughly between Grahamstown and Port Elizabeth, and as such is one of the most restricted of South Africa's numerous antelope, with only a handful of permits available annually. I had taken just one oribi in my life, up in the flood plains surrounding Zambia's Bangweulu.

In South Africa oribi are expensive as well as restricted, and I didn't think I needed another. McGillewie thought otherwise. A previous client had missed a really big one, so the permit was available and Larry was certain we could find him. We did, and quite easily. He was with a female up on top of one of Adrian's grassy ridges. Larry knew him instantly, so we made a quick stalk and I lay down with the rifle over my backpack and shot him at about two hundred yards.

The afternoon was still fairly young, so now we got serious about looking for bushbuck. Truly, it was the craziest thing I've ever seen. We'd seen a few bushbuck while hunting blue duiker, but now that we were concentrating on them, they seemed to be everywhere. In part it was because we were now looking for them in the right places, but more important is that bushbuck like to feed in late afternoon, and this was a perfect sunny afternoon just starting to turn cool. We saw more bushbuck rams in the next couple of hours than I have ever seen in one place. We didn't see any monsters, but with the sun just starting down, Debra stalked and shot a fine old ram, putting a wonderful finish to our day along Adrian's beach.

Wednesday was our bontebok day. The bontebok is an open-country animal that, like his close cousin the blesbok, is usually not particularly spooky. Originally he occupied a fairly small range that, unluckily for his tribe, lay square in the path of the Boers as they brought their oxwagons north to escape what they considered English oppression. The quagga and the blaubok similarly occupied small ranges and became extinct during the nineteenth century. The bontebok could well have followed, but forward-thinking farmers saved a few individuals. Today they have bred up well and are readily available, but they interbreed freely with the drab and far more common blesbok. So they must be farmed separately, and today are found in registered herds of pure stock. Interestingly, although bontebok must be kept apart from them, all that's required is a low sheep fence. Bontebok are one of several antelope that simply will not cross a fence, so game-fencing is not required, but no bontebok today are truly free-range.

We took a fine ram with little difficulty, and the following day Debra shot an enormous black wildebeest. Also called white-tailed gnu, the black wildebeest was also saved at the very brink of extinction. The only one I have ever shot I took clear back in 1979, when black wildebeest were still very uncommon and quite expensive. Today they are plentiful, and are a common sight on many (if not most) well-stocked farms in both their native South Africa and in Namibia. The black wildebeest, by the way, is another animal that is readily confined by a low stock fence.

We had accomplished almost all of our objectives and had time to spare, a real rarity in my African experience. One thing Debra wanted badly that we'd failed to obtain was a bat-eared fox. This may seem a little odd, but Debra has a magnificent trophy room on her Wyoming ranch. Originally it was a legacy from her late husband, Weatherby Award winner Basil Bradbury, but today it's mostly filled with her own animals. What sets it apart is that she has lots of smaller animals along with the major trophies, and she wanted one of the pretty little bat-eared foxes to go with her wolves, coyotes, jackals, hyenas, and so forth.

We spent several afternoons and evenings trying to find one without success, but on the last day she got a wonderful bonus. The caracal or African lynx is extremely plentiful in the Eastern Cape and is hated by sheep and goat farmers. On any given day packs of hounds are pursuing lynx in the deep canyons and thick thornbush, and on our last day Larry finally got a call: A houndsman he knew was running a lynx in the deep canyons above the Great Fish River. We pounded up there, made it to the tree, and Debra shot a nice lynx. It was her shot and I was happy for her, but also a wee bit jealous. Although I'd looked for one often, I had never seen a lynx. So I knew I'd have to come back.

Boumba River

We flew into Mouloundou, a big village on the Ngoko River, a muddy stream dividing Cameroon from Congo. From there Cameron Hopkins and cameraman Garrick Cormack went one way to hunt with Geoffroy de Gentile while Tim Danklef and I and Howard McCutcheon went the other to hunt from different camps with professional hunters Steffan Ndongwa and Guav Johnson. Our mentors took us a short distance to a mud boat ramp on the Ngoko, where we boarded a long, narrow wooden boat fitted with, thankfully, a fairly new outboard. We traveled down the Ngoko just a short distance, then turned north up the Boumba River, a smaller and even muddier stream that serves as the primary geographic feature in Mayo Oldiri's Boumba and Upper Boumba concessions.

The trip upriver was uneventful, save for gathering clouds and the occasional sprinkle that clearly heralded a serious storm. The river narrowed and our boatman steered us through some rocks, and then the stream flattened out again, with heavy forest encroaching on both sides. I recalled the trip upriver in Joseph Conrad's *Heart of Darkness*, so ably updated by John Milius in his screenplay for *Apocalypse Now*. I wondered if Joseph Conrad's renegade trader or Milius's rogue colonel, both named Kurtz, awaited us. But there were no drums along the way, and no arrows or blowgun darts were launched from the dark vegetation. There was only the obvious urgency: If we didn't get to camp soon, we were going to get soaked!

We were almost in sight of camp when the rain started in earnest, and after we arrived it pelted down in sheets for hours. This was very good news. I hadn't been in the forest for nine years, but I remembered the rules: No rain, no bongo. We were getting good rain, and conditions would be excellent for the next two or three days. What I didn't fully appreciate about the forest, but would learn soon enough, was this more general rule: No rain, no forest game at all!

The camp we pitched up at had been built by Steffan some years earlier. During the forest hunting season it was his home and his kingdom, as was Geoffroy's camp far to the southeast, where Cameron was now, probably sitting under thatch watching the rain as we were. This was quite a camp, given that it was situated in the middle of nowhere, if not actually in the heart of darkness. Forest hunting is done in the rainy season, so the camp was built on stilts, with comfortable rooms adjoining a riverfront lounge and dining area, all joined by raised walkways with thatched roofs. Howard would be staying there to hunt with Steffan while in a day or two Guav, Tim, and I would head farther upriver to hunt from a fly camp in the newly opened Upper Boumba hunting block.

We understood that the fly camp wouldn't be quite as comfortable, but there was good reason to go there. Steffan's long-established area was very good for bongo, probably better than the Upper Boumba. But bongo are plentiful in the forests of southern Cameroon, and they weren't the issue. I had taken a wonderful bongo in 1997, not far east from where Cameron was hunting. I knew I wouldn't beat him, and I didn't really care whether I got a bongo or not. That said, I did expect to get one: The bongo is far and away the most plentiful animal in this part of the forest, and Mayo Oldiri is pretty much a hundred percent successful on bongo. So, to be honest, that part of the hunt was for the television camera. What I was really there for was the forest game I hadn't taken: dwarf buffalo and forest sitatunga. I knew both were iffy, less common and harder to hunt than bongo, but these were my real goals. The Upper Boumba block had only recently been opened to hunting after cessation of logging. Guav hadn't been up there, but Steffan had, and he believed there were fewer bongo but more buffalo and sitatunga.

We could have gone right away, but it took most of a long day to get there, and it was raining now, not tomorrow. It was May, beginning of the rainy season, and showers were still unreliable. Wherever we were, we needed to take advantage of the wet conditions and hunt now. We could switch camps on a dry day.

Hard rain continued through most of the night. The river rose visibly, lapping at the supports underneath our elevated camp and pounding on the roof, but the rain stopped well before dawn, creating perfect conditions. Shortly after daylight Steffan and Howard went one way while Guav, Tim, and I went another. We took a boat north, almost to the navigable limit of the Boumba, and walked west to a series of salt licks. During and just after the rain bongo had visited each and every one, leaving more bongo tracks than I have personally ever seen in one day. But they had come in herds of a dozen and more. Although wonderfully encouraging on the first day, this was a useless situation. It was impossible to isolate a bull track, and in the climax forest that surrounded us it was clear folly to track a herd of bongo because if we closed on them, there would be almost no way to identify a bull.

Natural mineral licks like this are scattered through the forest, kept open by game movement and the locations passed down by local hunters through generations. It had rained the night before, and there were too many bongo tracks to follow.

We started our hunt with a boat ride up the Boumba River, brooding forest on both sides. It started to rain just before we reached camp, setting up perfect conditions for the next few days.

So we looked wistfully, started to sweat, and traveled on to the next salt lick. That one, too, held the tracks of a herd of bongo. Clearly the animals weren't scarce, and just as clearly they had roamed freely during the rain. The last lick held more bongo tracks, but also the fresh tracks of a small herd of forest buffalo. Since dwarf buffalo was supposed to be a main event, it seemed to me that we should follow them. After all, buffalo are buffalo and you follow the tracks. But it was the first day, so I kept my mouth shut. Good thing, else I'd have shown my ignorance. By the end of the hunt I knew that following a herd of buffalo in climax forest is even sillier than following a herd of bongo.

Finding nothing we could go on, we returned to camp for lunch and a jet-lag-induced nap, and in the afternoon we traveled a short distance from camp and tried to call duiker. We actually had a blue duiker come in, but I was hoping for a duiker I hadn't taken, a bay or a Peters. It wouldn't have mattered. I heard a quick scampering and saw a small gray flash, and that was that.

In the forest, the day after a rain is critical. Forest game moves when it rains but hunkers down when it's dry and forest is noisy. Rain day plus one is when you are most likely to find tracks, and we did, but they must be tracks you can follow. We weren't so fortunate, but Howard was. He and Steffan found what we were looking for, the tracks of a single bongo bull, and after a couple of hours of tracking Howard took a fine bongo bull on his first hunting day.

The next morning we could have moved camp, but it was the second day after a hard rain, almost as good as the first. We talked about it and elected to take advantage of favorable conditions. It was a good move: We found the big tracks of a single bongo bull hardly a half-hour from camp. I didn't yet understand the strategy, but our head Pygmy, whom we called Sergeant (he could lead my squad any day!), took point with a small

Tim Danklef and I after several hours of tracking bongo. No, it hadn't rained on this day, but it doesn't need to rain for you to get wet. After a couple of hours of walking you will be soaked with sweat.

That's Sergeant and Corporal, with Guav Johnson and me behind. The Pygmies track
with their little dogs on leashes, releasing them only when an animal is jumped.

terrierlike dog on leash. His Number 2, whom we called Corporal, followed
with another leashed dog. Then came Guav, me, Tim and his camera, and
then our retinue—three more dogs and twice as many Pygmies.

A short way into the dense growth we learned we were following not
one bongo bull but two, and a merry chase they led us. By eight o'clock it
was hot and muggy. By nine it was oppressive. After that it wasn't worth
worrying about. From the few roads the tall trees generally obscure the
topography, so I was surprised when the tracks led us up one precipitous
ridge after another. Late in the morning we took a water break, and Tim
and I looked at each other and laughed. Gander Mountain had just come
on as a sponsor, and we didn't yet have the cotton safari clothing we were
developing. But we felt obligated to wear the Gander logo, so we had
tough, well-made shirts in a polyester blend, sort of like wearing plastic
bags. Guav had a couple of small sweat spots on his shirt, but Tim and I
were soaked to the limit of our shirttails. The things we do for television.

An hour later, we were clearly getting close. We had climbed a
nasty, thorny, brushy ridge, then descended it and climbed again as the

Guav Johnson, me, and our full retinue of Pygmy trackers with my bongo, a good bull for anywhere and perhaps a bit above average for Cameroon. My rifle hadn't yet arrived, so I used outfitter Antonio Riguera's .500-3" double rifle.

bongo wandered back and forth, seeking a place to lie up. We stopped to take a drink and catch our breath, and Tim checked the camera. The digital readout showed "moisture," and nothing else worked. He had been carrying it slung, and sweat and ambient humidity had fouled the electronics.

We set the camera in a small patch of hot noonday sun, hoping it would dry. A half-hour didn't help, nor did another half-hour, though we kept moving the camera into that fast-moving patch of sun. Tim, to his credit, passed the baton. It was my bongo, my call. But if we were serious about our TV series, there was just one answer: We had to wave off. I asked Guav to explain it to our Pygmies, but I knew they were perplexed. These bongo were right there, and I know we'd have jumped them in another half-hour. The lesson was invaluable: From that point we kept the camera bagged until things got serious!

Next morning we moved up to fly camp, which turned out to be a serious journey. North of Steffan's camp were rapids that a boat couldn't traverse, so we had to drive south nearly to the Ngoko and take the hand-cranked ferry across. Then we drove north for several hours, eventually taking another ferry to the west to reenter our hunting area. It was that day, our third, when Cameron got his bongo, although a couple of days passed before we learned of his success via satellite phone.

Mayo Oldiri had secured this Upper Boumba block a couple of years earlier, but logging operations were underway and they weren't allowed to hunt it until the loggers moved farther west. Now the area was quiet, but an intricate network of logging roads remained in the wake of chain saws and logging trucks. This conjures up images of clear-cutting, of destruction of the rain forest, but in Cameroon this couldn't be farther from the truth. In this area at least, logging operations were obviously sensible and selective. Other than the roads, the forest seemed almost untouched. Giant stumps were there, but we had to look hard to find them. I've seen clear-cutting, and this area was logged by using good forestry methods. Of course, logging roads have had a tremendous impact on hunting in Africa's forests. They give access, not only to legal hunters but also to poachers, and they provide a clean, clear medium to look for tracks. Logging is partly the reason modern bongo hunting is more successful than ever before . . . and it perhaps has opened up the

The most common animal on the Upper Boumba is the Peters duiker, so common that we actually saw several every day scampering along the verge of the forest roads. This is a very good male.

forest to allow more food to grow and is thus equally responsible for high populations of forest animals.

We covered a lot of ground that first day, with local guides Sergeant and Corporal showing us the way. Bongo tracks were much less plentiful than around the main camp, but it seemed there were plenty of bulls around. We saw old tracks of three or four lone bulls made just after the rain, and older tracks of buffalo as well. Interestingly, there were lots of duiker and, unique in my forest experience, they were visible. Most common were the reddish-tan, medium-size Peters duiker, and we saw several picking their way along the forest roads every morning and every afternoon. In fact, this was the only small duiker we saw any evidence of at all, and Tim described the area as the "house of Peters duiker." But there were also a lot of the square tracks of the much larger yellowback duiker, the most tracks of this elusive animal that I have ever seen.

That night it rained again, hard, and we were grateful for well-thatched roofs. This "fly camp" was well designed and well laid out, with a covered dining area and separate thatched sleeping areas for the PHs and their clients. The shower was marvelous, as good a bush shower as I've seen. But, after all, it was a fly camp and wasn't perfect. Within the thatched hut was a mosquito-net tent for sleeping, and that was just fine. The camp beds were not so fine. Actually, they were lawn chairs laid flat, with sheet and blanket on top. I made the terrible mistake of attempting to sleep in this torture device the first night. I guess I slept too well, because to this day my right shoulder hasn't recovered. Thereafter I slept on the floor, which was much better!

We awoke to yet another day of perfect tracking conditions; a rain had made the forest game move. Not a half-hour out of camp we found fresh, heart-shaped tracks where a big bongo had crossed the road. The tracks had been made after the rain, but the rain had stopped early. We took the spoor in the same order as before, but Guav cautioned that the tracks didn't look real fresh. It could be a long day.

It was not. The bongo led us through horrible second-growth that the Pygmies call "green forest," only ten feet tall but almost impenetrable. Then the tracks took us up an overgrown skid road, down another logging road for a few hundred yards, and then into tall-tree "dark forest," where the undergrowth is less thick but little light penetrates through the distant canopy.

It wasn't clear to me that we had gained much, and the tracks were still more or less straight. There was no meandering as if the bongo was feeding or looking for a place to lie up. If Sergeant had an opinion, he didn't share it. But just a few hundred yards into the dark forest we heard a heavy animal crash off ahead of us. Now I would see the Pygmy way of hunting. Sergeant and Corporal released their dogs and dashed off after them. Behind us the three other dogs were unleashed, and they swept past us as we struggled through vines and thorns. Within a couple of minutes the shrill barking turned sharp and stabilized, and Guav hissed over his shoulder, "They've got him!"

We ran forward, and I was instantly breathless and covered in sweat. The barking was close now but hidden behind a wall of gray brush. Then I could see movement and a flash of white-striped red hide. The dogs were there, barking and darting in and out, and in their midst was a great bongo bull. I saw the horns as he swept them down and swiped

We failed utterly and miserably on forest buffalo, and I never even saw a fresh sitatunga track. At the end of the hunt I got a fine bonus with a good yellowback duiker, the largest duiker in that part of the forest and one of its great prizes.

at a dog, and there was no reason for further evaluation. Guav said something that ended in "good bull," but I already knew that. A few steps more and I was almost clear enough to shoot, hardly ten yards from the bull.

My own rifle, a Ruger rebarreled to .416 Taylor, had failed to arrive in Douala. In its place I had a Krieghoff double .500, loaned by Mayo Oldiri's owner, Antonio Riguera. Honestly, my hands were so soaked with sweat that I fumbled the safety and had to try a second time. By now the bongo was leaving, stepping away, but that .500 was plenty of gun. I took the going-away shot and the bull went down, and as soon as the dogs were clear I stepped to the right and finished him with the solid in the second barrel.

Not too many years earlier I had hardly dared to hope that I might someday take a bongo, and now I had a second bongo, a beautiful bull with perfectly shaped horns, this one taken in the Pygmy fashion. There are those who say that this technique, using small dogs, is not sporting. As I said in the first chapter, my suspicion is that those who say this are of a previous generation who hunted their bongo in the more open finger forest of southwestern Sudan and eastern C.A.R. Without the dogs, there is very little chance of seeing a bongo in the incredibly dense forest of Cameroon. But sheer difficulty doesn't justify a hunting technique, so that isn't the point. Without dogs you might see a flash of red, but you will not see the horns. I saw the horns before I shot and thus knew what I was shooting. Unless you've personally hunted the true climax forest and tried to see into it, you should not judge this technique.

Between Cameron, Howard, and myself we now had three good bongo bulls in five days. And now things got difficult. In fact, to end the suspense now, no other major trophies were taken among the three of us. Howard actually saw a big sitatunga but didn't get a shot. Neither Cameron nor I ever saw one. Nor did either of us see a buffalo bull, although Cameron had a close encounter with a truculent cow. I did see the bushes move a couple of times, and I learned a great deal along the way.

Two things I learned were that rain makes all forest game move—and that there is little movement during dry conditions. There were actually quite a lot of forest buffalo in the area we were hunting. Several times after a rain, we saw the tracks of small herds that we might have followed but

The African forest is not truly a rain forest, but a genuine climax tall tree forest. It is incredibly difficult to hunt, and a safari to an area like this is not for everyone and certainly not for beginners in Africa—but it is dramatically beautiful country.

did not. Then we had no rain for a week and saw almost no tracks—of anything. At the tail end it rained again, and we had tracks to follow.

Four times in two days we found good tracks of buffalo bulls, and these we followed. I quickly learned why we did not follow any herds. It is so thick that without incredible luck it is almost impossible to track an animal and gain visual contact. Twice, on consecutive mornings, we tracked a big-footed bull until he crossed a river and left our hunting area. I assume he knew that sanctuary lay on the other side. The two other times we tracked the bulls to their beds, and they jumped up at a matter of feet and took off. I never saw even a patch of red hide, although I did see bushes moving in their wake. Both times the Pygmies released their dogs, and I learned a third thing: It is much more difficult for the dogs to stop a buffalo than a bongo! It does happen, and beyond catching one crossing a road or feeding in a rare clearing, this is the most likely way to take one. But I have no idea how many buffalo you must track before you actually see one! I do know that I'll have to do it again, because I really want one of those short-horned, small-bodied, and incredibly elusive forest buffalo.

The forest is different, and certainly not for everyone. Despite the frustrations, I enjoyed it. Tim had never seen it before, and although we spent a lot of time griping to each other, I think he enjoyed it as well. We got some good footage of gorilla, and an amazing amount of video of Peters duiker scampering along. And we enjoyed this fly camp deep in the forest, complete with its lawn-chair beds. We ate well for a few days after we took the bongo, and when the meat was gone we discovered that our cook's real specialty was beans and weenies out of a can. I got a very good Peters duiker, and that, too, was tasty, but it didn't last long, and then we were back to beans and weenies.

The forest is pretty much feast or famine, with little opportunity for "camp meat" along the way. You have to capitalize on what opportunity there is. This area had the greatest concentration of yellowback duiker that I've seen. Not only were tracks in evidence, but also every few days we would actually see one. If the truth must be known, I missed not one but two! The first was forgivable. It was about four in the afternoon—after a shower, of course—and as we came around a curve the animal stood in the middle of a forest road, maybe 150 yards away. My rifle hadn't arrived yet, so I grabbed what was closest, Guav's open-sighted Model 70 in .416 Remington. A few days earlier I'd taken a fine Peters duiker with this rifle, so I know it was sighted in. However, the front sight covered the entire animal with plenty of countryside to spare, and I just plain missed.

I couldn't kick myself too hard under the circumstances, but even so I was sick. The yellowback is one of three giant forest duiker, weighs over a hundred pounds, and is a rare and desirable prize. My buddy Joe Bishop has done something like five forest safaris and has never shot one—though not for lack of effort. Judging by the tracks, we were clearly in an unusual concentration of yellowbacks, but I didn't think we would see another. Two days later we did. It was almost dusk and raining, and we were just cresting a hill on a forest road when a dark animal crossed the road below us and stood on the verge. By now my rifle, a Ruger Model 77 rebarreled to .416 Taylor and topped with a Trijicon 1.25–4X scope, had finally arrived by road from Douala. We had checked zero and it was perfect. So I have no excuse other than that the road was straight, the light was poor, and I had no idea how far off this thing was. I missed again, and knew it was over.

Early on the next-to-last day I got a reprieve. A big yellowback duiker stood in the middle of the road at maybe two hundred yards. I held the tip of the Trijicon post high on the shoulder, just below the backline, and was almost amazed when the big Hornady bullet smacked home. The animal went down hard, then got up and made it into the brush. We all ran, the Pygmies streaking ahead, and they had him long before I got there. By now I understood that my chances for a dwarf buffalo were very slim, so I accepted this yellowback as a fine consolation prize. We took the full skin and, after having endured several days of canned rations, carefully peeled out the backstraps and looked forward to a fine meal. Not quite. Our hungry crew devoured the entire duiker, and it was beans and weenies again!

At the end we packed up and retraced our steps to Steffan's Boumba River camp. It started to sprinkle as we crossed the first ferry, and the rain came down in wind-driven sheets the rest of the drive. The narrow track ran rivers, so going was slow and we got stuck two or three times. It was the wettest, coldest, most miserable drive I can remember. That's a funny thing about hunting in the forest. It can be incredibly hot and muggy, with sweat running in rivers—and then comes the rain, and suddenly the temperature drops twenty degrees and you go from very hot to very cold. But that's part of the deal, because you need rain, you want rain, and after three or four dry days you pray for rain.

In the evening at Steffan's camp, with wet gear hanging everywhere, it was pleasantly cool after the rain. We drank some good French wine, and after dark our crew treated us to the bongo dance. I had hoped for the rare prize of a dwarf buffalo or a forest sitatunga, but those required more luck than I'd had. No matter, the main prize from the forest is always that reddish, white-striped wonder, the bongo. We had taken our bongo, and we'd done just fine.

Sapi and Dande North

Whh at a difference a little rain makes! In June 2006 the Lower Zambezi was back to normal, meaning lots of water out in the bush, the game widely scattered, and the animals behaving as they should. We needed a normal year, because we had a major agenda in the Lower Zambezi. We—partners Tim Danklef, Dave Fulson, and me; and my own partner, Donna Grey—gathered in Harare in early June, joined by Steve Hornady, L. L. Bean's Bill Gorman, and Cameron Hopkins. The purpose was to film segments for *Tracks Across Africa,* and the schedule was ambitious. Tim and Dave, assisted by South African videographer Bruce Parker, would be doing the filming. Steve Hornady was hunting buffalo, leopard, and sable; Bill and Cameron were hunting buffalo.

Initially Donna and I were along for the ride, she literally and me to do some on-camera stuff. At the conclusion of this hunt we would jump in a boat and travel farther down the Zambezi to Dande North, on the far side of Chewore and the last Zimbabwe area before the Mozambique border. There we would meet a new set of sponsor–clients, and off we'd go for a second round of buffalo hunting.

ONCE MORE IN SAPI

Steve Hornady actually had a dual mission. The leopard portion of his hunt would be filmed for *Petersen's Hunting Adventures;* his buffalo and sable were earmarked for *Tracks.* My mission was to shadow him and smile on Dave Fulson's camera. Tim paired up with Cameron, and

Bruce Parker filmed for Bill Gorman. I'm not much of an observer, but Steve and I go back a long way, and we had a lot of fun.

Actually, Steve Hornady is an interesting case study in African hunting. Excepting a short plains-game hunt with his kids, Steve had not hunted Africa since 1983, when I was with him on a hunt in Zambia. This in itself is not so remarkable until you put it in this context: Since then, Steve Hornady has hunted more mountain game, sheep and goats, than anyone else in the industry before or since. I can say that because after Steve, I've hunted that stuff the second-most! He likes it rough, and although we never discussed it, my suspicion was that even Zambia was too easy for his liking (he probably believed the buffalo he took on that trip had been standing a bit too close to the road). Clearly, for a guy who has hunted Marco Polo sheep and markhor (and loved it), a South African game ranch had not been to his liking.

He wanted a leopard and a sable, and he was willing to hunt a buffalo. The previous year Steve and I had done an incredibly tough mountain hunt together for Dagestan tur in the Caucasus Mountains of Azerbaijan, the most up-and-down country I've ever seen. I couldn't match that, but part of my mission here was to ensure that he had a real hunt. In the end, I succeeded far better than I'd hoped!

We started out shooting impala for bait, Steve using the only rifle he'd brought, the very first Ruger Model 77 in .375 Ruger, a joint development between Hornady and Ruger. Steve was hunting with Paul Smith, and every time Steve pulled the trigger, Paul simply shook his head. Steve was shooting brilliantly, the kind of shooting I'd expect from a serious sheep hunter, but of a quality that Paul had rarely seen. After a couple of days we had promising trees festooned with impala. The weather was relatively cool, so it would take a couple of days for the baits to ripen (ugh!) properly and a couple more for them to go off. So we had time to hunt buffalo.

I like Steve Hornady a lot. A few years older than I, he's occasionally prickly, often funny, and extremely tough. In Zambia in '83 we all went to the Lusaka hoosegow because he insisted on photographing a bridge. That was a bit too soon after "external operations" by the Rhodesian forces, and things almost got out of hand. We were in our thirties then. In 2005, in Azerbaijan, we were well into our fifties and

I had a helluva time keeping up with him! I wanted him to have a tough buffalo hunt here, not as tough as Wayne Holt's the year before but tough enough to be appreciated. I don't think we accomplished that—but maybe we came close.

We picked up the tracks of a good herd relatively early in the morning, not far from the Mana Pools National Park boundary, and they were headed the right way, deeper into Sapi. We followed for a couple hours, and Wanda and Coffee showed the magic they were capable of: With a big herd moving through the mopane, they pointed out the outsize tracks of a bull on top of the rest. This, they explained, was a *dagga* bull shadowing the herd. He was probably too old to mess with the herd bulls, but it was June and there would be cows in season. He would shadow the herd and wait for an opportunity, sort of like the old joke about the young bull and the old bull. The young bull wanted to run down the hill and cover a few cows; the old bull advised that they should walk slowly down the hill and cover all the cows.

So we tracked the herd as the morning heated up. The wind remained good, and when we hit them we moved to the right, where this outsize track had consistently been. Wanda knew what he was looking for, and when he saw the scabby, balding, and taller back of an extra-large buffalo shadowing the herd, he led us in at an angle. We were lucky, catching him in relatively open mopane. We were luckier still in that his horns matched his tracks—exceptional bosses, exceptional drop to the horns, reasonable width. We could have kept looking, but it would have been foolish. This was a very fine buffalo.

Paul took Steve forward the last few steps, set up the sticks, and then moved them and set them up again as the bull drifted to the right. He was standing in the lee of a stout tree, and at the last moment he sensed something amiss and turned, almost facing us. Steve's shot, with one of his 300-grain Interbond bullets, dropped the bull instantly. Too instantly. As we ran forward, the bull got to his feet and moved to the left.

It was at this point that I forgot my role and screwed up completely. I was maneuvering to the left to get clear, which was not my job. Steve shot again and Paul shot, but the buffalo was still on his feet, moving left into cover at maybe seventy yards. I had no right to shoot—a most important point—but I had the shot and I took it. I apologized profusely on the

Paul Smith studies his topo map, ably assisted by tracker Wanda, Steve Hornady, and Tim Danklef. When a leopard track is found, the site is GPS'd, then the map comes out so they can try to determine where the leopard might be coming from or going to.

spot, and do so again now. The buffalo passed behind a couple of trees and I lost him, but he went down right there. We approached him carefully and Steve paid the insurance. Then we could admire the first buffalo to fall to the brand-new .375 Ruger. By the way, the first shot was absolutely fatal, and I'd give anything if I'd simply left my rifle in the truck!

Steve's buffalo was superb, but it was nothing like the monster Cameron Hopkins took, a heavy-bossed old bull with deep hooks and a wide spread, the kind of buffalo he had always wanted. This year the rains had cooperated, and plenty of buffalo roamed Sapi. This didn't mean it was easy. Bill Gorman had bad luck almost until the last day, when he and professional hunter Mike Payne finally came up with a dandy old bull.

Steve and Paul were baiting for leopard in a far-flung circle, some placed baits on trees that had produced previously, while others targeted two big tracks that we'd located. We had a couple of females feeding, and in fact one, in the Upper Sapi, jumped from her bed under the tree when we ground our way up the sandy riverbed to check the bait. But as the days went by we had no hits from male leopard at all, despite seeing large tracks in the neighborhood.

Other than impala to feed the kitties, there was little other hunting to be done and little time to do it, except for the hippo that Steve wanted to take. We had heard of a big bull hanging out in Hyena Pan (named for the hyena I had shot and a leopard had carried into a tree there two years earlier). Fortunately, this pan was on our baiting route, so we checked it a couple of times. There were reasonably fresh tracks but no sign of a hippo in the pool, so we made the assumption the hippo had left, as they are wont to do as the water starts to recede.

A couple of days later we took another look, just in case and because it was the right time of day, with all baits checked and nothing going on. We were pretty certain the hippo wasn't there, but Wanda and Coffee circled the big, irregular pan to check for tracks. A few minutes later Coffee came back. The hippo was in the bush, and Wanda was watching him.

By agreement, I handed over the other new Hornady development, the first Ruger Number One single-shot chambered to and stoked with Hornady's reintroduction of the great old .450-400 three-inch Nitro Express. This would be a job for solids. We crept up to Wanda's position near the bank, and indeed there was a bull hippo standing thirty yards into the thorn. Unfortunately, there was too much brush for a shot, so the only option was to try to approach until the shot was clear. We almost made it, but not quite. At the last moment the bull drew the line. Rather than charging, as we expected, he broke and ran to our left. We ran with him, trying to beat him to his water sanctuary.

We lost, but once in the pan he made a mistake, turning to face us. Steve had the Ruger up instantly and fired one shot centered on the forehead "V." The bull sank, and except for the recovery, that was that: the first animal taken with an American rifle and an American load for tiger hunter Jim Corbett's favorite cartridge.

Steve had a few more hunting days, but at the ten-day mark it was time for most of us to move on. At that point we had a good male leopard feeding along the Chewore, and I would have bet money Steve would be successful. I would have lost. On the eleventh day, if not the eleventh hour, a good male came in late, and Steve, who had shot so perfectly throughout the hunt, shot a bit low and a bit far back as

Steve Hornady and Paul Smith with the first buffalo taken with the new .375 Ruger cartridge. This is a fine old dagga bull caught shadowing a herd, a common occurrence in May and June, which is the primary breeding season for buffalo in this area.

the cat took one fateful step forward in fading light. They backed off that night, and the following day tried to follow a fading spoor in thick riverine bush, one dwindling drop at a time. Dave traded his camera for a shotgun as they peered into every bush along the Chewore, but this cat was gone forever.

Hearing about it on radio, none of us believed it. We thought it was a bad practical joke, but regrettably it was real. There was nothing to be done about it except to move on, and Steve, Paul, and Dave moved on to the Douma area just north of the Escarpment, where Steve took the kind of sable antelope he had dreamed of for more than twenty years.

DANDE, ROUND ONE

Dande North is a different deal than Sapi. For the past decade it has been the exclusive concession of Swainson Safaris, run by the Meredith brothers, Cyril ("Squirrel") and Daryl. Starting in 2006, in a typically complex African arrangement, Chifuti Safaris' dangerous duo of Andrew Dawson and Paul Smith joined in with a management and marketing role in Dande North. Blessed with perhaps the densest buffalo populations in southern Africa, and a large quota to match, Dande North is altogether different from relatively flat Sapi. It has high, well-watered hills and sand rivers that hold permanent water throughout the season—at least in a normal year.

The original plan had been for us to go downriver by boat, but the timing didn't work, so Tim, Donna, and I shot over the Chewore Hills in Andrew's Cessna while Bruce Parker took the long way by road, bringing in one of the Land Cruisers we would need. We met our next victims, Gander Mountain's Mike Schoby and Ruger sales rep Flint Virgets, at Maruru Camp on the western side near the Chewore boundary. Both were set up with big Rugers in .416 Rigby and were raring to get after their first buffalo. And although it wasn't exactly my first buffalo, I was raring to go as well, because I'd get to hunt on this segment!

I would hunt with Andrew Dawson, Flint would hunt with Squirrel Meredith, and Mike Schoby would hunt with Mike Payne, at least at first. When Paul Smith finished Steve Hornady's hunt, their group now moving on to Douma, things might change.

The shift to Dande didn't please, at least at first. I'd long heard it was wonderful, but I had gotten very comfortable in Sapi. I was starting to understand that area and I'd seen the quality of its buffalo, at least when conditions were right. Had I been calling the shots, I'd have stayed in Sapi. I held this opinion for my first couple of days in Dande. The country was exceptionally beautiful, with high, green hills and lush valleys, but I guess we were hitting it wrong because, although we got into a couple of crazy-wild herds of buffalo, we didn't see much. I had it wrong, and since my mind was made up, it took me a few days to see the error of my ways.

No area produces on any given day, but Dande actually does have one of the greatest concentrations of buffalo I have ever seen, rivaling the Selous Reserve in numbers and exceeding the Selous in trophy quality. It is, in short, awesome for buffalo, with big herds wandering at will and most sand rivers holding *dagga* boys. Our problem, which turned out to be no problem at all, was that it had been an exceptional rainy season, opposite the previous year. Every valley was lush with water and grass, so the buffalo didn't have to

There were several firsts on this safari and this was another. Steve's hippo was the first animal taken with the new Hornady loading for the great old .450-400-3", chambered in a Ruger No. 1 single-shot.

move very far—and if they didn't cross a road, well, you had to go dig them out.

On the third day we started digging. We left the truck on a long ridge and took a big swing along the Chewore boundary. We saw plenty of old spoor, but the only buffalo we actually saw was a lone bull that cameraman Bruce Parker almost stepped on when he went ahead to film our approach. He got away without a good look at the animal, and it was well into afternoon and very hot when we finally reunited with the truck. Of course, Andrew's driver informed us that a very nice herd of buffalo had walked right by a few hours earlier.

We had lunch in the shade, found the tracks, and started after them. Not surprisingly, they'd only gone a few kilometers before lying down. We caught them about four o'clock, already up again and feeding along a brushy *gwacha* (ravine). It was a good-size herd, more than a hundred, and they were quite calm, as are most of the buffalo in Dande North, I would learn. We maneuvered on them for an hour or more, circling this way and that. There were a couple of nasty old bulls with poor horns, and a couple of promising youngsters, but with sunset approaching we had seen nothing of interest. Andrew grinned, looked at me, stretched his calf muscles, and said, "Are you ready?"

I nodded and looked at Bruce Parker. "Get ready to run," I told him.

We dashed along a low ridge, me barely keeping up with Andrew, Bruce and Donna just a few steps behind. The first buffalo were caught unaware, and we almost passed them before they spooked. They led us on to the main group, and the stampede was on. But it was almost sundown, and the herd wouldn't splinter. The main group thundered across a ravine and up the far side, then stopped and milled while the best bull, heavy-bossed but narrow of horn, stepped forward to challenge us. Against the sunset it was a magnificent picture, but I had no camera, only the rifle I had no intention of using.

That was the day Mike Schoby, hunting with Mike Payne and with Tim Danklef on the camera, had some excitement of his own. They got into a small herd, and Mike got a good broadside shot at a very nice bull. The shot was good, but the effect was not. The bull went into thick vegetation—too thick. They were unlucky in that the charge came from just a few yards, but they were lucky in that they were in a tiny clearing. Mike Schoby managed to jump aside. So did the lead tracker, but he jumped the wrong way—right into Mike Payne, fouling his shot. Payne got clear and lifted his double Krieghoff just in time to have the grim realization that he was out of time to stop the onrushing buffalo. Wisely he tried to jump clear, and he almost made it. The flat of the buffalo's horn swiped him on the leg, doing little damage but knocking him flat. Tim got it all on camera, and then did his own duck-and-dive.

The buffalo kept going into the next patch of cover. Payne, prone and with the wind knocked out of him, still held his rifle. As the buffalo disappeared he fired both barrels into the broad backside, desperate shooting that almost certainly prevented serious mayhem. They gathered themselves and took the track once more, and as they approached the thicket the buffalo charged once more, perhaps a bit slower. Both Mikes fired, and this time the buffalo went down.

On our way back to camp that evening, after a day that took us twenty-six kilometers on the map, we ran smack into a herd of buffalo in the dark. We let them pass, and a couple hundred yards farther we ran

A herd of buffalo moving through mopane forest on the Dande. While most buffalo were located by tracking, the buffalo density is such that, over the course of several days, you will almost certainly bump into buffalo now and again.

into four bulls shadowing the herd. They all looked pretty good in the dark, so at first light next morning we were back at the spot. Although it had been twelve hours since we'd seen these buffalo, we caught them within an hour. This, I was learning, was the magic of Dande. With plenty of grass and water, the animals had little reason to move vast distances. If you couldn't find tracks, you might have tough sledding, but once reasonably fresh tracks were found, the buffalo wouldn't be far.

This herd was bedded right on top of a ridge covered with stunted mopane. It was early and cold, and the breeze was steady. At first we saw just one buffalo ambling across the skyline, but Mukassa led us to the left, and in a few moments we were within forty yards of a dense mass of buffalo, some bedded and some standing. On the far left, at the tail end of the herd, were several bulls. Maybe they were the same bulls we'd seen the night before, maybe not, but the pale light of dawn showed that most were clearly immature. And then we spotted an older bull, distinctive

There were several shootable bulls in the herd, but this is the one Donna wanted. His bosses are exceptional, and his horn tips are fantastic. He was at maximum horn growth and hadn't yet started to wear down—a truly exceptional buffalo.

This rear view shows the conformation and long tips on Donna Grey's buffalo. She used the first Ruger No. 1 in .450-400-3", firing 400-grain Hornady solids.

with heavy, polished horns, a big body, and gray, patchy hide. He was close but was pressed in with other buffalo, and there was no shot, even when he moved off.

"Look for the white bull," Mukassa said as he led us alongside the herd. A bull so gray he was white passed at twenty yards but still wasn't clear for a shot. We circled once more, then again, and I wondered how long the wind would hold. The buffalo had come down off the ridge and were working their way across a deep, sandy wash. Mukassa led us in, and we stood on one bank while, forty yards away, buffalo filed around a little point and climbed the opposite bank.

I was on the sticks, ready, and Andrew and Mukassa were watching. "He's in the bottom," whispered Andrew. "He's climbing up the bank. He's going to come out next."

A cow stepped forward, and then that bull so gray he was almost white, with worn, polished horns, stepped onto the opposite bank and into the clear. I was shooting the Ruger single-shot in .450-400 three-inch, the old .400 Jeffery with new Hornady loads. For once I followed my own advice, carefully dividing the bull into horizontal thirds and bringing the Trijicon post up the center of the foreleg one-third into the body. The bull took the 400-grain solid hard; a post-mortem would show the bullet entered the on-shoulder, crossed the top of the heart, and exited the off-shoulder. I knew instantly that the shot was good, but the buffalo was still going, and he was too mixed up with the herd for a second shot.

Andrew and I rushed along the bank, hoping for a better angle, while the buffalo stampeded up a gentle rise above the creek. As we ran I stuffed another round into the single-shot. This all took perhaps three seconds, and by the time the buffalo were reaching the top, not 150 yards away, our bull's back legs started to go, and he fell over before I could fire a safe second shot.

Although he'd been with the herd, he was a classic *dagga* bull, with wonderfully worn and well-polished horns. Flint Virgets shot his bull that day as well, also a grand old *dagga*. He took his out of a group of seven bachelor bulls that paraded down a sand river toward the hunters. What a sight that must have been!

DANDE, ROUND TWO

Now we all had our buffalo, and plenty of time remained. What to do? That depended on a man's individual interests. Technically, Dande is a better area for plains game than Sapi. There is a small quota in Dande for sable (almost nonexistent and not on license in Sapi), a larger quota for both kudu and warthog, and bushpig and bushbuck, both off-license in Sapi, are fairly plentiful. Still, it's a valley area. Only buffalo roam there in herds upon herds. Even impala can be hard to find. But if you dig around, it's amazing what you can find. Flint Virgets was on his first African safari, and he dug around well, taking impala, bushbuck, and warthog, and on his last day a fine greater kudu.

Mike Schoby had incredible luck, quickly taking a really big warthog and an exceptional bushpig. And then he went down to Andrew and Paul's new fishing camp, Tafika, on the Sapi-Chewore boundary. He wanted to do some tiger fishing, and with Tim's help shoot a fishing segment for Gander Mountain's own television show. I didn't have much interest in the plains game, but I asked around a bit and found that, unlike Sapi, where every animal is spoken for and allocated, they did have a couple of buffalo still available. It occurred to me that Donna had now tracked more buffalo than most guys who have shot several. She enjoyed the walking and the tracking, and I had a feeling she'd like a crack at a buffalo of her own.

I took Andrew off to the side and we struck a price for a second buffalo, and he radioed Harare and got her the required "TR-2" hunting license. Getting the license and getting it into camp with a resupply run took a day, while we did the onerous work of "recreates" and interviews for the TV show, as well as filming some product stuff for the sponsors. With that stuff done, we agreed that Andrew should go to Tafika with Mike Schoby and Tim. Mike Payne went out as well to guide an incoming elephant hunter, and Paul Smith, having finished Steve Hornady's safari, came in to finish my hunt. Please note that this kind of switchee-changee stuff isn't normal for Chifuti Safaris; in both 2005 and 2006 we stretched their camp capacity to the breaking point so we could gang our "television safaris" together, and accommodations were necessary. Flint Virgets alone held solid as he continued his hunt with Squirrel Meredith.

Once all the film work and the changeovers were accomplished, we announced to Donna that it was her turn to go look for a buffalo. We had four full days and a partial fifth if we needed it. We wouldn't need quite that much time. . . .

We started fresh with a sight-in session at first light. Back home I'd had Donna spend a little range time with the Ruger .450-400 three-inch, just in case, so it wasn't altogether a cold start. We knew that the stock was a bit long, which is OK off shooting sticks, but we also knew that with its straight stock and heavy barrel the rifle was a real pussycat to shoot—but at the same time plenty of gun for buffalo. Paul had never seen Donna shoot, so actually the sight-in business was more for his benefit than hers, and that's pretty normal. Every initial sight-in on a safari is a lot more about the professional hunter finding out how his client shoots and handles a rifle than about actually checking zero!

With a couple of shots near the center of the bull's-eye, we were ready. It was late morning, but on the way back the previous evening Flint and

Paul Smith in the trophy shed at Maruru Camp in Dande North. Dande is a huge hunting area with several permanent camps.

Squirrel had crossed the fresh tracks of a big herd not far from camp. We took the tracks at ten o'clock, figuring we'd hit them some time in the afternoon. A half-hour later the tracks led us to a big, open knoll studded with buffalo dung. The herd had spent most of the night here, and when Wanda unraveled the spoor and led us onward, it was much fresher.

Big herds tend to travel very slowly if undisturbed, but in this year of exceptional grass I guess they didn't need to move much at all. A half-hour later, not suspecting we were even close, we almost walked into the herd. They were already bedded again in a shaded little valley, and Wanda got us down before we were spotted. So far this was about the easiest buffalo hunt I'd ever been on. Shifting a bit between trees, we could glass several buffalo in the near edge of the herd. Paul grabbed me and said, "Look at that bull!" The hulking animal was bedded in a little knot of its kind, with many more dark forms beyond, but at this weird angle we could see big bosses and wonderful curving horn tips that seemed to almost meet in the back. We needed to get closer, and even that was amazingly simple.

Paul led us out to the right, the steeper side of the valley. With Wanda checking the wind at every step, we duck-walked part of the way and then scooted along a rocky trail in that funny butt-crawl with feet forward, hands back, rifles across knees. It can be hard on the seat

Donna Grey and Paul Smith with our Dande buffalo, five good bulls taken by four hunters in about a week.

of your pants, but it beats the heck out of hands-and-knees. Slowly we circled back toward the herd and got in behind a tree. Paul put up the sticks, and Dave got his camera rolling.

I stayed back out of the way, but I could kind of see what was going on. We were about sixty yards above four bedded bulls, with plenty of other buffalo to the left and right. The wind was great, our position was perfect, and the buffalo were completely unaware, at least for the moment, but their position was awful. A young bull, wide-horned but soft-bossed, lay facing us on the left. To his right was a better bull, facing away. The big bull we'd seen was to that one's right, quartering away with his head to the left. Tight behind him was the fourth bull. A pass-through was almost certain, so there could be no shot until the target bull stood up and was clear.

It was not yet noon, and at this point the shortest buffalo hunt in history. Before we were done, it would become one of the longest in my experience. At 2:30 Donna was still standing on the sticks, rifle rested, waiting. A couple of times one of the young bulls had seen or sensed something, and he'd stood and played the "look-away" game that buffalo resort to when they aren't certain: He would stare at us for long minutes, then look away—and then quickly look back to see if we'd moved. We managed not to spook them, and somehow Donna managed to keep her cool and stay on the sticks, refusing offers to take a break. Finally things started to happen. The youngest bull, on the left, wandered away. Then the bull next to him got up and slowly followed. Our bull struggled to his feet, the other bull still tight behind him. Ours was facing left, and needed to take just two or three steps forward to be in a clear shooting lane. Instead he turned and ambled off to the right, out of our narrow shooting window.

We were all sick, and I guess we knew our chances now were very slim. This was a very big herd, and although they were still undisturbed, finding that bull and getting him clear in the press of bodies was most unlikely. But we had to try, and we had just one small advantage: This bull's horns were distinctive. But that isn't enough when there are multiple mature bulls to sort out in a moving herd. You must find some other identifying factor. With my bull a few days earlier it had been his gray, patchy hide, as well as horns that were oddly polished and shiny in the slanting morning sun. With Donna's bull it was a hand-size red patch on his right hip, maybe a horn wound or a close call with a lion.

We followed that red patch for another two hours, getting several glimpses. There were other good bulls in the herd, and Dave was dying: "How about that one?" "What's wrong with that bull?"

Technically he was right. The herd held other good bulls. Too, we had great film, and, after all, it was a first buffalo. But Paul, too, was right. He was fixated on this bull with the red rump patch, and if we didn't get him, we'd still have lots of time. In fact, we'd started out that day intending merely to look at some buffalo and have some fun with the herd, and then hunt *dagga* bulls until we got one. This bull had the unique combination of huge bosses that were fully hard, plus magnificent horn tips. We would get him or we wouldn't.

The herd numbered more than two hundred buffalo, and eventually we spooked them pretty bad and split them up. We thought the group with our bull had gone up over a ridge, so we decided to give it one more try. Amazingly, when we topped the ridge we had buffalo spread out in a grassy valley below, feeding peacefully again. We moved down to the last bit of cover, a huge antheap with trees growing from it. Below us, just over a hundred yards off, were three or four trees with buffalo scattered around. So began another waiting game.

We thought our bull was on the far side of the biggest tree, just a shape through the branches. And then he stepped forward, and his horns were obvious. For long moments he had a buffalo behind him, and then another in front of him. And then, at long last, he was perfectly clear, quartering slightly to us with his head down. I have no idea how she had remained so calm for so long, but Donna was still ready. She pasted him on the left shoulder, the bullet exiting the right flank, and he turned and was gone behind the tree—along with the rest of the herd.

We waited a few moments for the dust to settle. The herd was gone, but one buffalo bull stood with head down a little way up the next ridge and almost hidden behind the tree tops. We moved down under the trees and could see it was our bull, very sick and apparently locked up. Donna shot him again, and he broke free and ran, but not far. In less than a minute we heard his death bellow, and we approached carefully.

Good thing. The grand finale to this unusual hunt was that after Donna's bull bellowed, the rest of the herd came back! Elephant are known to do this, but few people I've talked to have ever seen this with buffalo. They weren't particularly aggressive, so we didn't shout or wave or shoot over their heads. We just stood there in awe until finally they moved slowly away and we could walk up and claim Donna's most excellent prize.

I had a tuskless elephant on my license, so we dug around the next few days and tried to find one. Interestingly, tuskless elephant are too common in Sapi, with multiples in almost every herd. Here in Dande they were far less common. We saw a few, but they were all either two-thirds grown or, if mature, had calves at heel. Just one would have filled the bill perfectly—and she came in a full-out charge, ears pinned back. However, the grass was so high that as we scrambled to get clear, we didn't know she was tuskless until it was too late. So we left that permit for someone else to fill and finished the hunt with a wonderful boat ride up through the gorge to Tafika.

Eastern Cape

I don't consider myself a trophy hunter, at least not in the negative sense. I happily take the good with the bad, the average with the superlative. I rarely carry a tape measure in the field and abhor the concept of defining the quality of a hunt by the size of the trophy taken. By extension, I don't consider myself a collector, either, although I suppose I really am. Primarily I collect experiences that I can write about. In the last few decades I could certainly have "collected" a lot of species I haven't hunted (and, in many cases, never will) had I not expended my time, energy, and resources repeatedly hunting animals that I really enjoy pursuing. In Africa these include buffalo, greater kudu, and bushbuck, and there are others I could name in different parts of the world.

On the other hand, there's only so much time and, for a gunwriter, even less money. I get a huge kick out of hunting an animal I've never hunted before—or continuing the search for an animal that has previously eluded me. At the start of my African hunting career this was easy because everything was brand-new. Today, especially in southern Africa, not much unplowed ground remains! Even so, whenever I plan an African hunt I take a hard look at the game list. If it doesn't match what I think I know, I check references and try to figure out if there's something new I should look for. I don't make this a firm rule. Other than a serval cat, which is often not on quota, there's nothing in the Zambezi Valley I haven't hunted—but that certainly doesn't mean I won't go there again! On the other hand, as we do more and more hunts for the television show, where I'm present with sponsors and such but not actually hunting, I do try to figure out if there's something I really want that I can spend some time looking for, whether it's bigger, better, or just unfamiliar.

This is more difficult in some areas than others, as witness the brown hyena I tried to get in 2005, which you'll hear more about in later chapters. One place where I'm finding it more difficult to come up with reasonable excuses to keep hunting is the Eastern Cape. Technically this encompasses South Africa's southeastern Indian Ocean coastline centered around Port Elizabeth, with what we think of as "Eastern Cape" extending inland through the coastal mountains and on to the windswept Great Karoo desert. I guess this difficulty reflects a lot of successful hunting over the years, because this region has perhaps the most extensive game list of any one area in all of Africa. There are indigenous rarities like Cape grysbok, bontebok, and vaal rhebok. There are localized races like the southern bushbuck, Cape eland, and Eastern Cape greater kudu. There are animals found nowhere else in South Africa, like blue duiker and oribi. And there are widespread animals like impala, springbok, zebra, wildebeest, warthog, and more. It's even a great place to hunt certain common animals that can be the devil to hunt elsewhere, like steenbok, common duiker, and bushpig.

During the 1980s and early 1990s I made several hunts in the Eastern Cape with good outfitters like Lud de Bruijn, Noel Ross, Al Spaeth, and the late Lew Tonks. Honestly, I worked my way through that extensive game list pretty darn well, leaving few gaps. In 2000 I made that quick hunt for one of the Eastern Cape's lovely black bushbuck, and in 2005 I hunted with Larry McGillewie expressly for a Cape grysbok and a bontebok. The hunts for these animals were successful, but what I really gained was a better appreciation for how wonderful the Eastern Cape really is. Back in the eighties and even into the nineties I didn't have the points for comparison that I would have a decade later.

The Eastern Cape is, well, a fantastic area. It has a wide variety of habitat in a relatively small area, from dense coastal thorn to high mountains to semidesert. Unlike much of South Africa, a lot of hunting properties in this region aren't game-fenced, and the average property is much larger than is common in areas to the north. Port Elizabeth is a beautiful little beach city, a good place for a genuine vacation, and it's easily accessed with good connections from Johannesburg or Capetown. For those who care,

Donna Grey, Larry McGillewie, and Baku (half beagle, half Jack Russell terrier) glassing for kudu in typical Eastern Cape thornbush at Hellespoort, west of Grahamstown. This heavy bush supports a lot of wildlife, but is very difficult to see into.

there are no tsetse flies and it's a malaria-free area. There isn't much left there that I haven't hunted, but that is no excuse to ignore a great area. By the conclusion of that 2005 hunt I had made plans to return to hunt with Larry McGillewie in 2006, and before the end of the hunt I'm about to tell you about, I'd made plans to return in 2007!

At least for 2006 I had several good excuses to hunt there again, if not actual reasons. Some were obvious. I really liked Larry McGillewie's blend of a calm, easygoing demeanor mixed with serious, no-nonsense hunting. Certainly I liked the Eastern Cape. I thought if we tried it just one more time, I might be lucky enough to get a good caracal. Donna would go with me this time, and with the Eastern Cape's profusion of game I thought it would be a great place for her to get her feet a bit wetter on plains game. On the business side of things, we need dangerous game for the television series, but buffalo, elephant, lion, and leopard are costly to hunt and time-consuming to film. We also need plains game, and I knew that given the variety of game available and McGillewie's determination, we could tape several good and affordable shows in just a few hunting days. To add to the variety and opportunity, Donna and I were joined by SureFire's Derek McDonald, with Bruce Parker coming in to do the filming. This would be Derek's first safari, and I knew he'd be hooked on Africa after a few days in the Eastern Cape.

Larry brought in his partner, Russell Lovemore, to spread the load a bit and also to free up a bit of his own time. Larry and his wife own a print shop in Grahamstown, and our timing couldn't have been worse, coinciding with the big Grahamstown art festival in early July. So Derek would hunt with Russell full-time, with Bruce's camera concentrating on him. Donna and I would mix and match, spending some time with Larry and some with Derek and Russell.

My primary goal was a caracal, but this was a feast that might take time to prepare, and bugging the cook wouldn't speed it up. Larry had a couple friends doing predator control in the area, and they'd call us if and when they struck a good track. If we were close enough, we'd drop whatever we were doing and head that way. There weren't a lot of other ways to play it. So that part would be a waiting game, and in the meantime we could concentrate on other game. Donna and Derek wanted kudu first and foremost. Derek and I wanted to hunt nyala, partly for the camera and partly because they're so gorgeous. And then, of course, there's the "M" factor, for McGillewie. Once again he had one blue duiker and one oribi permit available. Of course we had to take them—and of course we wanted to, because this time we could get these unusual hunts on camera. So the game plan for the week evolved. We'd start on Hellespoort, that big, brushy series of ridges west of Grahamstown, primarily looking for a kudu for Derek. Then we'd spend a day in the hills hunting nyala, and then a day on the beach at Adrian Ford's place . . . and then we'd see where we were.

Actually, we started out slow. Hellespoort literally crawls with kudu and, realistically, is probably overstocked. It's brushy and difficult to hunt, and it's also harsh country. Typical of Eastern Cape kudu, the horns of mature bulls there tend to finish their second turn in the mid-40s. But we were looking for a bit better. Better is there, but not common. So over our first couple of days we saw a lot of kudu and passed up a lot of kudu, and a couple of really good bulls gave us the slip. On the second

Donna's bushbuck is a superb specimen for these small, dark Cape bushbuck, but what really makes him stand out is the wide horns, a most unusual configuration for any bushbuck.

morning Larry and Donna were glassing from a big ridge to the south while Russell, Derek, and I combed a couple of deep canyon systems. We saw one of those better bulls, wide, heavy, and beautiful, and he almost gave Derek a shot at about three hundred yards, but just as we set up he turned, went into the brush, and slipped over the ridge.

We waited a bit and then followed, hoping to catch him again. Nothing doing. We saw a number of kudu on the next ridge, but not that one. After glassing for a bit, we turned right and worked our way along the crest. A half-mile farther along we were glassing some kudu on the far crest when Derek said, "What's that thing with a red head?" Russell and I were looking at something else. We didn't have a clue what he was looking at, and I couldn't conjure up a redheaded animal. Then we saw it in a tiny clearing, a jackal sitting up like a dog, the morning sun glowing red on his head.

In South Africa's game-ranch country a jackal is always fair game, but this one was 250 yards away, with the small target cut at least in half by the presentation. I was really glad I wasn't carrying a rifle! Derek got on the sticks, found the jackal, and center-punched it with his Ruger

.300 Magnum. Up until then we didn't have a clue whether Derek could shoot or not. From this point on we had no doubt, and he never disappointed us.

We spent yet another day at Hellespoort looking for bigger kudu than we were seeing, and then we had appointments to meet. We'd get back to the kudu in a couple of days. Russell and I each hoped to take a nyala, and our fourth day was designated Nyala Day. The nyala is not actually native to the Eastern Cape; its original range stops considerably to the north, in the warmer, thicker thornbush up along the Durban coast. Some of the first nyala in the Eastern Cape were introduced by my old friend Lud de Bruijn, in the Bedford/Somerset East area off to the southwest. Given adequate riverine cover and a comparative absence of parasites in the cooler country, they've done extremely well and have spread considerably, confounding the individual ranchers' efforts to confine the breeding stock. It was to this area that we headed, with

Donna Grey with a fine oribi, an old ram with exceptionally heavy horns. This is one of South Africa's most limited prizes.

Russell Lovemore leading the charge. Typical of these guys, they fully expected to take two nyala in just one day!

This area isn't what you think of as classic nyala country. The riverine bush is plenty thick enough, but the ridges are taller and much more open than in dense, rolling Zululand. The nyala didn't seem to mind. In the early morning chill we worked our way along a winding watercourse, spotting a few of the red females and a couple of young males. Then, well up a big ridge, we glassed what seemed a very nice bull feeding with several cows. Derek had never seen a nyala, so he gave me first shot.

The approach was fairly simple, up to a point. A branch of the creek gave us good cover to reach a windmill at the base of the ridge. A couple of good patches of brush allowed us to slip a bit closer, and then we ran out of cover with a longish shot remaining, perhaps 250 yards. Russell set up his sticks, and when I had a good broadside presentation I took the shot, holding a bit high on the shoulder with the .30-06. The first shot hit him well enough to drop him, but as we approached, he stumbled up and tried to run. Another shot got the job done. He was a beautiful nyala, not as big as the best Zululand trophies but perfectly shaped and very good for the area.

Russell knew the secret to these nyala, but I did not: In this area they apparently tend to move very late in the morning, perhaps because of the cooler climate. While skinning my bull, we had a bird's-eye view of the valley and counted at least a half-dozen bulls stepping out of the thick stuff to sun. I'd had quite a saga with my nyala trophies. The mounted head of a fine bull I took in Zululand in '79 was ruined in one of California's earthquakes, and an even better bull that I took in 1991 came into the U.S. with a ruined cape and just one horn. I wanted a life-size skin for this nyala, with no mistakes, and with the day heating up, Russell correctly decided to do the skinning on the spot. This took a lot of time, and with midday nearing I was worried that the delay would mess up Derek's chances.

By the time we got off the hill with my nyala, the bulls we'd seen along the creek had indeed vanished, but there was no reason for concern. Our intention was to hunt the upper portion of the same river, but long before we got there we spotted a lone bull slipping along the edge of some thick stuff ahead of us. We jumped off quickly and eased through the brush to cut him off. Just a few minutes later Derek and Russell caught

It was nearly dark when we made a long running stalk on this bat-eared fox. I shot him from about 200 yards with Larry McGillewie's .222 with a Trijicon scope. Honestly, this was one of the best or luckiest shots I've ever made.

him standing right on the edge of the riverine growth. Derek took a fast shot, and though the bull took it hard, he dashed into the streambed. We found him around just one bend, hit perfectly and stretched out as he died in full flight.

It had been quite a full day. We had two really beautiful nyala bulls, and on the way back we made a slight diversion to see if we could find me a white blesbok. We found a herd right away, but although blesbok are trusting animals and usually don't offer much of a hunt, these didn't want to cooperate. Russell and I spotted a very good ram and followed the herd over hill and dale on foot before finally getting a shot right at sunset.

The next day was our day at the beach, or rather above the beach at Adrian Ford's place. We agreed that Derek would first hunt blue duiker with Adrian's little dogs, and if we got lucky, Donna would try to take an oribi. We hunted some of the exact same thickets Adrian had taken me to a year previously, but it was an altogether different hunt. Though we moved blue duiker on almost every drive, we saw only flashes of movement, more like flitting shadows, or heard the little animals dashing through the thick stuff. We were looking down a brushy slope on the sixth or seventh drive when a blue duiker scampered past just at the limit of vision, allowing no chance for a shot. The terriers passed below us a couple of minutes later, and that was the end of that. Adrian stood up, dejected. But then the barking changed and grew shrill. Adrian grabbed Derek's shoulder and pointed, and a blue duiker charged right through the middle of us. It was much too fast for an inbound shot. I was sitting ten feet behind Derek, and the little animal passed me almost close enough to touch. The duiker jinked away as Derek turned, allowing a safe shot. Derek's first barrel was clearly behind. The second looked good, but the duiker went on into the brush. Adrian's terriers found him a few moments later, a big male. In late afternoon we found a really big and extremely old oribi ram feeding in an open valley with a couple of ewes. Larry took Donna on a slow, careful approach, and she shot it nicely, finishing a fine day at the beach.

At this point we separated, sort of, Russell taking Derek to some big country adjoining the Addo Elephant Sanctuary to the south. This was flatter, brushier country and difficult to hunt, but Russell felt the kudu genetics there were the best in the Eastern Cape, thus offering a chance for a better bull. He was right. Donna and I joined them down there a couple of days later, and there were indeed some spectacular kudu. A lot of the property adjoined Addo's double boundary, and lots of big kudu were on the wrong side of the fence! One afternoon, glassing from a high ridge, we counted more than twenty bulls feeding in an open valley in the park, and several were kudu you'd shoot anywhere, well into the mid-fifties.

There were good kudu on Russell's side of the fence as well, and that thick cover is good for bushbuck as well. Derek took a nice bushbuck ram along the way, and after four days of hard hunting he was finally rewarded with an excellent Eastern Cape kudu. Donna took her kudu on Hellespoort, one of the better bulls we saw there, and she also made a fine shot on a beautiful bushbuck with thick, unusually wide horns. During this period I was sort of along for the ride, waiting for a caracal call that never came. One evening just before dark, however, we slipped over to Russell's home place to look for a group of bat-eared fox that he claimed he saw every evening.

Although I had tried many times, I had never actually seen a caracal (African lynx) until the last day of this hunt. Larry McGillewie had faith and kept telling me it would happen. It did.

You've heard that before, haven't you? This time it was the straight scoop. Dusk was approaching, and we were just heading to the area where these creatures were supposed to be when we ran headlong into the pack, running right down the road toward us. I got out of the vehicle and got a rest as the little animals ran, then stopped and looked back, but I was much too slow. We caught them again just at dark, not far from Russell's fenceline. Larry and I made a quick running stalk, and I, using Larry's Brno in .222, shot one in dim light at about two hundred yards, easily one of the best (or luckiest) shots I've made in years.

That brought us to our last day, which became probably the most action-packed day I've spent in Africa as we tried to cram in much too much. I had given up hope of taking a caracal, but right in the middle of trying to get Donna a nice blesbok, the call came. The dogs were running a lynx (another name for the caracal), and the tracks showed it was a big male. We changed horses in mid-stalk, heading north to the big canyons of the Great Fish River. The dogs pushed the lynx up a brushy tree at the bottom of a straight up-and-down ridge, and as we scrambled our way to them I was still convinced that this was never going to work. It worked just fine. The cat was indeed a big male and he was well treed, no problems at all. I wondered how many days I'd spent hunting caracal, only to take a real monster in less than an hour!

Russell and Derek were hunting nearby, so they joined us to take a look at the cat. While there, with the camera still rolling, Derek took a beautiful impala. Then we returned to our starting point for the day, and Donna took a good blesbok ram. Now we were well south of Grahamstown and the afternoon was getting along. We could have called it a day, and should have. Or we could have gone to a private game park close-by and taken some footage of lion, another good "should have." But no—oh, no—I had to keep pressing right up until the last minute. The third option, which seemed the best but was by far the worst, was to go on south to one of Russell's honey holes for bushbuck.

By the time we got there, little more than an hour of light remained, but Russell wasn't in the least concerned. The area was a huge expanse of ridges covered with that thick, nasty, prickly Addo thornbush, bordered by relatively open valley. The thick stuff was stiff with bushbuck, and in the evening Russell was certain we'd see a good male feeding out into the open. Unfortunately, he was right.

We spotted an old, heavy-horned ram feeding along the edge and stalked within about 150 yards. I could have stood on the sticks, and maybe I should have. Instead, to reduce movement, I crawled into a good sitting position and took the shot. It felt OK to me, but Russell called it correctly: "A bit far back." I agreed, but I thought the shot was close enough behind the shoulder to be into the lungs. Russell was right and I was wrong.

At the shot the buck ran hard into that nasty thorn. We found blood right away and were just starting to follow when Larry rolled up in his truck. He shouted for us to wait—he was going to put the dog in. His wonderful little dog, Baku, is half-beagle and half-Jack Russell. At night Baku goes from lap to lap, lying on his back to have his belly scratched. In the day he's the best blood-trailing dog I've hunted with. During two hunts with Larry I'd scratched his tummy often and had seen him turn several potentially tough tracking jobs into quick

This is the bushbuck that gored Baku, and it was my fault because my first shot wasn't as good as it should have been. Baku bit me severely while I was holding him, but I didn't care. He's a great dog, and he survived to hunt again.

recoveries. He is Larry's best friend, and, like Larry, I consider him my friend as well.

Baku streaked past us and had the bushbuck within fifty yards. Since I'd already messed up by fluffing a perfectly easy shot, albeit by just a couple inches, it was a good thing Larry sent in the dog. The bushbuck was waiting along the trail, facing toward us, and the only way Russell and I could get there was by crawling. Without the dog, those sharp horns might have stuck one of us. The dog was to the left, darting in and barking, and the bushbuck was facing us with his head down, frozen.

I shot him on the point of the shoulder. That should have killed him outright, but the impact broke him loose. As a puppy Baku had been lightly gored by another bushbuck and now was usually careful. This time, though, he was too close, and in a flash of movement the bushbuck was on him, pinning him to the ground with a rapier horn. I shot again into the body, and Baku broke free, screaming. Lord, what had I done?

The dog came to me, and I saw a shiny loop of intestine blooming from his flank. He would have gone on to Larry for help, of course, but long before he got there the cruel thornbush would have gutted him, so I grabbed him as gently as I could and started pushing his insides back into the gaping wound. Baku was fighting mad now, and instead of struggling to get free, he reached up and bit my face. I felt the sharp teeth enter and rip, but both my hands were busy, so I let him chew on me.

Russell had gone forward to check the bushbuck, and in a few moments he came to me. Baku was calmer now, and everything was back in place. I handed him off to Russell, telling him it looked very bad—but to watch for his teeth! As he went off through the bush, I hollered to Larry that Baku was badly hurt. "Shot or the bushbuck?" came the response. Honestly, it had happened so fast that for a terrible few seconds when Baku was coming toward me, I hadn't been sure. "Bushbuck, all the way through," I hollered back.

We had both vehicles with us. Larry drove off to the vet, with Baku, calm now, on Donna's lap. At this point nobody knew I'd been bitten, which was just fine. I watched my blood drip onto the ground for a few moments, mopped my face as best I could, and when Russell came back we dragged the bushbuck out of the brush. We took a couple of pictures, and I said some words for Bruce's camera. We assumed Baku was dying, and I figured he deserved the truth: That I'd messed up and this was my fault.

We joined Larry and Donna at the vet's place in Grahamstown. Larry's wife, Sharon, was already there. Everybody loves Baku. The poor little guy was on the operating table, tubes everywhere. The horn had entered the small of the back and exited the flank, opening the body cavity but not penetrating the intestines. His injuries were severe, but he would live to hunt again. I felt a huge wave of relief, and then we drove around the corner to Larry's doctor's office. This poor guy left his dinner and met us there, stitched up my face, and gave me a tetanus shot and some antibiotics. I looked like hell on the plane the next day, but I was a lot better off than Baku. Of course, as Larry said later in an e-mail, Baku's scars are covered by fur. I'll carry mine as a reminder that it isn't always smart to push too hard—but if you do, you'd better shoot straight.

Erindi

E rindi is a huge private holding, the largest contiguous private ranch in Namibia. Lying about two and a half hours by good road north of Windhoek, it occupies much of the triangle formed by Okahandja to the southeast, Omaruru to the southwest, and Otjiwarongo to the north. I'd seen Erindi's beautiful ads in *Safari* magazine for some time, but I'm not much impressed by big ads. My friend Jim Crawford had been, well, bugging me to hunt there. But honestly, I knew Jim and his wife, Tammy, had done their first African hunts at Erindi. They did extremely well, but I knew their perspective for comparison was limited, and I know from personal experience that none of us is capable of objectivity when evaluating our first few safaris.

Also, I wasn't looking for another hunt in Namibia! There was very little game there that I hadn't hunted, and what remained seemed either unlikely to be taken, like brown hyena; too costly, like southern roan; or not importable into the U.S., like black-faced impala. Perhaps more to the point, over the previous few years Dirk de Bod had become a really good friend, and he was still managing Bishop Hills for my buddy Joe Bishop. I didn't need another place to hunt in Namibia, and I had concerns about being disloyal to Dirk by hunting with one of his direct competitors. But Crawford was insistent, and he knew how to set the hook: According to him, the folks at Erindi were using a great pack of hounds, and their leopard-with-dogs hunts were non-slip successful.

I got the green light from Dirk. Other than a couple of openings reserved for friends, he was booked up two years out and so wasn't

Willem Roux's hounds are some of the best-looking dogs I've ever seen, friendly and in great shape. On the trail, they're all business. He trains his dogs to bark rather than bite, and canine injuries are extremely uncommon while leopard hunting.

worried. Also, and of equal importance, I got the recommendation I needed. Dirk de Bod is that rare outfitter who has enough confidence in himself and his business to worry little about good competition. I knew he'd give me the straight scoop about Erindi, and he told me it was a good place and that its young professional hunter, Corné (short for Cornelius, pronounced Cornay) Kruger, was a good man. I should check it out, Dirk said. So on the last day of the Safari Club convention I met Jim Crawford at the Erindi booth. He introduced me to Corné and Erindi's manager, Paul Joubert, and we set a date for the end of July. OK, at this point I didn't really think we had much of a chance for leopard, but the timing was such that both Donna and daughter Brittany would be with me, and I thought we could have some fun with the other game.

Like most of Namibia, Erindi is best known for its plains game. I'd hunted the Omaruru District in the late 1970s, at least fifteen years before several ranches were gathered together to create Erindi. I knew it would be good for native species such as kudu, gemsbok, and hartebeest, and I figured that the game had been developed so that the place would offer a lot more than that. Even with impeccable recommendations, I was skeptical about the leopard thing. This was purely a case of me being outdated. It was literally a generation ago when I hunted that area with Ben Nolte. Only a very few leopard were there then, mostly living in the forbidding spine of the Erongo Mountains and occasionally coming down to raid livestock. In those days nobody actually hunted leopard in Namibia!

In due time (meaning when I got around to cleaning up and sorting the stuff I'd picked up at the convention) I thumbed through Erindi Hunting Safaris' truly spectacular brochure. I was dumbstruck by a two-page spread showing nothing but leopard. Most were obviously big males, purportedly taken the previous year. Apparently the folks at Erindi considered leopard a specialty, and, just as apparently, the leopard situation had changed in this part of Africa.

Indeed it had, and I should have been paying attention. For years leopard had been officially on license. Instead of being hunted, trapped, and even poisoned by farmers as soon as a track was seen, they now had value and, within reason, were tolerated until a professional hunter could bring a client. The most recent CITES convention had more than doubled Namibia's export quota of sport-hunted leopard, from just 100 to 250. The reason was they could document that 150 leopard were still being taken for non-export, meaning for depredation.

There were other clues as well. I'd noted in a couple of chat rooms I occasionally visit that several correspondents reported taking leopard in Namibia. This didn't register. Joe Bishop reckoned that at any given time he had three or four leopard operating on his relatively small farm. This didn't register, either. I knew that Dirk, in a recent hectic season, had taken some absurd number of leopard, like nine for eleven hunters, as good an average as anywhere in Africa. I figured he'd had an exceptionally good year (which was true), and that he must be an exceptionally good leopard hunter (also true). Somehow it didn't occur to me that one reason for all these reports was that Namibia had a whole lot more leopard than it used to.

Slowly, though, the lights were going on. Erindi's brochure was a real eye-opener. Then, in May, Debra Bradbury did a leopard hunt in Namibia and shot a big tom over bait in daylight. I was getting the message: I was outdated, and a lot more leopard were roaming in Namibia than when I first hunted there. The increase hadn't happened overnight.

My Erindi leopard was a big-bodied, big-headed leopard, but he was very old and had no body fat whatsoever. His weight on good scales was just under 150 pounds, yet his track was 10 centimeters, the same as Allan Skruby's much larger cat.

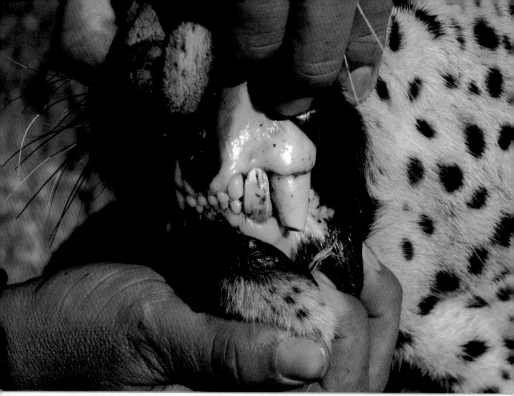

I have no idea how long leopard live in the wild, but this one was about as old as a leopard can get. Note how both incisors and canines are badly worn and broken.

Besides increased value on individual leopard, Namibia had become a much more popular safari destination. Increased costs and political instabilities elsewhere have resulted in a greatly increased safari industry in stable, inexpensive Namibia. Because of the increased market, more and more Namibian farmers are paying attention to their game. After hunts there in 2003 and 2005, I had stated that there must be ten times more game in Namibia than was the case back in the late 1970s. Oddly, it just never occurred to me that this applied to leopard as well, but by the time we arrived at Erindi, I was starting to believe.

This time, oddly, our guncase made it in, but our bags were delayed by a day. This, you will probably understand, was more traumatic for Donna and Brittany than for me. It was also more traumatic for Corné, as you'll see below. Resident on the ranch was Eastern Cape houndsman Willem Roux, a couple of his dog handlers, and more than a dozen really fine dogs. In order to hunt leopard with dogs, you must have fresh tracks. You can look for them, or you can bait for them. After years of careful management and fairly light hunting, Erindi was overstocked with several species, particularly gemsbok and warthog, so bait was readily available.

During the several months he spends annually on Erindi, Willem Roux baits constantly, not just when a leopard hunter is inbound. This practice, rather than being wasteful, makes sense if you think about it. He can cull older gemsbok and non-trophy warthog and feed them to the cats, making no impact on game populations and just possibly saving some of the scarce or prized prey animals like klipspringer and Damara dik-dik. His baiting circuit is huge and every morning he's out early checking baits, so of course he has a pretty good idea of what's there at any given time. At one point he had something absurd like twenty different leopard feeding on various baits.

That, of course, was before I arrived. When we got there, the leopard scene was relatively quiet, with little activity. This wasn't critical. We didn't need twenty leopard; we needed just one good male to leave a fresh track. Willem did in actual fact have a good tom feeding, and he wanted to move on it the first morning. I put my foot down. Bruce Parker was already there to do the filming, and even jet-lagged I certainly could have gotten up early if a leopard was on the menu. But this was at least partly show business. Not surprisingly, Corné had .30-06 ammo for Donna's rifle and, amazingly, a box of 7mm-08 for Brittany's Kimber. But there was no ammo for my Ruger in .416 Taylor. We hadn't checked our rifles, and trapped in our delayed bags were key items that various sponsors would expect to see in the finished film product. If the luggage was just plain missing, as my gun case had been for more than half the Cameroon hunt a few months earlier, I could have borrowed what was needed and carried on. That situation didn't apply here. South African Airways in Windhoek had called Johannesburg, and we knew our bags were there. They'd be in the next day, and, incredibly, SAA had pledged to deliver them to Erindi before dark. I didn't believe it, but we had to play the hand, which meant sleeping in the first morning.

So we did, in one of the most comfortable lodges I've ever enjoyed. The guest rooms at Erindi are essentially hotel-style under a real roof, single-story, either looking out onto a small water hole or positioned around one of the two pools. We looked out onto the water hole, which was perfect. Wildebeest and springbok came in frequently, and several times a black rhino with an enormous front horn made an appearance. The pools, by the way, were pretty but useless in the Namibian winter! While we were there it was unusually cold, mornings below freezing and jackets worn all day on some days, and August in Namibia is often windy.

Lazily late that first morning, we checked the rifles with Corné's ammo. The range was good, with a covered benchrest and genuine movable target frames, but even on the first day I wasn't surprised. Everything was first class at Erindi. Then we started looking around the countryside. Erindi is something over 160,000 acres in one piece, dominated by several significant mountains with brushy plains below. It is classic Namibian game country, with well-developed water, and is stiff with plains game. On this exceptionally cold and windy first day, though, you couldn't prove it by our productivity. We made a couple of desultory stalks on gemsbok and hartebeest, and in late morning we ran into sturdy Willem Roux while he was out making his rounds. Yes, his big leopard had come to call, but their efforts to make me feel guilty about sleeping in failed.

When Tim and Dave and I had first started filming, I had a bad tendency to forget about the camera when there was hunting to be done. By now, though, it was a part of normal life, albeit a part I'd never planned. If things weren't right for the camera, I was ready, willing, and able to back off.

That afternoon, just as promised, a van delivered our bags. We even had daylight remaining to check the girls' rifles with the correct ammo and shoot my .416. The rifle was, to use a new term we'd coined, sponsorally correct. It was a left-hand Ruger M77 rebarreled to .416 Taylor (a .458 Winchester case necked down to .416) because at that time Ruger offered no large calibers in left-hand, and the only left-hand action was limited to .30-06-length cartridges. It wore the Trijicon 1.25–4X scope with tritium-illuminated post. I was finding the bright Trijicon post exceptionally fast, but not as precise at longer range as a more familiar cross hair. So I breathed a sigh of relief when my first and only sight-in shot was perfectly centered and just slightly high at a hundred yards. Bring on the leopard!

We were out the next morning at half past four in freezing dark, checking baits. Donna and Brittany got up that morning, but they

Unlike so many private ranches in southern Africa, cheetah and other predators are welcome on Erindi. There was a radio-collared female cheetah with three nearly grown cubs, and we were able to get some rare close-up photos.

wouldn't make that mistake again. Ours is not much of a spectator sport even under the best of circumstances, and in subfreezing dark in an open vehicle it was downright miserable. But I was learning. Baiting for a dog hunt is different because the only object is to locate a good track. There is no intent to build a blind, so the baits are hung simplistically along likely movement corridors. The cats favor the rugged hills as security cover, and they tend to follow arroyos or *gwachas* when they come down for their nightly hunt. Given a choice, cats like to follow roads at night. So the baits were generally along roads at the bases of hills or at the intersections of dry streambeds.

With Willem working one set of hills and us another, we could check a lot of Willem's seemingly innumerable baits before dawn. Of course, you would never, ever do this on a baited hunt. Bait checking shouldn't even start until late morning, when it's extremely unlikely that a cat will still be present. With dogs, it doesn't matter if you spook the cat off the bait, so long as he leaves a track. More important is the fact that warm, dry conditions are the worst for scent, and Namibia in winter is very dry.

Fox, Donna, and Corné with Donna's excellent steenbok. That's Ruger, a fine Jack Russell terrier, in Fox's arms.

The hunting on Erindi is done by Corné and his younger brother Nick, and by PH Basie Marais, another young hunter. Those three together have taken more than thirty leopard in the last four years, with Corné accounting for more than half. Willem was only in his second year there, but he and his dogs had corralled more than a dozen. These guys knew the game, and they understood that their best chance for a successful chase was to find a track in the dark and run the hounds at very first light, when the scent was freshest and, of equal importance, the air was damp with dew.

We found no signs of feeding leopard at all that first morning. The vast "herds" of spotted cats of the previous week had vanished into the hills. Willem and Corné weren't concerned. This happened, and we had time. We'd have leopard feeding. Me, I figured it was par for the course. Boddington's leopard luck was striking again.

The sun was well up when we returned to camp for blessed hot coffee and a warm breakfast, and then we went out to see what we could find. Once again it was windy and cold, with the animals in the brush and nervous. Not much happened that day, or the next morning. From experience I knew that conditions were as bad as they could get, and that when it calmed down and warmed up, game would come out of the woodwork. On the other hand, I had to wonder if Erindi was really as good as I'd been told!

That third afternoon Corné took us in a different direction, hoping to find some of the normally visible blue wildebeest that so far had remained completely hidden—as had most everything else. He had it pegged. We ran headlong into a herd of mountain zebra, the first we'd seen, and a little while later Fox, Corné's driver, tracker, mentor, and friend, stopped and pointed up a gentle rise. A good wildebeest bull was feeding up in the brush, totally unaware.

Corné took Donna on a careful stalk while the rest of us watched. They closed to less than a hundred yards, put up the sticks, and at the shot the big bull dropped like a rock. Only then did we see the second bull! Corné motioned for Brittany to come quickly with her rifle while this second bull reluctantly drifted over the ridge. He hadn't gone far, and in a few minutes we had a second wildebeest down. We took care of Brittany's first, a really huge-bodied old bull. Then, with the sun starting to slip, we retraced our steps to Donna's bull.

She had shot him again for insurance, which is a good thing since wildebeest aren't supposed to drop like that. I had assumed she'd hit a bit high and clipped the spine, but not so. Her first shot, quartering slightly away, had taken out the top of the heart and broken the off-shoulder, magnificent performance from her .30-06. Her wildebeest was one of the best I have ever seen, also an old bull but with a tremendous spread, little wear, and exceptional points that came well around.

The next morning was bitter cold but calm, portending a good day. Fox, Corné, and I had barely left the ranch when Willem called on the radio. He had a track. We gathered around a well-chewed warthog below the first major hills north of camp. By now I understood that these guys had taken a lot of leopard. This was reassuring, but was in itself a concern. Erindi is big, but it's finite. They take the occasional stock-killing leopard on a neighboring ranch, but most of their leopard come from Erindi's rugged hills. I didn't understand how this area could keep producing big leopard. Most neighboring ranches raise

Donna sets up to take a shot at a Hartmann mountain zebra. This is almost the highest point on Erindi, which is one of the highest points in Namibia.

cattle, so the concentration of game is on Erindi. With numerous unmolested female leopard around, undoubtedly Erindi pulls in males, and without question the rugged mountains combined with plentiful prey offer ideal conditions. Whatever, after the *Boddington on Leopard* project, I knew leopard sign and I knew what I was looking at. So did Willem and Corné.

The warthog was smashed and the ribs completely eaten, a clear sign of the aggressive feeding of a powerful male. This alone would have been enough to spur us ahead, but in the carefully swept ground under the bait, amid indistinct scuff marks and tracks of small night predators, was the clear, clean print of a big tom leopard. I measured it—ten centimeters heel to toe. This would be a big cat. Willem and Corné knew the track. They had run this leopard before, twice to a property line they couldn't cross, once into rocky caves where the dogs had lost the scent. Maybe this time he would make a mistake.

The rule is that dogs can't be released until a half-hour before sunrise, so we waited, visiting while we shivered. I went to Willem's truck, where his dogs were eager, perhaps scenting the leopard on the night breeze. Even so, they were friendly and anxious to be petted, which is unusual for hounds. But I would learn that these were unusual hounds—Walker and bluetick mixed with English foxhound—and exceptionally well trained.

Now that we were ready to run on a leopard, I was glad the girls were back at the lodge. One of my concerns over this method of hunting is the potential for mayhem to the dogs. The previous year, when we ran Allan Skruby's wounded leopard, the dogs had sustained only a couple of minor scratches. I figured they'd gotten lucky, but as we discussed the coming hunt in the cold dark I learned I was mistaken once again. Injuries can happen, but these dogs had been trained to bark, not to bite, and to keep the leopard moving until it bayed or treed but to stay away from its razor claws and long teeth. A few months earlier they had lost a dog to a gemsbok bull encountered accidentally in the bush, but they maintained that a trip to the vet hadn't been required in the last dozen leopard run with Willem's dogs. In fact, the only injury had been to Willem himself.

That chase had taken them up over a ridge, and the cat was fighting the dogs in thick brush on a little shelf. They could only see flashes of the cat, with no chance for a shot. The safe course was to let the chase proceed; perhaps the cat would tree, but at least he'd come into the clear sooner or later. But Willem worries about his prized dogs, and in a stationary fight in thick brush the cat has all the advantage. They needed to descend a little rock face to get a closer look, and Willem went first. As soon as his feet hit the ground, he and the cat made eye contact and it charged instantly. This I understood: As soon as Allan Skruby's leopard had seen Abie Steyn, it realized the dogs weren't its biggest problem, and it came like a bullet. I assume this cat was the same. While in-bound, it was shot, but too far back, and it jumped on Willem, clawing at arms and shoulders and burying teeth into his scalp and face. Willem is a big, powerful man, and he gave the leopard a tremendous punch in the face, knocking it back to the ground, where it was shot as it tried to jump on him once more. That had been just six weeks earlier, and the scars were still fresh.

The morning was foggy, and a gray dawn slow in coming. Finally Willem and Corné deemed it light enough, and they took strike dogs on leash to the bait. At first the going was slow as the dogs—and their handlers—tried to work out the spoor. The spoor led east, to the boundary where this cat had escaped before. Given my leopard luck, I wasn't surprised.

Brittany's mountain zebra was enormous, with a perfect and unblemished skin. It was the largest zebra in a herd of mostly stallions, and we were surprised when "he" turned out to be an extremely old, almost toothless mare.

Then the chase turned north, toward a big, rough mountain. Now the pack had the scent clean and hot, and the strike dogs were unleashed. We scrambled through thornbush after the sound, rapidly losing ground, and then the sounds changed, growing more strident. The leopard had been much closer than we had guessed, and the dogs had jumped him. Now we trotted, as we could, and while topping a low ridge we saw several white dogs scrambling up the right side of the big mountain, just small spots maybe six hundred yards above us. The leopard was up there, probably just ahead of them, but we couldn't see him. The dogs reached the top and went over, and the barking died away. I was winded already, and I knew we needed to get up there quickly.

We were just starting up the slope when the distant barking grew louder. Dogs boiled over the top and started down the center of the slope right above us. Now there was a different sound, the deep grunts and angry roars of an enraged leopard. Willem was far behind now, but Corné knew the drill. Moving as quickly as we could, we headed for the sound, Corné shifting left to get ahead of the chase. For long minutes we could hear barking and growling, closer and closer. The chase had slowed down, and now the fight was on. We moved closer, and for some reason my legs seemed to carry lead weights.

Now we caught glimpses of dogs, and then a flash of spots and a long tail above gray bush. We were on the brushy lower slope, and very close. We maneuvered through some thick brush and froze as the din came nearer. For the first time I could see the leopard clearly. He was walking toward us, stopping to swat at a darting, barking dog and then stepping forward again. He wasn't twenty-five yards away, and the shot was clear . . . except that one of Willem's beautiful dogs was directly behind. I waited, believing that at any second the leopard would see us and charge.

This did not happen. The leopard, snarling all the while, swatted at the dog behind him, then turned to our left front and disappeared behind a bush. When he reappeared he was walking, broadside, at less than twenty yards, and all the dogs were clear for just an instant. His shoulder was partly covered by brush, but the lung shot was open. I put the Trijicon post on the back line of the foreleg, the tip about a third of the way up into the body, and the rifle went off. The cat leaped into the air, spun just once, and was still. The dogs, all perfectly unhurt, rushed in for just an instant, but they knew their job was done and they had only passing interest in the dead leopard.

When he stepped out, I knew instinctively that this was a big male, even though I have seen relatively few leopard. Close inspection showed he was also extremely old. One canine tooth was broken, and an incisor was completely missing. With a ten-centimeter track, he could have been as big as Allan Skruby's leopard, but he was not. He had no body fat whatsoever, and my guess is that Namibia's desert leopard tend to be rangier. At Erindi all leopard are carefully weighed and measured, and this one went 148 pounds, with a length of 7 feet, 2 inches. They have taken a lot of leopard on Erindi, a few a bit bigger, most a bit smaller. So long as they still have old leopard like mine, they're doing a darn good job.

Now we had the luxury of time on our hands, and could pace ourselves and enjoy Erindi. This we did. Gemsbok are seriously overpopulated, and we all took nice bulls. I lucked into a very good warthog, and Donna took a huge common zebra stallion. Brittany took a nice springbok, and Donna made a brilliant shot on a bat-eared fox with Corné's little Marlin

.17 HMR. The black wildebeest continued to elude Brittany, but in the midst of incredible plenty she wasn't the only one getting skunked.

Corné maintained that he knew where we could get a brown hyena on bait. He was right. We got a hit the very first night, the track of a huge hyena clear in the swept earth. This was a conventional bait site for leopard, complete with a good blind, and Corné said he had seen a brown hyena here every time he'd sat for a leopard. Maybe, but not this time. We sat for three nights until we nearly froze, but after that first good feed, the hyena never returned. On the fourth morning we discovered that a lion had taken over the bait, and that was that.

We had some fun along the way. Erindi has plenty of native game but has no high-dollar species like sable and roan. Cheetah are tolerated, within reason. We caught glimpses of several while out and about, and one afternoon we caught up with a radio-collared cheetah with three half-grown cubs. The mom had been raised in captivity and released, and it was amazing how close she let us approach. There is truly no animal in the world as beautiful as the cheetah.

On another day we watched the release of seven white rhino brought in from South Africa. There are something like thirty-two black rhino on Erindi, and about half that many white rhino. There are a few elephant as well, and in the course of our hunt we saw all three species.

On the last day Corné took us up to the highest mountain, one of the highest points in Namibia. On the way up we got a quick glimpse of a really big warthog, and when he stopped on a low rise, I took a quick shot with the big .416. I didn't hear the bullet hit and saw no reaction as the pig ran over the ridge, so I assumed a miss and, at two hundred yards and change with a .416, didn't feel the least bit bad about it. Fox thought differently, as did Corné. We went out to check and found a wide swath of lung matter and blood that led us to a very big and very dead warthog.

Pictures taken, we headed on up the mountain. The road was an amazing engineering feat, perfectly safe but very steep and thus very scary. No way would I take the wheel! No sooner had we topped out than we saw a big herd of mountain zebra, almost all stallions. They were a long way off, so we took the vehicle around the ridge and made a long and difficult stalk. The herd was in a little pocket and we came in above them, closing to perhaps

175 yards. We watched them for a while, trying to pick the right one, and Brittany, with a steady rest over a boulder, shot the largest zebra beautifully with her little 7mm-08.

The herd ran downhill only a short distance, then started back up the mountain, crossing about two hundred yards behind us. Why not? We picked out another fine stallion, and Donna shot him with her .30-06. There is no more typical Namibian animal than the Hartmann mountain zebra, and to take two on foot in their natural high-country haunts was a perfect end to a truly wonderful safari. And it had an equally wonderful postscript: The ranch had a road crew up there, and we stopped by their camp to give them some zebra meat. They were concerned about a big leopard that had been coming near their camp every night. We found a track, and it was yet another big tom with a ten-centimeter spoor. At that time that mountain had never been baited or hunted for leopard.

Lemco

The land once known as Rhodesia, now Zimbabwe, was rich in game when Cecil Rhodes's Pioneer Column came north in 1893. The country's fertile interior became productive ranchland and farmland while the harsh, dry border areas remained wild. For three-quarters of a century farmers and ranchers waged a war of attrition against the buffalo, elephant, and great cats. Rhodesian hunters of my age and older cut their teeth hunting buffalo almost at will on the great lowveld ranches, or on hunting holidays to the Zambezi Valley. The literature of Africana is filled with accounts of hunting buffalo and elephant in what is now Zimbabwe, penned by John Taylor, Ian Nyschens, Fletcher Jamieson, Richard Harland, and others.

However, there are no accounts of classic safaris in old Rhodesia. Although the occasional guest might be invited out for a "shoot," "sport hunting" was specifically illegal in Rhodesia until the mid-1960s. In 1965 Rhodesia issued a Unilateral Declaration of Independence (UDI) from Great Britain. One of the early acts of Ian Smith's government, made initially as an experiment, was to specifically authorize nonresident hunting and legalize export of trophies. So Zimbabwe's entire history of safari is just forty years old, a history as turbulent as it has been brief.

The long bush war that ended with the creation of Zimbabwe started with UDI. It was a small fire at first that, as the years passed, turned into a conflagration. As the hunting experiment got started, security risks were a minor irritation at first, but by the mid-1970s many prime areas, including most of the Zambezi Valley, were too hot for hunting. Still, pioneer outfitters like Ian Henderson and Brian Marsh, Peter Johnstone, and Geoff Broom began a fledgling industry that grew in spite of worldwide sanctions and security concerns.

Even at the beginning it quickly became apparent that there were two distinctly different types of Rhodesian safari. There was a classic hunt that included some mix of buffalo, elephant, and the great cats, done mostly in the peripheral areas like the Zambezi Valley and areas adjoining Wankie National Park in the northwest and Gonarezhou Park in the southeast. In much of the interior the great game and cats had long since been eradicated to make way for cattle and crops, but thanks to developed water and agriculture, many varieties of plains game flourished. So the second type of Rhodesian safari was a "ranch hunt," not a trip in a fenced game ranch but a hunt on a working cattle ranch that also held a lot of game. I can well remember the advertisements of early booking agents like George Daniels and Paul Mertzig: "AFRICA FOR $1,995" proclaimed the ads. During the bush war it was possible to take kudu, sable, and a whole lot more at these prices. In the late 1970s, when security risks were at their highest, I was one of Roger Whittall's first clients on his Humani Ranch, now part of the Save Valley Conservancy. He charged me the princely sum of $25 per day, plus trophy fees at a small fraction of today's rates.

The stage was set. When the bush war finally ended and Rhodesia became Zimbabwe, her outfitting industry blossomed. With an eager market waiting, more and more ranchers converted from cattle to game, and wildlife prospered. During the 1980s and 1990s hunting in Zimbabwe generally continued to follow two tracks: Dangerous game on the periphery and plains game in the interior. It was, of course, relatively easy to combine the two, so a fairly typical Zimbabwe safari included a few days of buffalo hunting in the valley, either followed or preceded by several days of plains-game hunting on private land. Buffalo were more costly and more limited, so the majority of safaris were for plains game.

During this period Zimbabwe competed well in price, success, and overall experience with both South Africa and Namibia on the plains-game market. Regrettably, that is ancient history. The Mugabe government's "land reallocation" that began in 2000 turned innumerable

Blue wildebeest are one of the most common sights on Lemco, and are one of several species that are definitely overpopulated. Really large herds seem uncommon, but small groups are almost everywhere. The plains-game density is like nothing I had ever seen.

prosperous ranches and farms into small subsistence plots and destroyed much of the long-nurtured plains game. It is believed that between 2000 and 2006 Zimbabwe lost as many as 80 percent of her invaluable sable antelope. The great buffalo and elephant hunting on Tribal Trust Lands or controlled by Zimbabwe's Forestry and Parks and Wildlife departments has been largely unaffected and remains fantastic. But the disaster is so widespread that today Zimbabwe no longer competes with South Africa and Namibia in the plains-game market.

There are exceptions, primarily the large conservancies. One such is the Save Valley Conservancy. I hunted there in the mid-nineties and it was wonderful. It is far better today. Another is Lemco, nearly a million acres of classic lowveld game country.

It isn't appropriate to say that hunting in these areas is like the good old days. During the good old days, when the Save Valley was a collection of neighboring ranches and when Lemco was Liebegs Ranch, plains game was grudgingly tolerated as a food source. Buffalo and elephant were eradicated as dangerous, disease-carrying nuisances. Lion were all but eliminated as well, and leopard would have been except that, in ideal lowveld habitat, they are too numerous and far too clever. Liebegs Ranch was established by Baron von Liebegs near the turn of the century, and at one time it grazed tens of thousands of cattle. As a young man my old friend and mentor Geoff Broom learned to hunt leopard on Liebegs, and many other top Zimbabwe professional hunters fondly remember hunting buffalo and elephant there in their youth. With no safari industry (and thus no value placed on the wildlife), access was easy, and the ranch essentially wanted help in getting rid of the nuisance animals.

After World War II the ranch was acquired by Lever Brothers. Best known for soap products, the company in the 1990s decided to concentrate on its core creations. Veteran outfitter and visionary Charles Davy gathered a consortium of investors, primarily foreigners, and the Lemco Conservancy was born. Thousands of miles of internal cattle fencing was rolled up and a huge double perimeter fence was created, enclosing more than 600,000 acres in one area, with adjacent satellite areas totaling more than a million acres. As was the case with the Save Valley Conservancy, this was to some extent like closing the barn door after the horses were gone. There were no elephant, no buffalo, and no lion on all those acres. These animals were brought back at great cost, as was the long-vanished black rhino. Today, and perhaps forever, both the elephant and rhino are token herds, a proper and essential part of the lowveld landscape.

Lion are not plentiful; in 2006 they numbered about 150, though they are well-established and increasing. Since no known lion remained early on, Charles Davy started with a clean slate and introduced Kalahari lion. Today a few are taken every year, and those few are among the best-maned lion in Zimbabwe. Buffalo have also done well. In 2006 the numbers were at about 2,500, and the animals are now increasing rapidly and dispersing, with a current quota of forty bulls. Leopard remain endemic, with the annual quota averaging twenty, and those usually include some of Zimbabwe's biggest leopard.

There are many good buffalo and leopard areas in Zimbabwe, but what intrigues me about Lemco is that, along with its dangerous game, it still has the incredible density of plains game once found throughout the lowveld. In this regard a visit there is a trip back in time, to before 2000. Baron von Liebegs developed an extensive network of boreholes as early as the 1920s, so of course the wildlife prospered. Today there are boreholes, dams, and watering points gravity-fed by miles of pipe. There are no cattle and no internal fences, and the wildlife density is unreal.

Andrew Dawson's own farm, now mostly gone, is in the north. As a young man he did most of his hunting in the valley, and as a professional hunter he's mostly a valley man. He had never been to Lemco, but he and Charles Davy are longtime friends and Andrew was considering doing some safaris there. In 2005 Andrew had a few days between clients and Tim, Dave, and I had a few days between filming commitments, so we jumped in a plane and came down to take a look. We were there just two days, and I was enthralled. We saw plenty of buffalo tracks, but the density of plains game was like nothing I'd seen in years. There are thousands of wildebeest, zebra, eland, and giraffe. Warthog and impala are legion. In proper habitat there are plenty of kudu, waterbuck, and bushbuck. There's a good population of sable, and even a few nyala. We saw cheetah, rare in Zimbabwe, and some of Lemco's famed lion. I wanted to spend more time there.

It was later that year when Brittany had her last-day disaster with a buffalo. Clearly we needed a return engagement, and Andrew suggested Lemco. Honestly, as much as I wanted to go there, I didn't jump on it. I understood the numbers game: Lemco is more than twice the size of Dande North, for instance, with considerably fewer buffalo. On the other hand, quota being as it is, a valley hunt would be for buffalo and little else, and we could have some fun on Lemco. I agreed, hoping I wasn't signing Brittany up for another tough hunt.

Lemco is a hard six-hour drive straight south from Harare. Andrew's truck met us there, while we—Brittany, Donna, and me; Andrew, his wife, Heidi, and two of their children, Rolf and Briny—took the easy way and flew in. Garrick Cormack drove over from Bulawayo to do the filming. We all gathered at Charles Davy's headquarters, then drove up to Dyers Camp. Overlooking the Bubye River, Dyers is the northernmost of several camps in the main conservancy, near where Charles believed the buffalo were concentrated.

We arrived in time to sight the rifles and take a short drive, and, yes, there were buffalo. We saw none, but fresh tracks pockmarked the water holes, and more crossed the roads. I breathed a sigh of relief. We'd get into buffalo, and fairly quickly.

The mopane thornbush of Lemco is dominated by massive monoliths, some several hundred feet high. Climbing them is good exercise, and they offer fantastic views down into the bush.

Yes, indeed. We were on tracks by eight the next morning, and looking at buffalo little more than an hour later. It was a small herd, and I think there was a pretty good bull in there. We never quite isolated him, but a couple of good-looking youngsters stood in the clear, and Andrew got Brittany on the sticks for practice. "For God's sake, don't shoot," I heard him whisper. Eventually they all spooked, and we didn't press them.

Lemco is mostly flat thornbush, but it's spiked by the occasional massive monolith, some rising to several hundred feet. That afternoon we practiced a slightly different technique, struggling our way up one of these steep mini-mountains so we could glass the surrounding bush. I was glad it was a cool day. Every time I get near a kopje, I get the black-mamba heebie-jeebies! We sat for a while, and actually glassed what appeared to be a very nice lone buffalo bull moving through the thornbush about six hundred yards out. After clambering back down the rocks, we found his tracks easily enough, but he must have been on some kind of bovine errand because we followed until nearly dark and he just kept walking.

The next morning we got on the tracks of what we thought was a different herd, but the distance wasn't great, so it could have been the same group. This time they led us on quite a merry chase, and it was midday and getting warm when Mukassa finally spotted buffalo moving ahead of us. We glimpsed what appeared to be a really good bull—wide, heavy, and clearly mature. Andrew started circling ahead, but by the time we got around in a tricky breeze, they were already lying down. We were in open mopane, much more open than most of the Zambezi, so we could see the top of the bull's horns at much too great a distance to shoot. Andrew and Brittany crawled forward while the rest of us waited, me chewing my fingernails. They got plenty close enough, but there was brush in the way. And then something happened, probably a cow catching movement. In an instant they were all up and moving, and the bull was lost in the group.

We gave them a bit of time and tried again, but this time we blundered into them in some thick stuff. Sensibly, Andrew called it a morning. We marked the spot carefully, then backed off and had lunch and a quick siesta. At three o'clock we took the tracks again, and in a bit more than an hour we had them, still bedded tight. And, miracle of miracles, the big bull was on our side of the herd and the wind was perfect.

This was, of course, just our second full day at Lemco, but for Brittany this was a direct carryover from the previous year, essentially her thirteenth day of buffalo hunting, and she had only one not-so-good chance to show for it. Andrew had never hunted buffalo here before, so we didn't have a particularly good idea of what kind of animals the area held or how difficult it would be to locate bulls. I could see his hesitation, but I think he made the right call. This was a very good buffalo, big-bodied and old, and I was pretty sure his spread was at least forty inches, maybe a bit more. Given his position, he was also a gift horse, and although my opinion wasn't sought, I didn't think we should walk away from him.

The wheels were turning in Andrew's head, and I guess he had the same thought. We got in behind some winter-brown mopane scrub and moved forward, first to one bush and then to another. At about fifty

I'm not sure who was happier, Brittany or her dad. We caught this bull napping on our side of the herd, and Brittany got all set up at close range. When he got up, she pasted him perfectly with a 400-grain solid from her .405 Winchester.

yards Andrew set up the sticks and Brittany got set. She was using her Ruger single-shot in .405 Winchester, stoked with the same hopped-up Hornady loads as the year before. She was shooting the same 400-grain solid at the same velocity as the .450-400 three-inch loads both Donna and I had used on buffalo earlier in the year, so I knew what that little cartridge would do. But right now she had to wait. The bull was still lying down facing right, apparently fast asleep. The other buffalo were off beyond, so our bull was completely clear, but most of his body was hidden, and, in any case, shooting a buffalo while he's lying down is a really bad idea. These are tense moments, and the longer they go on, the worse they get.

This time it didn't take very long. He started to stir, slowly at first, and Andrew whispered to get ready. I don't think the bull heard the whisper. It was late afternoon, really past time when the herd should be up and moving, but we were plenty close enough to be seen, and I'm sure that as he came out of his stupor he checked the area and saw something he didn't like at all. Instantly he was on his feet, quartering to us and staring, poised for flight. In that moment Brittany shot him very precisely on the point of his on-shoulder. The impact rocked him back on his heels, a perfect shot, but he recovered just as fast, and as he turned, both Andrew and I fired. I was certain there was no need, but this time we wanted no problems. He disappeared into the mopane and was down within forty yards. As soon as we cleared the brush and could see him, Brittany fired again, but there was no reaction at all. She had her buffalo, and he was all the buffalo anyone could ask for—ancient and grizzled, with a spread of 42 inches on the button.

We had plenty of time left to hunt, and we were hunting in a land of plenty. But it was late in the season, after a couple of months of intensive pressure, and the plains game was extremely spooky, as spooky as anything I've seen. I'm sure we made half a dozen stalks for every shooting opportunity!

The three animals considered overstocked on Lemco are blue wildebeest, zebra, and giraffe. These zebra were educated, and even the wildebeest seemed to understand the game. But we all managed. Brittany took a nice wildebeest bull just at dark one day. Donna flattened yet another one, her .30-06 and a plain old Hornady InterLock knocking it off its feet with a shoulder shot. I love the .30-06 and have tremendous confidence in it, but body-shot wildebeest don't behave like that. It was a bit intimidating, and Brittany I were both starting to wonder how she was doing that so consistently.

Me, I was playing with Brittany's .405 and its heavy-bullet loads. I shot a zebra and a wildebeest, both taken cleanly with one shoulder shot each, but neither went down to the shot. I was glad that happened on a morning the girls slept in; otherwise, I'd have taken a terrible ribbing. I also did something I've never done before and probably will never do again. Charles came by our camp a couple of times to check on us, and each time he insisted that we shoot giraffe. I had never shot one of these gentle giants and didn't really want to . . . but neither did anyone else. So I got elected, and it actually wasn't quite as easy as I'd thought. Imagine stalking within close range of an animal that, with its head way up in the air, can see every step you're taking!

Giraffe are gentle and fairly trusting creatures, and I'd never wanted to take one. Because they are grossly overstocked on Lemco, it seemed the thing to do. Having never shot one before, I had no idea how huge a big bull giraffe really is!

Donna started out really hating the camera. She probably still does, but she's learned to deal with it. She made a brilliant shot on this impala, and now she and Andrew have to do a recap for Garrick Cormack's camera.

Garrick, our filmer, was born on Lemco, and he alone had some experience with them. He suggested we stalk at an oblique angle, approaching slowly and indirectly. He was right. We got within sixty yards, and I tried for a heart shot with my .416 Taylor. The bull ran and took a second bullet, and then he cartwheeled, one of the most spectacular things I've ever seen. This was a huge, dark bull, and although I've been close to many giraffe, I had no idea they were that big.

Most of this wasn't serious stuff, but a couple of serious items were on the agenda. Lemco is one of the best places I know of for big Livingstone eland, and I wanted one. We just couldn't make it happen. We saw several cow herds with no bulls, and once we glassed five bulls from a tall hill. At least three were mature, and two were very big. They were far, far out beyond a brush line, feeding their way through some open patches. The wind was good, so it could have worked. But we lost our line on the approach, and we had one look only at more than three hundred yards. Two miles later they were still running. And that was that as far as eland were concerned.

The other serious pursuit was a waterbuck that Brittany wanted. Certain areas held lots of waterbuck, and some were good ones. We turned down a bunch, and one really good bull gave us the slip several times. Once, after a long and tricky stalk, Brittany had a shot at him. He was moving across a clearing, but she wasn't steady. She missed, which I think was probably good for her. She probably wouldn't agree, but it hasn't happened very often and it is part of the game.

It was the last evening, maybe a half-hour before sundown, when we located a really nice bull feeding with some cows. I tend to think it was the same one she missed, but perhaps not. This time she didn't miss. I am constantly amazed at how deadly her little 7mm-08 is. She uses 150-grain Swift Scirocco bullets, and there's something almost magic about that bullet at the 7mm-08's moderate velocity. A big waterbuck is a lot of animal for such a light cartridge—as are zebra and wildebeest and such—but in the right place it works wonders. This waterbuck was nearly broadside, and she took him squarely in the shoulder. He spun to go and then went down. And that was that.

Lemco is truly an amazing place, the lowveld at its very best. It's a place I want to see again, but preferably earlier in the season. Or, as Charles Davy implored me to write as he showed me his too-full calendar from the previous two months, "Tell them August and September are really good months. April and May are good, too. Please tell them that not everybody has to come to Zimbabwe in June and July!"

Never Enough Namibia

Namibia, then South-West Africa, captivated me when I first saw her rugged mountains, thornbush valleys, and grassy plains nearly thirty years ago. Perhaps this was because I grew up hunting the U.S. West. I didn't do so well the first time I hunted then-Rhodesia's heavy thornbush. A serious whitetail hunter would love that country, and I've grown used to it (and better at hunting it). Back then I'd done almost no close-cover hunting, and it confounded me. Namibia was much more my style, country where we could climb rocky hills and glass to our hearts' content, then plan a careful stalk.

I loved it, and I loved my professional hunter, old Ben Nolte (not so old then). When I came home I sang Namibia's praises, and although I was very much a fledgling writer then, I wrote quite a few stories about it. Nobody cared. In those days Namibia had a very small safari industry, with just a handful of genuine professional hunters and quite a few farmers who took hunting guests under a more restrictive license. German was one of her three languages, probably almost as widely spoken as Afrikaans, with English a distant third. It remained a playground for German-speaking European hunters, and although it was inexpensive and held plenty of game, very few Americans went there. Until the end of World War I this sparsely populated, arid land was called German Southwest. From 1918 until 1990 it was South-West Africa, a protectorate of South Africa. Upon independence it became as it is today, Namibia, still sparsely populated, still arid, still beautiful.

Slowly over the past twenty years, though escalating quickly in the last decade, Namibia's outfitting industry has burgeoned. More and more farmers have converted from livestock to game, or at least are actively managing their game. South African species like blesbok, impala, and black wildebeest have been widely introduced. As mentioned earlier, leopard have come back strong and so have cheetah (which are on license only in Namibia, although they are not currently importable into the U.S.). More and more ranches are actively breeding roan, sable, and waterbuck, and although the trophy fees are frightful, the quality is superb.

If there's a downside to Namibia, it's that it is primarily a plains-game destination, plus leopard. Other members of the Big Five are very restricted. Quite a lot of elephant rumble in the far north and Caprivi, and although the number of permits is small, the ivory is good. Buffalo, however, are limited in both range and numbers, with just a handful of annual permits, and less than a handful of permits are offered for lion. These limitations have not stopped Namibia from becoming, after South Africa, the second-most popular safari destination in Africa.

Today hunters numbering in the thousands get off the plane in the Windhoek airport and disperse throughout the country. And why not? Namibia is clean, safe, and rich in game. The road network is good, so charter flights are required only to the most remote destinations. There are dozens and dozens of competent professional hunters, trained and tested under a rigorous PH licensing system that is, after Zimbabwe's, the second most difficult in Africa. To hold a PH license in Namibia means something, as it should (but does not always) in every African country.

It can be a bit chilly in the winter months, and August is often chilly and windy, but the days are normally glorious and sunny, the country is magnificent, and as the years pass the game just gets better and better. Namibia is a place I never tire of. When my buddy Joe Bishop told me he was considering buying a ranch there, I told him Namibia was the only African country in which I would consider investing. Indeed, although I doubt I could ever afford it, if I could swing it I'd own a small ranch there myself.

But on a gunwriter's income this is most unlikely, so I have to content myself with occasional visits. We brought in Ruger's Randell Pence and Dave Regula of the giant distributor AccuSport for a plains-game hunt for the TV show, with Bruce Parker coming in for the filming. We'd just come from Lemco, so Donna and Brittany were still with me. Now, we obviously had a lot more hunters than we did cameras, meaning that Bruce could focus his camera on our guest-sponsors Randell and Dave, hunting with Pete Kibble, while the girls hunted with Dirk de Bod without camera pressure, and I could just sort of flit back and forth as I pleased—and even take a couple of days off to work on this very book. The itinerary was exactly the same as for our "TV safari" in March 2005: We'd spend the first few days at Bishop Hills, then transition to Pete Kibble's "Kenya Camp" a couple of hours away.

Now that both Donna and Brittany were interested in hunting, I had to get better at my "role reversal" as an observer. I don't think I ever actually shot anything at Bishop Hills on this trip. This would please Joe Bishop immensely, who always accuses me of poaching whenever I'm on his place. Unfortunately, while I was as pure and innocent as the driven snow, the girls weren't quite so blameless. I was writing away one morning when Donna shot a good kudu bull. The horns were well into the 50s and beautifully shaped. More importantly, this kudu was very old, just skin and bones and almost certainly destined to check out before the rains came. I tried to explain this to Joe, but of course he didn't believe me. Once again, Donna dumped the kudu in its tracks with a perfect shoulder shot at about 170 yards.

I was also pecking away at my electronic mistress one afternoon when Brittany shot a really nice old warthog, thus scratching an itch she'd had ever since turning down, on that very ranch, a couple of dandies because they were "ugly." I was absent, too, when she took one of the biggest blesbok rams I've ever seen, but I did manage an appearance for her black wildebeest. This was actually a bit of a saga.

After failing to take one on Erindi, Brittany now figured she had a score to settle with the black wildebeest of the world. Joe and Dirk's herd has bred up dramatically, and there are quite a few really good bulls on Bishop Hills. After a couple of failed stalks, we finally got her on a dandy, just at midday. The shot looked good and the reaction was perfect, but by dark we'd totally lost the spoor and were trying to isolate this same bull out of several groups in a brushy valley. The chore looked impossible to me.

This is a fabulous black wildebeest, and also a bit of a miracle. The day before, Brittany had taken a difficult shot and wounded this bull, and we'd pretty much given him up as lost when Dirk recognized him in a herd. This time she flattened him.

The next morning we tried again, getting into several groups but seeing no bull that looked similar and no bull that appeared injured in any way. That afternoon, with the wind perfect, we stalked down into a little group of black wildebeest bedded in a tight valley. We were no longer looking for that wildebeest.

We were on a little hill, with just bits and pieces of black animals visible behind a thick, green screen. Dirk had Brittany on the sticks, and eventually the wildebeest grew suspicious and started to file out one at a time. Dirk had her focused on a darn good bull, but then another, hidden bull stepped into view. Dirk instantly recognized the warty growth central on its muzzle, and told Brittany to shoot that one. This time the shot was perfect, right on the shoulder. He dashed out of sight but was down in less than ten yards. A small miracle—it was the same bull of the day before. Her first shot had been just a couple of inches back and low, not quite into the body cavity. As we'd guessed after following for so long, the animal might well have recovered otherwise—but now we had him.

My lack of shooting wasn't altogether the result of not wanting to, or trying to. I was hoping for an extra-good kudu, but we didn't make an all-out effort because we knew the chances might be a bit better on Pete's place. Also, we got sidetracked once more with a brown hyena. Dirk maintained that this was one of the wariest of animals and most difficult to get on bait. He did something I have never seen done, and although it didn't exactly work, it makes sense: We hung baits by working right from the back of his Toyota so that our feet never touched the ground. We checked baits in the same way, thus avoiding depositing human scent near the bait. True, we put diesel, oil, and rubber scent near the bait, but these hyena live on active ranches and must hear and see vehicles much more frequently than they do humans. At least that was the theory, and it seemed to work . . . up to a point.

There were tracks around, and we got a hit on the second night. In a rocky outcropping up above the bait was a little depression where we could set up the rifle, lie back comfortably, and sit up soundlessly. It was about seven o'clock, just an hour after dark and only slightly freezing, when we heard faint sounds coming from the bait. We sat up very

This is the track of the brown hyena I was hunting. I think we would have had a very good chance at him if a leopard hadn't run him off the bait—but at least I learned a bit more about hunting these cagey animals.

Pete Kibble's tent camp isn't quite as fancy as Dirk's, but its design is straight from Pete's Kenya upbringing. How could it get better than a tent on a plain under an acacia?

carefully, I leaned into the rifle, and Dirk put on the light. A big animal was underneath the bait, but something was very wrong. This animal had short hair and spots, not long fur with stripes. It was a big female leopard, and she left only reluctantly.

Later we theorized that she must have had cubs nearby, because for the next couple of hours we heard her moving around in the brush beyond the bait, and she had obviously claimed this bait for her own. We froze out at about 10 P.M. The leopard came back and fed, but the hyena didn't come back until the following night.

When he did, the leopard was waiting for him, scuff marks from the struggle appearing clear in the road about fifty yards from the bait. It looked like a short altercation, with the hyena's running tracks heading away and the cat's stately pug marks returning to her meat. That was my last chance at a brown hyena, but just maybe I'd learned a trick or two.

Dave and Randell were taking their time as well. They both shot nice gemsbok, and by the time we'd packed up for Pete's they had a couple of blue wildebeest as well, but they were holding off on kudu. I wasn't too worried. This had been an exceptionally wet year, and the brush at

Brittany had quite an afternoon. First she took a fine steenbok, then a jackal with her first-ever running shot, and she capped it off with this really big southern bush duiker, a relatively uncommon trophy in Namibia.

Joe's was lush, with water everywhere and kudu hard to see. Pete's place doesn't necessarily have more kudu, but the country is a good deal more open and every year he produces some very good bulls.

Pete's country is something like a hundred square kilometers, several ranches grouped together in a big block, much of it fairly flat but dominated by a system of big ridges. Most of it is unfenced, but there is a big fenced area that holds a number of black rhino as well as offering some sanctuary for good breeding herds of both roan and sable. We spent most of our time on the open ground because at this time of year kudu tend to be migrating through. Multiple bulls are likely to be seen every day, and usually they will be different bulls than those seen the day before.

Though looking for kudu, we were also just hunting in general, especially since I had both my "shooters" along. Brittany had quite a lot of luck one afternoon. We spotted a big steenbok standing on a little raised spot above brush that could have hidden an ocean of these small antelope. She and Dirk made a quick stalk, and she shot it handily. An

Donna came through again with this exceptional warthog, massive in body as well as tusk. He was at a cattle trough at midday, right in the middle of some cattle. Dirk took her on a stalk, and when the warthog squirted out and was clear she took the shot.

The African wild cat could well be the ancestor of our domestic cat because it can readily breed with your Fluffy. It has distinctive barred legs and a black tail tip, and it's just a bit larger than most housecats.

hour later she shot a big jackal, and then just at dark she dropped a huge common duiker, an animal not common in that region.

Donna had a couple of good days as well. One afternoon we stalked a water trough, and a fine warthog squirted out from among the cattle. She took the only shot she had, quartering away, and a few minutes later Dirk's little Jack Russell had him. On another afternoon we glassed a good springbok ram bedded up on a low ridge with his ewes. We had good cover to 317 yards, according to the Leica rangefinder. And then we had no cover at all.

We'd already been seen, and the ewes were moving off. The ram got up last, and we were in a quandary. Donna is deadly off shooting sticks, but she had never practiced offhand at that distance, let alone shot anything. Her .30-06 had a Leupold scope featuring the Boone and Crockett reticle, with additional stadia lines. I happened to know that the way the rifle was sighted, the first stadia line was dead on at just a bit over three hundred yards. Dirk looked at me, I looked at Dirk, and we shared a mutual shrug. There was no harm in trying; we certainly weren't getting any closer.

The conversation would have provoked some laughs in certain circles:

"See the stadia lines?"

"The what?"

"See those extra lines below the cross hair?"

"Oh, those . . . OK."

"Wait for him to stop, and put that first line under the cross hair where the black stripe stops on his shoulder."

The ram took a few more steps and stopped almost broadside. The rifle went off, and the distant animal fell over, pole-axed. Donna hadn't heard of a stadia line, but she knew exactly where to put it. Without question it was the best shot of the hunt. Better than a couple of mine, because I missed a perfectly simple shot at a warthog and messed up an equally easy shot on a nice gemsbok.

It would get much worse than that, but before it got worse it got better. One evening during the Erindi hunt, while coming back to camp after dark, we'd seen an African wild cat cross the road in the headlights. This little night cat looks a whole lot like a tortoise-shell housecat but is bigger and has longer legs and a slightly shorter, black-tipped tail. The only other one I ever saw stood on a ranch road in broad daylight in northern South Africa, and it was just too far for a shot. I hadn't known they occurred in Namibia, but now that I knew, I asked about them. Dirk didn't think there were any on Joe's ranch, but he believed Pete's area held quite a few. So one night we went out looking, and apparently they aren't scarce if you look in the right place. We saw three, and I took a really nice one.

Late in the hunt I borrowed Randell Pence's Ruger Number One in 9.3x74R, a new chambering for Ruger, and used it to take a heavy-horned gemsbok bull. Randell and Dave, too, were getting in their licks. Both took really nice kudu, and I was with Randell when he shot his, a super bull taken with a lovely shot at beyond three hundred yards. He didn't do that with the hard-hitting but short-range 9.3. When he got as close as possible, he swapped the big single-shot for Pete Kibble's bolt-action Ruger in .338 and dropped the bull in its tracks.

On another afternoon I shot the biggest jackal I've ever seen, a perfectly placed frontal shot. So my shooting was very much on again, off again, and I have no idea why. But I thought I had things straightened out by the last afternoon. We'd seen and bypassed an awful lot of kudu up to this point, and since everybody else was pretty much finished, I had Bruce Parker and his camera with me. We would take a kudu, even if we had to settle for less than what I had in mind.

We didn't have to settle. Very late in the afternoon we spotted a huge bull feeding in some tall black thorn. From a distance it was easy to see his horns above the brush, but closing for a shot in that stuff was a different story. Several lesser bulls blew out, but this guy was cagey. He knew we were there, and he knew that safety lay in the thick stuff. So we played cat and mouse for quite a while, Randell and I just glimpsing his horns as he slipped carefully from one thicket to another. And then we had him. He was behind a tall bush, completely safe—but there was lower bush on either side, and he had to show himself when he moved.

It was under a hundred yards, and I was up on the sticks with Randell's 9.3. The cartridge is a lot of smack for kudu and, with its slow-moving 286-grain bullet, not a bad choice for a shot in thick cover. The bull moved left, and just his top third showed over the

We took a couple of mornings off to shoot sand grouse over a water hole. This is some of the most difficult wingshooting on earth, and doing it with a borrowed shotgun that doesn't fit doesn't make it easier. Dirk did a lot better than I did!

This is the biggest jackal I have ever seen. Generally speaking, the jackal is considerably smaller than even our California coyotes—but not this one!

I borrowed Randell Pence's Ruger No. One in 9.3x74R to take this lovely heavy-horned gemsbok bull. It worked wonderfully and perhaps gave me false confidence, because I used the same rifle when I messed up on a fantastic kudu!

brush. It wasn't a good presentation, at least not good enough as events proved. But I was shooting a big gun and it was a kudu, an animal not known for toughness. I put the Trijicon post as far down into the brush as I dared, and knew I was holding high on the shoulder when the rifle went off.

The kudu dropped to the shot, clearly flattened by the impact, and lay still. Dirk and I rushed forward, crossing a low spot that took us out of sight for just a moment. When we could see the kudu again, he was already up and moving, maybe sixty yards away. I got the rifle up, but just as I got the sights on him, Dirk, out of long habit, set up the sticks and in doing so pushed the rifle barrel out of the way. The kudu's gray rump vanished into the thorn, and that was the last we saw of him.

We had good blood, but it was getting dark fast and too many other kudu were in the area. The right call was to mark the spoor and come back in the morning, which we did. Normally I'd toss and turn all night worrying about an unrecovered animal out in the bush, but this was a kudu, knocked flat and leaving lots of blood. I fully understood I'd hit him a bit too high, but I slept soundly that night in absolute certainty that we'd find him in the morning, probably stone-dead.

Dirk's tracker, David, is one of the best. Pete Kibble's excellent trackers came with us as well, so we had plenty of competent help. It was just as well we hadn't followed the night before. The blood led us more than two miles, and the tracks showed he was still running. It would have been long since dark before we reached that point—and it wasn't much farther before the blood petered out, then stopped altogether. The tracks were lost in a maze of other kudu tracks, so we sectioned the ground and kept looking. We searched until nearly dark, never finding another trace or another clue. That was the end of that hunt—not the ending I would have chosen, but the truth.

Pete had another hunt scheduled in that area immediately following, and he saw no vultures. We knew I'd hit the kudu too high. That was all I'd had to shoot at, and I took the risk. It was a stupid mistake, and wishing I'd missed him clean or, better, not taken the shot at all doesn't do that poor kudu a bit of good. We had assumed that I'd hit him underneath the spine, high enough to drop him from shock to the spinal cord. If I had, we probably would have found him. More likely, I creased him on top of the spine. If so, there's a reasonable chance he survived, and I'd prefer to think that. Maybe I skipped the bullet on a tough black thorn branch, or maybe I just fluffed another shot. If so, it wasn't my first such shot, or the first on that safari. It was the final shot of that safari, in fact, but I'm sure that, unfortunately, it won't be the last shot I ever miss. Come to think of it, since I'm certain I'll never have enough of Namibia, it probably wasn't even the last shot I'll miss in that country!

Zambezi Delta

There are two strange psychological syndromes associated with exposure to Africa. Oddly, almost every hunter returning from a first safari becomes an instant expert, waxing eloquent and authoritative on the sights, sounds, and hunting conditions of a vast continent after experience in just one small corner with one outfit. This one is generally quite harmless. Those of us with multiple safaris under our belts simply smile and nod, realizing that we were exactly the same after our own first safaris. This syndrome may, however, negatively impact hunters contemplating their own first safari. Word of mouth is always the very best reference, but make sure you evaluate any recommendations in the context of the experience level of the person offering them.

The second and more insidious malady is a strange phenomenon I like to call the "gloom-and-doom syndrome." I wrote about this in chapter four when talking about mountain nyala hunting. Again, we all succumb to it. Clear back in 1909 Theodore Roosevelt complained about some parts of Kenya being "shot out." Hemingway voiced the same complaint about Tanganyika in 1933, and Ruark's "high cost of lions," clear back in 1953, is one of his most often-quoted one-liners. I, too, fell into the trap easily, and have fallen into it more than once. Kenya closed hunting shortly after my first safari, and in 1977 the demise of African hunting seemed truly imminent. As you may have noticed, this did not come to pass. After my first mountain nyala hunt I truly believed there would be little future opportunity to hunt these animals, and prospects certainly couldn't get better. Once again I was wrong.

Mahimba Reserve is surrounded by tidal rivers and swamps, an area that was ignored by the long bush war and, until fairly recently, probably didn't have the diversity of species to be a desirable hunting area. In today's Africa it looks pretty good!

Some countries are not what they were. Others, like Namibia, are better, with more wildlife and more hunting opportunities. Ever since it became patently obvious that the closure of Kenya was not the end of the safari, I have tried to keep a positive outlook, not always with success. I was wrong about mountain nyala, although I was right that the habitat was shrinking. Yet another country that I have failed utterly is Mozambique.

I didn't see Mozambique in the 1960s, when her safari industry was at its peak. I wish I had, because I'm sure it was spectacular. Big kudu, lots of sable, huge leopard, legions of buffalo, tons of elephant, plenty of lion, not to mention nyala, waterbuck, and all the rest. With a few exceptions, Mozambique was never known as the place to get the biggest and the best, but between the beginning of her safari industry in 1959 and its collapse in the early 1970s she offered one of the largest and most varied bags in Africa at that time. The rapid Portuguese pullout began in 1973. A long and bitter civil war began almost immediately, and sport hunting became untenable not only because of safety but also due to lack of infrastructure.

I first saw Mozambique in 1988, shortly after the long bush war finally ended. I took a very nice elephant on the southern shore of Cabora Bassa, so the safari was successful. But up until that point in my African hunting career I had never seen such a wasteland for game. There were the occasional kudu and bushbuck in the thickest bush. We saw a few tracks of sable and buffalo, and one day we saw a herd of roan. There were plenty of cats around, but what they were finding to eat I haven't a clue. It might take three days to find an impala to use for leopard bait, and if we saw a duiker or grysbok by midday we'd joke, "This area is stiff with game."

This part of the Zambezi Valley had been truly hammered during the war, with AK-47 hulls on every trail and human skeletons frequently encountered in the bush. My belief was that the game was so depleted it might never recover, and ever since I've been cautious about recommending Mozambique. I had succumbed to both syndromes. At that time I had never been in the Zambezi Valley, so I was ignorant of what the valley is supposed to be like. This area had been ravaged, true, but the Zambezi Valley doesn't hold great concentrations of plains game. Hard hunting is normal—but I didn't have enough experience to understand that.

I also fell into the gloom-and-doom pitfall. As the years passed I was aware that game populations were rebuilding and that numerous good outfitters had set up shop in Mozambique. But I had seen it at its nadir, and I had little desire to see it again. Once more I was dead wrong.

MAHIMBA RESERVE

In 2005 Eastern Cape outfitter J. P. Kleinhans made an experimental trip to Mahimba Reserve, a privately owned chunk of country about fifty miles north of the Zambezi and fifteen miles inland. Owned by a large farming and mining concern, Mahimba was once grazed for cattle and planted for sisal and coconut. It is surrounded by swamp and unbridged rivers, and is accessible only by light aircraft or barge from the coast. During the war the farming and ranching were abandoned, but the area is so inaccessible that the conflict had little impact. The game built up well and has been hunted for more than a decade by outfitter Sandy McDonald. McDonald wanted to concentrate on his Lower Zambezi Valley area near the Zimbabwe border, so Mahimba was available. When J. P. was a boy his dad took him on buffalo hunts to the valley, and he'd long wanted his own dangerous-game area to augment his South African operation. He liked what he saw, and in 2006 Mahimba became his concession. J. P. is like a brother to my filming partner Dave Fulson, so before I really had time to think about it, I was suddenly committed to two back-to-back ten-day hunts in Mozambique, a country I had little desire to see again.

My buddy Joe Bishop came in for the first part to hunt with J. P. and me. Donna was also with us for the first part. SureFire's Cameron Hopkins and Greg Rader came in for the first shift, and both Tim Danklef and Dave Fulson were there to do the filming. Cameron and Greg would hunt with Dominique Marteens, a very good young professional hunter who had been the "resident PH" at Mahimba for several seasons. We would film that hunt for our *Tracks Across Africa* show. Then the SureFire boys and Tim and Dave would depart, and I'd stay on to hunt with Ruger's Ken Jorgensen and Hornady's Wayne Holt. We'd film this part for the new *Petersen's Hunting Adventures* TV show, with Primedia's Conrad Everts coming in to do the filming. Oh, Lord, we had put a lot of eggs into the Mozambique basket. I hoped it would be OK!

We met up at the Johannesburg airport and caught the flight up to Beira, on the coast just south of the Zambezi. It was hot and humid in the airless customs office, and things got a little rocky with the gun permits. The bush pilot sent to collect us had a faxed copy, and, miraculously, all the serial numbers were correct, but the customs officials wanted the original with all the right stamps and it hadn't yet arrived from the capital city of Maputo. I admit to having a terrible temper, but most of the time I can control it. Not everybody present seemed able to do that, so, sensing imminent disaster, I bit my lip and sent everyone else away. After endless haranguing on both sides, I got the import permit and we were on our way.

At least, some of us were. Tim and Dave had flown in a few days earlier, so they were already in camp. By now it was too late in the day for multiple trips, so Joe, Donna, and I flew in with all

Buffalo tend to group in large herds at Mahimba. We saw relatively few bachelor groups, but we encountered plenty of big herds, and most herds seem to have mature bulls.

the guns while Greg and Cameron unloaded their jet lag in splendor (relatively speaking) in Beira. It was September, when it should have been getting hot as blazes. It was not. A weird ocean system was hanging over coastal Mozambique, bringing high winds and—in September!—occasional showers. Our first day was cold and blustery, and J. P.'s pilot judged it too windy and the ceiling too low for his little Cessna. So Cameron and Greg were stuck for a full extra day in Beira. They took it better than I would have. They figured out where to find good Portuguese-style seafood, and a friendly taxi driver took such good care of them that they bought bicycles for his children.

There didn't seem much point in waiting around, so Joe and I checked our rifles on the runway, then headed out with J. P. and Dave. The country was very different—lots of tall grass, some burned and some just plain long, and studded by tall palm trees and stubby palmettos. Along the watercourses grew thick stands of papyrus, perfect sitatunga habitat—though no sitatunga exist as far east as Mozambique. The country was dead-flat, with small belts of thornbush on almost imperceptible rises. Frequent and incredibly tall termite mounds offered the only vantage points. This was a different Africa than anything I had seen. In some

Joe Bishop and I have done some of the world's toughest hunts together: bongo, Derby eland, mountain nyala, Marco Polo sheep. Oddly, this was the first time we've hunted buffalo together, and this was a great day.

J. P. Kleinhans and I are happy with my first Mozambique buffalo. I hit this bull a bit high, and we followed him through some really scary Capstickesque long grass. I was really glad he didn't stop there.

limited ways it reminded me of the Okavango's palm islands, but was far from the same.

BUFFALO, BUSHBUCK, BUSHPIG

An unusual fact about this part of coastal Mozambique is that there are virtually no large predators. The occasional lion might wander through in the dry season, but the area is black cotton soil, flooded much of the year, and, so the story goes, animals with pads (rather than hoofs) get foot rot and cannot survive. I can neither confirm nor deny this, but there are no leopard, no lion, not even any hyena or jackal. A few servals and genet cats are around, but that's it. In the heyday of Mozambique hunting, this area probably wouldn't have been worth an outfitter's time without the great cats. Today, with perhaps thirteen hundred resident buffalo and a fair selection of plains game, it's a desirable concession. When J. P. first told us about it, one thing that made our ears prick up was that, given the absence of predators, the game, especially the buffalo, were the calmest he had ever seen. We, of course, were thinking, *Great conditions for television!* But I'd have to see that to believe it.

I saw it, and I believe it. As far as I saw, the buffalo of coastal Mozambique are rarely huge. Ken Jorgensen's bull was squarely on 40 inches, a lovely bull. Later, south of the Zambezi in Gert Saaiman's trophy shed, I saw a couple of bulls in the low 40s. But in the main the buffalo seem a bit smaller in the body than the animals farther up the Zambezi, and the typical mature bull is perhaps 36 inches in horn width, with few noticeably bigger. That was the bad news. The good news was that there were plenty of buffalo, plenty of mature bulls, and they were indeed some of the calmest buffalo I have ever seen. Over the next twenty days we took seven, and every single one was captured perfectly on camera. Getting buffalo is one thing; getting them on camera is another. We have never enjoyed this kind of hunting and filming success anywhere else.

We saw it for the first time on Joe's buffalo on the first day. Both of us were hoping for an easy day so we could get over the jet lag and see the country, but the buffalo—and J. P.—had different ideas. About nine o'clock J. P.'s local trackers, Illian and Gomez, stopped us and pointed out fresh tracks crossing the road. The herd had been feeding as it passed, milling about, and the trackers were trying to age the spoor and get direction when they saw white cattle egrets over tall grass just a couple hundred yards away. The buffalo were right there.

Now, just because they're calm doesn't necessarily mean they're easy. In fact, it might mean you stay with a herd—because you can—long after it would be patently hopeless in other areas. We quickly uncased rifles and gathered ammo, knowing we'd be on the herd in just a few minutes. This led to a fundamental error, and everyone present knew better: We took no water. Thank goodness it was a cool, cloudy day broken by several rain showers.

The herd was moving, and we were on their tracks more than an hour before we caught them the first time. I stayed back with the trackers and was able to see just the black, undulating backline of a mass of buffalo while Joe and J. P. maneuvered behind palmettos. The first approach is always the best, and I think they'd have gotten a shot except that a family group of warthog came in from behind, got

Dense papyrus groves are common along Mahimba's watercourses. Buffalo love to bed in this stuff, and you do not want to follow a wounded buffalo in there! Come to think of it, if a herd goes into papyrus, best leave it alone!

our wind, and dashed right into the middle of the herd. The buffalo exploded and dashed off in a cloud of gray dust with white egrets trailing overhead.

"Calm" is a relative term. Illian and Gomez knew their buffalo and knew they wouldn't go far. So we waited a bit and took their tracks. An hour later we caught them again. And an hour later we caught them again. And so forth. It was a good-size herd, over a hundred buffalo, and sorting them out in half-burned grass was difficult. We knew after the first sighting that several mature bulls were in the herd, but I think Joe was up on the sticks six times, maybe seven, without a clear shot. In this country the antheaps are a blessing; when there's an antheap within shooting range of your target, you have a good chance. But there isn't always an antheap when you need one.

About noon, waiting yet again for the buffalo to settle, J. P. asked if we were OK. We were. He apologized (again) for not bringing water and suggested we give it another hour. The day wasn't hot, and we'd been cooled by a couple of showers. Nobody wanted to give up. So we pressed on and the hour passed, as did an additional half-hour. And then a nice bull stepped clear of a termite mound and gave a frontal presentation at about a hundred yards.

The bull whirled at the shot and was into the herd, but the reaction looked good. Joe Bishop is perhaps the finest field rifle shot I've ever seen. He almost never flubs, but he also has an uncanny ability to call his shots. He came off the termite mound shaking his head. "I pulled it a little bit right."

We followed the herd across a dry streambed, and just then another hard shower caught us, strong enough to force Dave under palm fronds to protect his camera. Not good, I thought. But the shower passed quickly, and just on the other side of the streambed we found the first blood. Joe's bull was already lagging behind the herd, and after a few dozen yards he turned away, leading us through patchy grass toward a thick treeline a few hundred yards away. Now there was lots of blood, and we were certain he would be dead, though Joe kept saying, "He's hit a bit to the right." I knew we'd find him in that thick treeline, one way or the other.

Just a hundred yards farther, in tall grass, Illian jumped back as if he'd stepped on a cobra. Oxpeckers jumped, but the black silhouette, low in the grass, didn't move. The buffalo was dead. Joe was a bit left and able to see nothing, so several seconds passed while he shifted right to fire an insurance shot, a .375 solid somewhere in that dark profile. At the shot the buffalo was no longer dead at all. The head came up and turned to us, the body followed, and he was on his way. He was met by J. P.'s .470, Joe's .375, and my .416, and he made little forward progress, but it was a classic example of the old adage, "It's the dead ones that get up and kill you." Joe has taken a lot of bigger buffalo, but I'm not sure he's ever had a more memorable buffalo hunt. By the way, his first shot was maybe two inches right of center—and on a frontal shot that's enough to cause trouble.

J. P. and Illian took a jog to get the truck while the rest of us, thirsty now and tired, settled in for a wait. Soon we were wet and cold as well. Another shower came in, a hard one this time, and we huddled under palm trees darn near shivering. Eventually the clouds passed, and J. P. maneuvered his truck in so we could take pictures, load up, and head back to a most welcome camp.

The camp at Mahimba was built by the Portuguese some years ago, all the materials brought in by barge, and handed down to today's concessionaires. It's a beautiful camp, a well-spaced row of A-Frame huts facing a papyrus-lined watercourse. To some degree it wasn't as beautiful as it looked. It was a dry year, and the well in the riverbottom was playing out. The water in the huts was, well, brown and muddy. Drinking water was filtered, but the camp proper was tired and needed work. As far as logistics were concerned, J. P. had bought a pig in a poke and had some work to do.

The camp wasn't perfect, but on that night it was most welcome. And there were plenty of buffalo. On most days, whether we were hunting buffalo or not, we would run into a herd somewhere along the way. And on any day we could surely find tracks to follow. Ken Jorgensen's buffalo two weeks later was probably the classic. We got into a small herd in late morning, closing to just a few yards, but there was no good bull in the herd. We regrouped, had lunch, and took a nap in a shady palm grove. That afternoon we got sidetracked by a herd of sable, but they gave us the slip. Then, in late afternoon, we saw the cattle egrets and dust of a great herd of buffalo.

Joe Bishop with one of the finest bushbuck I have ever seen, taken with perhaps the best running snapshot I have ever seen. The problem is Joe often makes shots like that, and I wish I knew how he does it because he makes it look so easy!

Ken and J. P. stalked them until nearly sundown. At that time of day they were at their most placid. From a distance Wayne Holt and I watched them, and now and again a small group would spook, but the herd, 250 strong, never stampeded. Wayne and I were in the truck just three hundred yards away, and from that raised position we could see the whole circus. We could even see the knot of bulls Ken and J. P. were trying to get to. Earlier that very day J. P. had asked me about the mostly Zimbabwe technique of charging a herd at sunset. He had never seen it done. But now, with nothing left to lose, he and Ken charged into the herd. The animals ran a bit, raising a huge cloud of dust, and then the bull the men were looking for turned to challenge them. Ken shot it frontally with his new .375 Ruger, dropping it on the spot.

Come to think of it, my buffalo was also fairly classic for this country. We were driving through serious long grass when Illian spotted tracks of a medium-size herd, very fresh. Then I continued my education in advanced buffalo tracking. Long grass is the absolute

Joe Bishop and Donna Grey with Donna's beautiful waterbuck. Good waterbuck are also quite plentiful in this region. Just be patient, and you'll see a big bull.

worst stuff in which to track. These Mozambican trackers had grown up in long grass; it was all they knew, and they could track in it. I have never seen anyone else who could! At one point they stopped and backed up. Our herd of the morning was walking on top of the tracks of a herd of the previous evening. How they figured this out is beyond me, and I couldn't believe they'd gotten it right until, twenty minutes later, I saw fresh dung.

The tracks led us in a big circle for three hours, and then we saw the animals grouped under some shady trees a little distance ahead. Off to the right we saw something strangely white, which turned out to be J. P.'s Indian-made Tata 4WD! We maneuvered on the herd for another hour, finally getting the drop on them at thirty yards on the far side of a huge termite mound. The bull was there, but he wasn't clear, and the buffalo exited in a huge cloud of dust. This time we let them go, then walked maybe a half-mile to the truck. We had a leisurely lunch and a half-hour nap in the shade, and J. P. commented that we'd be back on them in an hour. He was only half right. In thirty minutes we had them feeding along under some trees, and a good bull pinpointed.

We crawled this way and that, finally reaching a low antheap within good range. The mass of buffalo was spread out in front of us, but the bull was hidden somewhere in the press. We waited for several minutes, then decided we should backtrack and crawl to another antheap to the left for a better view. Just as we backed off, the buffalo started to move. We scrambled back up the low mound, and J. P. set up the sticks as three buffalo walked off to the left, perfectly clear. The second was a good bull, and he stopped broadside at about eighty yards.

I'm not as good at calling my shots as Joe, but I knew I'd rushed the shot, hitting the bull center on the shoulder, a wee bit high. He went into tall grass, and suddenly I knew what Peter Capstick meant! The grass was long and luxurious, and the day was windy. The tops were blowing and swaying, and the wind covered all sound. Blood was smeared waist high on the grass, easy to follow, but if he came at us in the grass, our first clue would be when his horns appeared at bayonet range. I didn't like it, but I'd caused it, so we had to do the follow-up.

Two hundred yards of tall grass is an eternity. Then the spoor led us across a streambed into, thankfully, a partially burned area. Just on the other side, J. P. stopped us and pointed ahead. I wish I knew how he saw what he saw—maybe it was light reflection, maybe a blacker shadow. We were much closer before I could see anything, but he had seen what he thought was the buffalo lying at the base of an antheap. He was right. We moved in, and the buffalo was lying down, facing away, head still up. I fired into the broad back with a .416 solid, just missing the spine, and the buffalo was up and running, hard. I fired twice more and J. P. gave him both barrels from the .470, and in a few seconds we heard his death bellow. Mahimba buffalo are not only especially calm, they also tend to come back to life!

The variety of plains game in the delta region north of the Zambezi is limited. There are sable, waterbuck, warthog, and lots of reedbuck. A few elephant roam there, and quite a few hippo and some huge crocodiles are found in the surrounding rivers. Some of these, especially the sable and big crocs, are interesting, but after buffalo I reckon the area's real specialties are bushbuck and bushpig. Oddly, there didn't seem to be a

Dave Fulson and Dominique Marteens with Dave's wonderful crocodile, photographed on the mud flat where it was shot. There was a very big (and very decomposed, ugh!) bushpig boar in its mouth!

lot of bushbuck in terms of numbers, but I have never seen an area with bigger ones. I have also never seen an area where daylight sightings of bushpig were more frequent.

The bushbuck are the reddish Chobe variety, generally smaller in the horn than Limpopo bushbuck to the southwest and East African bushbuck to the north (but not in coastal Mozambique). In a period of just six weeks, four bushbuck over eighteen inches were taken. Unfortunately, I didn't get one of them!

Hunting bushbuck specifically, along riverine thickets for example, seemed to me to be almost impossible because there were no obvious habitats and you never knew when a bushbuck might pop up. Joe wanted one and I didn't care, so he had first shot. Thank God! We were going through some burned grass with scattered palmettos when Gomez spotted a bushbuck sleeping in the shade. He'd no sooner pointed him out than the bushbuck was up and running hard. In the same instant Joe had his rifle up and swinging, and he got the shot off just as the ram vanished among thick palmettos. It didn't come out on the far side, and we found it in there stone-dead. Carrying a bit over eighteen inches of horn, it was taken with a combination of the best and the luckiest shot I've ever seen.

A few days later, just at dark, we drove down a grassy watercourse that was one of the few known specific bushbuck haunts. A nice ram got up and trotted into thick palms along the edge. Beyond was burned grass, so J. P. thought we had a chance to take him. We left the truck and circled around, and saw him once moving ahead of us. It was getting dark, so J. P. left me with Illian and Gomez and headed back to get the truck so we could meet in the riverbed at full dark. We moved a bit farther ahead and unknowingly went past him. He came out behind us, running across a narrow opening. I dashed forward a few steps to get a rest on a palm tree and caught him just as he reached tall grass. Mine was a little one, "just" 16 inches. A couple of days later, in midafternoon, Greg Rader shot an 18-inch bushbuck as he was fighting another ram that seemed just as large. We never saw the other one again.

With bushpig, well, I was a little slow on the uptake. I had a chance, but I really hate to shoot from the truck and I let the moment pass. That was the only chance I got, although we heard bushpig fighting in nearby brush, and the big crocodile Dave Fulson shot had a good bushpig boar in its mouth. Joe never had a chance, either, but one morning Cameron and Greg took a bushpig each. Wayne Holt was also extremely lucky, taking a fine bushbuck and a bushpig. There were plenty around, and in coastal Mozambique they come out to play in the daytime.

A Sable Saga

There was a time in southern Africa when the sable antelope was a relatively common animal. No longer. Today sable are reduced in both numbers and range, and although game ranching is bringing them back in both South Africa and Namibia, they are a premium animal today. One of the attractions of Mahimba is a significant sable population. They don't get big there, and given their smaller bodies, shorter horns, and chestnut highlights in body and mane, they are probably Roosevelt sable, not the larger and darker common sable. But they are well south of where Roosevelt sable have been proven to occur, so at this writing they are officially plain old sable that don't get very large. No matter, a mature sable antelope is a great trophy, and there are fewer and fewer chances to hunt them.

Dave Fulson wanted one badly, so he came in a few days early just to hunt sable. I had one on quota, but it was in my mind for Donna to take it. Cameron wanted one, and the sable was the only animal Wayne Holt had come for. A year earlier, during his quick exploration, J. P. had seen lots of sable, including lots of bulls, standing around looking at him. He had ten on quota, they were allocated, and he anticipated no problem taking them.

When Dave and Tim arrived, a father-son team was departing. Both had taken sable, and they told Dave not to worry, that he'd get one in a couple of days with no trouble. In fact, he might have. Before we arrived he turned down a couple and, horrors, missed a big bull in a big open field not far from camp. Throughout the hunt he dubbed it the "field of shame," but the shame wasn't all his. He'd borrowed J. P.'s .458, and it had been in zero just a few days earlier. Between them they'd failed to check it, and after the debacle, they discovered it was shooting more than a foot low. The real shame wasn't a miss—that can, and will, happen to all of us. The real shame was that this was the last sable bull seen for a very long time!

I don't know what the deal was, but for some reason, during this particular period in September the mature bulls left the herds. Where they went in that relatively open country I have no idea, but they just plain vanished. Dave wanted a sable so bad that Donna and I agreed he should shoot the first one that popped up . . . but none did. Sable weren't in short supply. In one good day we must have seen a hundred, but all were cows, calves, and immature bulls. The days passed, and I grieved for Dave's sable, and for Donna's sable—she wanted one badly as well, and I'd promised she'd get one, no problem.

Most of all, however, I was worried sick about Wayne Holt's sable. Aside from being a good guy, he was, after all, a sponsor of our TV show, and the sable was all he cared about. With the first hunt slipping away—and tempers growing short from brown water and no sable—we held a summit conference to decide if we should call Wayne and tell him not to come. The one man who knew Mahimba, Dominique, convinced us otherwise. "They're here; we will see them," was his simple verdict.

He was right. They didn't show up in time for everyone, but they did show up. Cameron shot one right off the road on his next-to-last day, the same

While we were at Mahimba, the sable bulls had left the herds and seemed to have evaporated. Sable was all Wayne Holt wanted, and I was worried to death, but I should have had more faith. J. P., left, found this fine bull for him, and Wayne flattened it with his .375 Ruger.

road we'd all been traveling for days. They didn't show up in time for Dave, but he got a most acceptable consolation prize. He slipped out onto the river with Dominique and shot a really massive crocodile, another trophy he had long coveted. Joe took a nice crocodile as well. Time ran out altogether for Donna. One afternoon she shot a very good waterbuck, but she left with the rest of the first group without ever seeing a mature sable bull.

Come to think of it, I hadn't seen one, either. So I sweated bullets the first few days of Wayne's hunt, especially after we had two strikes against us. The first chance came in the heat of a hot afternoon. We were driving through a grassy plain when we bumped a big herd of sable, and a good, dark bull was in the herd. We could have gotten a shot, and should have, but we didn't, and even Illian and Gomez could not track sable through long grass.

The second chance was even more painful. Remember when Wayne and I were watching Ken and J. P. stalk Ken's buffalo? I was watching the buffalo when Wayne said, "There's a sable bull!"

Yes, there was one, about two hundred yards away in some palmettos, completely unaware, just messing around. He fed toward us slowly, passing

Natal red duiker are probably not as plentiful as suni, but you couldn't prove it by me. In one afternoon I saw several, and I took this fine male just a few minutes after I took my suni.

about seventy-five yards away. He was black and fully mature, probably thirty-six inches, a good bull for the area. We talked about shooting him, but we knew we couldn't. It would have been OK to mess up Ken's stalk, because there were lots of buffalo around. But Conrad and his TV camera were with Ken and J. P., so taking the shot would have defeated our entire reason for being there. We watched the sable walk away.

It was a very dry year and many of the rivers that usually held water were bone-dry. J. P. reasoned that the herd we had seen must be watering at a river not far from where we'd seen them, and sable usually water in the evening. So in late afternoon of the next day we worked our way along the papyrus-lined river. We saw a small herd right away, but it held no bulls at all and they slipped into the papyrus. To my thinking this was very un-sablelike, since these creatures tend to favor fairly open woodland. I wondered if those forbidding papyrus thickets were sheltering all the bulls we weren't seeing!

A half-hour later sunset was approaching. We could cut right and hit a road before dark, or we could continue along the river, where dark would catch us far from a road. J. P. talked to Illian in the pidgin Portuguese-Afrikaans mix that they somehow made work. We went straight along the river.

We hadn't gone a half-mile before we blundered straight into a big herd of sable, probably the same herd we'd seen two days earlier because it contained a big, black bull with tall horns. With light fading fast, J. P. and Wayne made a quick run to a termite mound and Wayne anchored the bull quickly with his hard-hitting .375 Ruger.

Suddenly, since Donna hadn't taken ours, I was the only person remaining without a sable, and of course I was the one who cared the least. During those scary days when we weren't seeing any bulls at all, we started calling them "fables" instead of sables, and this fable has a happy ending. On my next-to-last morning, after more than twenty days at Mahimba, we left camp in good daylight with no particular goal in mind. Ten minutes from camp, bedded on the edge of Dave's Field of Shame, was a lone sable bull, almost certainly the same bull he had found there three weeks earlier.

There was no one I could pass the shot to, and no hesitation. I needed only to clear a bit of brush to get an open shot. Perhaps I should have waited for him to get up, but I knew he'd get up running. I shot him in line with the shoulder, as low on the body as I could see in the grass. His great head dropped, and then came back up, and then he was up and running. I worked the bolt on the .30-06 and swung with him, and he rolled and stayed down. It was the end of a long sable fable.

COUTADA 10

Both the game and the country are different south of the Zambezi. That's where you find the huge flood plains of Marromeu, home to a hundred thousand buffalo long after the war ended. Then the Russians came in with gunships and waiting refrigerator ships, and in a short time those vast herds were reduced to as few as six thousand. In new Mozambique they're coming back, and on our way north from Beira, on the trackless flood plains of the Zambezi Delta, we saw vast herds of buffalo with clouds of egrets overhead. Much of the country there is divided into huge coutadas, government-owned concessions. Thanks to careful management the game

Dave Fulson wanted this sable, and I wanted it for him first and Donna second. He appeared after they both left, and I had little choice but to do business. I shot him ten minutes from camp, in the same place Dave saw him many days earlier.

has prospered, far better than I realized—not only the buffalo on the flood plains but also the varied wildlife in the bordering woodland.

South of the Zambezi the game is quite different from what I had seen at Mahimba. There are still waterbuck, warthog, bushbuck, reedbuck, and bushpig. The buffalo are much the same, modest in body and horn. South of the river the sable grow better horns, and mature bulls are coal-black. My guess is that if the DNA research were completed, the smaller, paler Roosevelt sable would be found to extend all the way down the coast to Mother Zambezi. South of the river, in suitable habitat, you find nyala, Livingstone suni, and Natal red duiker.

The suni and red duiker were of particular interest to me. Both are found from Mozambique's Zambezia on south and southwest into Natal and Zululand, but both are the very devil to come by in South Africa. There the saying goes, "I'm going looney looking for a suni." The red duiker is perhaps even more localized and less common than the suni. Years ago I had hunted where they both occur but had never seen either species. Honestly, I'd never specifically looked for them, but I'd long been told that if you could get in the right spot, both little antelope were extremely common in Mozambique. When we set up the hunt with J. P., my personal interests were suni and red duiker, and I was surprised and disappointed when he told me that neither occurred in Mahimba. But, yes, there were lots of them. At the end of my hunt, he said, he could arrange for me to go to one of the big coutadas south of the river, where I should be able to take them with no problem.

The plan was to take the plane and fly into Gert Saaiman's Coutada 10, not far north of Beira, and hunt for a couple of days on the way out. Communications were terrible, and although this had all been sort of arranged months in advance, as the days slipped away we had no firm plan and no coordinates for Gert's landing strip. So I got my sable (otherwise I wouldn't have made this side trip), and on the last morning, barely twenty-four hours before my flight out of Beira, we finally secured the GPS coordinates of the airstrip servicing several adjoining coutadas.

We landed in late morning, not really knowing if we were welcome, let alone expected. We were not expected. Fortunately, Gert's neighbor was there servicing his plane, and he took us to Gert's camp a few kilometers away. We were welcome there. "Thank God!" said Gert with a smile. "We couldn't get hold of you. How much time do you have?"

"I know it's a bit crazy," I said, "but I've got to be in Beira tomorrow morning, so I guess I've got today."

The smile faltered, then returned. "Well, I'm clear this afternoon. Let's have lunch, and then we'll see what we can do."

Before we left, Gert took me on a little tour of his trophy shed. That was the most educational part of the trip, and I quickly realized I'd been very wrong about Mozambique for quite some time. Most of his buffalo weren't huge, but there were lots of them, all good, mature bulls. There were two very good sets of elephant ivory plus a dozen good sable, among them a 43-inch bull taken by Texan Brian Bannister, still in camp. There were several very good nyala, huge waterbuck, big bushbuck, lots of warthog and bushpig and reedbuck and more. This was the trophy shed of an extremely successful outfit that had available an incredible range of game. There were even some Lichtenstein hartebeest, and I had no idea they occurred anywhere south of the Zambezi. Gert also had a unique assortment of the pygmy antelope, not only suni and red duiker but also common duiker, oribi, and, of all things, blue duiker.

Coutada Ten covers more than a quarter-million acres, vast flood plain surrounded by much woodland. Gert Saaiman had obtained the concession a decade earlier, and he admitted there hadn't been much game then. But he and his neighboring outfitters have nurtured the area and minimized the poaching, and what I saw was incredible. This comment from Gert spoke special volumes: "A lot of my colleagues and competitors complain about the governments they deal with. Honestly, the government of Mozambique has been wonderful to me. We work together on the quotas, and we have had no problems. As the game builds back, we've slowly brought the quotas up. Right now I take seventeen sable, but my sable hunting has gotten too easy. I think I should go to twenty." I didn't know that any outfitters got along with African governments—and I sure didn't know anyone in Africa had that many sable available!

Gert offered me a shotgun for the suni, suggesting that a rifle would be better for the red duiker because of the likely range. I gathered that he expected me to take a suni but wasn't so certain about the duiker. The suni occur in thick timber called "suni forest," where little other game occurs. Bush fires had almost leveled the country around his camp, so we drove for an hour and a half, fast, before he stopped and we uncased the guns. It was about half past three.

In the next half-hour we saw a dozen suni, females standing and watching us pass, a couple of young males, and unidentifiable forms scampering into the thick stuff. Then I saw a small, reddish-tan antelope standing in shadow. The horns looked totally outsize for so small a creature, and Gert confirmed, "Yes, shoot him!"

I did, and that was the end of my suni safari. The forest was in heavy shade, with no good place to take pictures, so we loaded him up and carried on. Twenty minutes later, far down the road, I saw a ray of sunlight glinting on something. We stopped and put binoculars on it, and it was a red duiker, walking slowly down the road—toward us. The distance was much too far, so we closed it a bit, and then we waited. The little animal walking straight toward us was a male with exceptional horns. So we waited a bit more, and I got steady. This was not a shot I wanted to blow.

I am all smiles after taking this beautiful Livingstone suni with professional hunter and outfitter Gert Saaiman. In South Africa the saying goes, "I'm going looney looking for a suni." Not so in coastal Mozambique; in proper habitat there are lots of them.

At something a bit over a hundred yards the duiker turned to my left and stood broadside for just a moment. He dropped to the shot, my .30-06 doing much less damage than I'd feared. That ended my long safari in Mozambique. I hadn't wanted to go there in the first place, but I'm awfully glad I did. And I'm sure I will go back. I can never see Mozambique as it was in 1973, but it's a lot better now than it was in 1988, and I believe that, with good outfitters managing their areas, it will only get better. Perhaps someday it will be as it once was, but since I wasn't there and have no frame of comparison, it's plenty good enough already.

Ruvuma River

In African hunting Tanzania is the grand prize, the big enchilada. Although often touted as the "birthplace of safari," it is not. Those honors go to long-gone Kenya. But Tanzania is the land of Kilimanjaro and the last bastion of the traditional East African safari. Realistically, given today's shrinking quotas, it is also the last outpost of the true general-bag safari, during which, on a full-length twenty-one-day safari, a hunter might have on license fully four of the Big Five—lion, leopard, buffalo, and elephant—along with an incredible range of plains game.

Pragmatically, Tanzania is also one of Africa's most costly countries to hunt, but once you get past the stiff daily rates and all the extras (government surcharges, charters, etc.), the trophy fees are enticingly reasonable. Once you get past the basic price of admission, for instance, the trophy fees for the three buffalo allowed on a Tanzanian hunt aren't much more than the current trophy fee for one buffalo in southern Africa. For dreamers like me, this fact, plus the mind-boggling list of species available, tends to make Tanzania seem a comparative bargain, and indeed it can be. These facts also combine to make it one of the most misunderstood safari destinations.

This is partly because Tanzania is a vast country with many different types of habitat. In Tanzania you must decide first what game is most important to you, because no matter how enticing that wonderful game list might be, ain't nobody gonna work their way through it—or even halfway through—on one safari. In general Tanzania offers two distinctly different types of game: traditional East African species like gazelle, gerenuk, lesser kudu, and fringe-eared oryx, mostly in the northeast, and "southern species" characterized by sable and roan, generally found in the central region and points south and west. There are opportunities to hunt multiple areas and increase the bag, and crossover species such as lion, leopard, and buffalo are found in varying densities (and trophy quality) in most areas. And then there are specialized safaris. In Tanzania, as anywhere else in Africa, one of the most specialized of all safaris is the search for a good elephant bull.

Over the years I have been fortunate to hunt in Tanzania four times, in 1988, 1993, 1994, and 2000. I understood all these things. And still, as I looked ahead to a 2006 Tanzania safari and even as it progressed, I mentally allowed myself to fall into the trap that ultimately must lead to disappointment. It was, after all, an elephant hunt. If we took elephant bulls that pleased us, then by definition we would have had a most successful safari. Anything else would have been icing on the cake, and yet, though I knew better, I led myself to believe that when the hunt concluded, oodles of rich, creamy icing would be dripping off the cake.

Clear back in 1988, in his early years as a professional hunter under Luke Samaras, I had a marvelous Masailand hunt with Michel Mantheakis. We became friends, and for years Michel would stay with me for a few days—sometimes a few weeks—at convention time. For no particular reason (except perhaps my wallet!), we never hunted together again, but I watched his progress from a young PH to a veteran and ultimately to a successful outfitter in his own Miombo Safaris.

In 2000 he obtained his Lukwika-Lumusilla Game Reserve concession on the Ruvuma River, which divides southern Tanzania from northern Mozambique. Because he had good areas in Rungwa, Selous, and Kilombero Valley, he was hunting in the Ruvuma area very sparingly, but he took some superb elephant there. We talked about it often when I saw him at the conventions, and I was fascinated. This was a hunt I wanted to do—partly because I wanted to hunt with Michel again and partly because over the years I'd picked up enough bits and pieces to realize the Ruvuma Valley was a stronghold for big elephant. I have a theory about elephant that may or may not hold water, but it makes sense to me. What is not theory is that ivory growth requires a mixture of diet, genetics, and age. Elephant don't grow tusks at the "pound of ivory per year" that Ruark and his contemporaries theorized. With good genetics and the right food and minerals, some bulls in their prime will grow ivory much faster than that; without these factors, tusks may grow much slower.

Ultimately, some areas have both the genetics and the conditions to produce the legendary hundred-pound tuskers but others do not. Many Zimbabwe tuskers, for instance, are fully mature as forty-odd-pounders, and only a few gifted bulls will double that or better. Northern Kenya was famous for producing heavy ivory. So was the area around Mount Meru and Mount Kilimanjaro. But whatever weight of ivory a given bull is capable of producing, it takes decades for him to reach his potential. An elephant that has lived long enough to reach this potential is a wise old man in elephant terms, and in hunters' terms. He has seen it all . . . and he's smart enough to know he needs to leave town when things get hot.

So my theory is that across the vastness that is still Africa, there remain unknown pockets of refugee elephant that have fled unacceptable pressure, and among them will be the oldest and wisest bulls. Most of these pockets, undoubtedly, are in areas that are no longer hunted. Somewhere in the huge Congo forest in both the former Zaire (now Democratic Republic of Congo) and Congo-Brazzaville, for example, there are hundred-pounders, and where there is one there will be more. But I doubt whether any outfitters will effectively penetrate the political and logistical barriers to find out.

Remember that smattering of huge elephant taken in southwestern Ethiopia in the 1980s? The Safari Club record book lists nine tuskers with ivory weighing over 100 pounds per side taken in Ethiopia between 1986 and 1989, the largest carrying 145 pounds in one tusk. In the entire annals of African hunting, this is a true surge of big elephant taken from one time and place, but it is especially noteworthy because this was the 1980s, before the ivory ban and in a time when widespread ivory poaching had reduced elephant to their lowest numbers. But wait just a moment: Historically, Ethiopia was not known for really big ivory, and her total elephant population is generally estimated at just a few thousand. Look at a map of Africa. As elephant travel, the heavy forests of Ethiopia's Gambela region aren't all that far from northern Kenya or from the White Nile region of Sudan. Both of these areas were known for

Sasawara's elevation is fairly high. The mangoes and cashews weren't yet ripe, so elephant weren't present in large numbers. There was some crop raiding of maize fields and grain bins, but mostly by cow herds.

big elephant, and in the 1980s poaching was rampant in both countries. I believe outfitters like Nassos Roussos, Tom Mattanovich, and my old friend Col. Negussie Eshete found a rich pocket of refugee tuskers, wise old elephant that had fled to a safer place.

In 1988, just before the ivory ban took effect, I hunted the Selous Reserve at a time when ivory poaching had decimated the elephant population. Even then there were lots of elephant in the dense thicket lines, but the magnificent bulls the Selous was known for had largely vanished. Selous elephant are small-bodied, and they are hard-pressed to grow really heavy tusks, but even so, that region tends to produce incredibly long, beautiful ivory. But in 1988 very few elephant were seen that reached Tanzania's legal minimums for either weight or length. During that decade it was believed that the ivory poachers reduced the Selous elephant population from over 60,000 to perhaps 30,000. Here's where it gets interesting. Later, when the ivory ban started to have an effect and the poaching was brought under control, aerial surveys of the Selous's *miombo* forest, relatively visible from the air, were able to locate only 15,000 elephant skeletons. That is still incredible carnage, but it means that something like 15,000 elephant went missing.

Today elephant are increasing rapidly in southern Tanzania, and there is also a huge herd in Mozambique's Nyasa Game Reserve just across the Ruvuma River. They go back and forth, with both an eastern and a western movement corridor now identified between the Selous and northern Mozambique. Tanzania's elephant have rebounded to an estimated 120,000 today while Mozambique's overall population, though probably healthy and almost certainly increasing, is much less certain (which is why, at this writing, Americans cannot import Mozambique ivory). But what of those missing 15,000 elephant? Surely some wonderful old bulls are evading discovery, and many of them almost certainly roam the Ruvuma drainage.

In Tanzania the majority of the elephant hunting is done in the Selous Reserve, where elephant can be hunted as part of a general bag, a situation that's almost unique in modern Africa. The Selous produces the occasional really big tusker, but Selous ivory is notoriously long and thin. Most elephant taken there make the legal minimum by length but often

Checking for tracks in the sandy riverbed of the Sasawara. Michel and I never came across fresh bull tracks, but Jim Crawford's team followed up a couple of bulls along the Sasawara. Despite such promise, we never saw a legal elephant.

We found several natural mineral licks, all showing recent elephant activity. Some were similar to this one, hollowed out at the base of a termite mound by generations of animals.

just barely meet the weight minimum of 37 pounds on one tusk. I had long believed it was possible to do much better down on the Ruvuma, and indeed Michel Mantheakis, as well as a few other pioneering outfitters, have produced some big ivory down there.

THE SASAWARA FOREST

At the Dallas Safari Club convention in 2006 Michel told me he had just obtained as a concession the Sasawara Forest Reserve and adjoining Muhuese Open Area, a bit north of the Ruvuma and well west of his Lukwika concession. The area was along the western movement corridor from the Selous, and his scouting just the month before had revealed plenty of good elephant sign. Would I care to be the first to hunt in the area?

Well, truthfully, I really wouldn't. I've been around the barn long enough to know that being first isn't always best. Besides, thanks to our TV series, by October, when the mangoes and cashews should be ripe and pachyderm crop-raiding at its peak, I would have spent more than four months in Africa. I figured one more hunt for the year would be the straw that broke the camel's back—and bank. But how could I afford not to? It was a chance to look for a really good elephant, something I wanted badly, in an area where I knew big tuskers occurred, with an old friend I'd wanted to hunt with for a long time.

I was still mulling it over a few days later when Jim Crawford called. I'd met Jim on a deer hunt in Mexico years earlier, and we'd stayed friends. Recently we had become even better friends when he became the primary investor in the John Rigby gunmaking firm, based in my little town of Paso Robles, but that happened after (and is unrelated to) our phone conversation. Jim began with little preamble: "Where can I go to find a good elephant?" I gave him the standard answer: Botswana for short, thick, and possibly heavy ivory—it's expensive but almost a sure thing; Zimbabwe for the best value—but not such a sure thing. But I added that just maybe he'd like to join me in southern Tanzania, take a chance on a new area, and find bulls with that long, lovely East African ivory!

He would. Turns out he was also a glutton for punishment. He and his wife, Tammy, would be hunting in Mozambique in late October, right next door to Coutada Ten, where I would hunt my suni and red duiker. They would fly up and meet me in Dar es Salaam for the elephant hunt. So, most of the die were cast. I sat down with Michel at the SCI convention a couple of weeks later and asked the fatal question, "What else do you think we'll find?"

He was honest: not much in the way of plains game, some sable, maybe some Lichtenstein hartebeest, a few buffalo. He rated the leopard in southern Tanzania as Africa's easiest to get on bait because prey was scarce, and thought there might be some of Africa's "ugliest lion" around, meaning not much mane. He told it straight, as he knew it. But that's the pitfall of Tanzania—it's the place of dreams, and you hear what you want to hear. We decided that since Tammy Crawford would be there, Donna might as well come along, and we'd get her a license so she could hunt leopard if we had the chance. Of course, I had images of leopard and buffalo and lion and tiger and bear, oh my!

We met up at the new Sea Cliff Hotel on the edge of Dar, a really beautiful place with good food, nice rooms, and a beautiful view.

Sasawara Camp was situated in a grove of shady trees along a gurgling mountain stream. It was as fine a tent camp as I have ever seen, and the nights were wonderfully cool.

Dave Fulson had flown in with us, and Garrick Cormack flew up from Zimbabwe to make it a two-camera shoot. Jim and Tammy had shot Mozambique flat the previous two weeks, but they'd had a tough hunt. Tammy was getting over a mild case of malaria, and Jim's malaria medicine, doxycycline, had given him serious sun poisoning. Down on the Sasawara, Michel was also recovering from a bout of malaria, so we spent an extra day in Dar and I think we all needed it.

We flew in to a dirt strip at a mission station north of the reserve, and Michel and crew were on hand to meet us. Jim would hunt with Bernard Sehabiague, an accomplished elephant hunter, while I would hunt with Michel. During the two-hour drive up through ascending ridges, we were surprised at the elevation and also delighted at the surprising chill in the air as evening approached. If Donna and I were pleased, Jim and Tammy were overjoyed. They'd been dealing with temperatures well over a hundred degrees just a few hundred miles

Our makeshift camp was right on the banks of the Ruvuma, with our dinner table on the sand. During the day it would be impossibly hot, but in this huge area we were never in camp in full daylight.

south and, worse, almost no cooling at night. They'd been dreading three more weeks of it.

We reached Michel's brand-new camp just at sundown, and I'd forgotten the wonderful conventions of East Africa. The entire staff was there to meet us, all smiles, and inlaid into the grass screening around the dining area was the split-bamboo banner, "Karibune Sasawara." Welcome to Sasawara. In the previous few days Michel's team had worked wonders, creating a camp that was neat, clean, and marvelously comfortable. We were home.

Our new home was amid some of the most gorgeous country I have ever seen, with high ridges dropping into lush, well-watered valleys. Michel's cook was wonderful, and it turned out we'd brought a couple of coolers of fresh seafood in on the plane. Camp life was fabulous, and the nights were marvelously cool. Unfortunately, as the days wore on we came to realize that the one ingredient that was sadly lacking was wildlife. I have never seen an area that looked so good and was so sterile.

On the second day we dropped off a ridge to walk one of the grassy valleys, looking for elephant tracks. We hadn't gone a quarter-mile, walking in line, when we ran into a beautiful sable bull. He stood and looked at us for a long time, and if we'd had the presence of mind to think about it, we could have brought Donna forward for an easy shot. But we didn't yet know, and we had elephant on our mind. We watched him trot away, and that was the only sable bull we ever saw. And we saw no other large antelope. Common duiker were plentiful, and every day we saw several, but that's about it.

Michel was nonplussed, and his worry deepened as the days passed. Just a year earlier, on his scouting expedition, he'd seen a lot of sable and buffalo and a smattering of other game. He'd had antipoaching teams in for six months. They'd found plenty of snares and snapped up dozens of illegal muzzleloaders from the surrounding villages, but it looked to me like this was closing the barn door after the horse was gone. Of course, Michel's concern wasn't just for our safari; aside from antipoaching and camp-building, his road crews had opened hundreds of kilometers of hunting trails, not to mention the government fees he'd paid to obtain a new area. He had come to stay, with the desire and business necessity to run three or four safaris a year in this area. So far it didn't look good.

There were a few buffalo in the area. One day, lacking elephant tracks, we followed three bachelor bulls, and on another day we tracked a small herd. Both times we closed with the buffalo, but both times they blew out without giving us a chance for a shot—they hadn't caught our wind, so they must have seen or heard us. I've hunted heavily poached survivor buffalo before, and these animals had all the signs.

There were a few elephant around, but not nearly as many as Michel had expected. Although this place was no more than a hundred miles from his Lukwika area, the elevation was much higher, and because of the cooler weather neither the mangoes nor the cashews were ripe yet. Some crop-raiding of sparse maize fields in villages bordering the reserve was occurring, but none of the reports yielded big bull tracks. Even so, Bernard and Jim were having pretty good luck seeing elephant, and in the first week they passed up two or three small bulls. In the same period we saw just two cow herds, both with small bulls.

The one bright spot was that there were indeed plenty of leopard around. One evening on their way back to camp, Jim's team saw two different cats. We saw tracks and scat in almost every valley we walked.

Sengi, Michel Mantheakis, and I pose with a really fine East African greater kudu. This bull belongs to old Sengi, one of the legendary Wakamba trackers. He saw him, he found his tracks, and he led me to him.

With so little game around, Michel sent his apprentice, Andy Warren, to a nearby village to negotiate for a few goats and a couple of cows. With a barnyard established and not much else going on, both hunting teams quickly got some baits up. Well, "quickly" is a relative term in this case. Michel believes in building the blind when the bait is hung, which is clearly a sound way to do things—but it takes a lot of time. On the other hand, we had little going with elephant or anything else, so we might as well try.

We got a hit right away, but the sign was a bit confusing—probably both a big female and a male. Donna and Michel sat two evenings, and then, after daylight on the third morning, they had the female on the bait for a half-hour. The male, if indeed there was one, never appeared, but later that day we had a hit on another bait. This one was clearly a male, no question, so we rolled the dice and decided to sit on the new cat. Well, "we" is also a relative term. Donna, Michel, and Dave sat for the leopard. Me, I hooked up my computer to the Toyota's cigarette lighter and worked on this book, hoping I'd hear a shot.

No shot came and there was still a bit of light left, so I was surprised to hear Michel's odd cat-scratching on the radio, which meant, "Come pick us up."

We did, and they were all smiles. The leopard had come and performed for the camera for nearly an hour. He was a male—not a small leopard but not a real big one, either. They could have shot him and everybody would have been happy. Or they could let him feed and hope for a bigger cat another day. They chose the latter . . . maybe a good call, maybe not, but only time would tell.

By now we were halfway through the hunt and had a decision to make. Actually, we were able to make a decision thanks to Michel. In addition to the Lukwika-Lumusilla Game Reserve, Michel also had an open area to the west, the Tunduru Extension. The reserve itself was available for the next few days, with no client, and for our last couple of days we could hunt the open area. It was hotter there and the crops were definitely ripe. After six years in that area, he also knew there were a lot more elephant. Our camp was not intended to be moved, but he had a big truck and a Unimog and was willing to move the camp, lock, stock, and barrel, a distance of 250 miles over bad roads to give us a better chance. Michel didn't owe us that; we'd taken a chance on an experimental area, knowing it was experimental, and we were big boys and girls. But we knew we were in trouble where we were, and with much gratitude we made plans to break camp.

LUKWIKA-LUMUSILLA

The move was a Herculean task, carried out with smiles by Michel's amazing crew. The last truck didn't make it in until nine o'clock the next morning, and the men worked through the heat of the day to establish some semblance of a camp. Situated in a beautiful spot right on the banks of the Ruvuma, it worked just fine, but it was sweltering hot in the valley of the Ruvuma and the camp could not be the equal of that fine camp along a little stream in the Sasawara highlands.

Lunch is a major event with Miombo Safaris—with table and chairs, no less! Left to right are Dave Fulson, PH Willie McDonald, PH Andy Warren, PH and outfitter Michel Mantheakis, and of course yours truly. Willie was between clients for a couple of days and joined us. Andy, recently licensed, apprenticed under Michel.

We made a good decision, though, because there were elephant here—lots of elephant. This was what the Sasawara could be, if it wasn't too late. Michel's antipoaching teams had patrolled this area for six years, and in that time he believed he had lost just one elephant to a poacher. That poacher had been apprehended and was now in Michel's employ. The animals showed it. I have never been around elephant that were so calm. Cow herds are always the great danger, and we avoided them when we could. But sometimes we found ourselves in the middle of them, and they always moved away with calm dignity, with no drama and no demonstrations. The bulls—and there were lots of them—were even calmer. If the wind turned, of course, they were gone, but rarely with screeching or running in blind panic. They were just gone. If the wind held, we could get close, and we did get close, almost every day.

The Lukwika area was clearly best for elephant, but it held a lot of other game as well. We saw quite a few herds of sable, but Donna's sable luck continued and we never saw another bull . . . well, another shootable bull anyway. We saw a spectacular bull with an incredibly long horn—yes, that's singular. His second horn was broken off at the base. There were a lot of impala wherever there was water, and bushbuck, and bushpig, and a scattering of duiker, klipspringer in the kopjes, and even some Sharpe grysbok (which I hadn't known ranged up into Tanzania). There were some buffalo as well, but what the country was probably best for, other than elephant, was greater kudu. Since we were on the north side of the Ruvuma, I guess they are technically East African greater kudu—not that the kudu care—but on the first afternoon we saw a half-dozen bulls that would look just fine in Zimbabwe.

On the second afternoon, along the mostly dry Upper Lumesule, we got into a big herd of elephant, a few cows and calves with more than twenty bulls, probably so grouped because of a female in estrus. We slipped around the herd in a good afternoon breeze, often as close as ten yards, and ticked off the bulls one by one. Several had long, beautiful tusks, but none was close to what we wanted, so we walked away and left them in peace.

The next day we saw the kind of bull we wanted, a beautiful hulk with short, thick tusks, and his buddy, thinner but with nearly five feet of ivory showing. They crossed the road in front of us, paying no attention, and we quickly grabbed our rifles and ran after them. This time the wind got us, switching 180 degrees and back again. We circled one way, then circled another, and they simply walked away from us. There was nothing to be done.

With elephant, Michel believes in hedging his bets. He always had multiple teams of trackers out, and his trackers were among the best. Leading my team was old Sengi, not only a Wakamba of southern Kenya but one of the famous Wakamba trackers. Sengi was of indeterminate age, probably near seventy. In the mid-1950s he started tracking for Dave Ommanney, the legendary Kenya hunter who was "Winchester's Man in Africa" in the company's long-running ad campaign. Sengi could still walk all day in the heat with a smile on his face. Late in the hunt we were joined by another legend, Makanyanga, also a Wakamba of Sengi's village. Makanyanga is even older; he started tracking for Ommanney in 1952, the year I was born.

My bull, taken on the seventeenth day, had the long, beautiful ivory you look for in an East African elephant. The Rigby double in .450-3 ¼" with Hornady solids performed wonderfully.

Both of these old men, like all Wakamba boys a generation ago, grew up hunting elephant with bows and arrows. In their day they hunted north to Somalia and Ethiopia, west to Sudan and Congo, and south as far as Zimbabwe. Their children are not hunters; they are schoolteachers, mechanics, and drivers. They are proud of their children, but they are equally proud of the young trackers, and they treat them as if they were their own children, sharing their knowledge with them and bringing them up in their ways. Thank God some of these great hunters are still with us, because theirs is a dying art.

It was hot in the Ruvuma, and the days were long. We would walk until nearly dark, then spend a couple hours or more bouncing back to camp in the vehicle. After a couple of days Jim got Tammy a flight out. She was still suffering from the after-effects of malaria, and bone spurs in her feet were giving her hell. Jimmy didn't look much better, but he hung in well, tracking day after day, all day, carrying his beautiful twelve-pound .500 Jeffery by Rigby. I was carrying a double .450 3¼-inch, also by Rigby, but this double was built light, about 10½ pounds, and I was grateful every day that I wasn't carrying a heavier rifle!

Jim turned down a lot of bulls, as did I. One day I was sorely tempted. We got into a herd of bulls, and just as we were getting close they caught the smallest swirl of breeze. They moved off, not in panic, and it was high noon and beastly hot. We thought they would stop soon, so we circled out of the wind and caught their tracks, and in just a mile they stopped in burned forest. These elephant on the Ruvuma are an odd mix of the smaller Selous elephant and the bigger-bodied southern animals, and one bull in this herd was a monster, towering above the rest. His tusks weren't especially long, but they were thick and carried the weight all the way. There was no issue about legality; each tusk probably weighed in the mid-fifties. The day was horribly hot, and we could have ended it there. I would have ended it there, but Michel remained confident we'd do better. We walked away, again.

On the fifteenth day, at dark, we glassed a beautiful bull just across the Ruvuma channel. He had amazingly long tusks with good weight—at least seventy pounds, maybe better. Technically he might have been in Tanzania . . . or he might have been in Mozambique. It didn't matter. We couldn't cross the deep channel to him, and in

Michel Mantheakis, Jim Crawford, one very pleased author, and Bernard Sehabiague with the fruits of three very hard weeks. My tusks, on the outside, are longer; Jim's, on the inside, are heavier. Take your pick!

any case Tanzania law allows no shooting within two kilometers of an international border. He was safe, and he probably knew it. We crossed the sand to the river's edge and watched him at three hundred yards until it was black dark.

I think it was the next day when, at long last, we had a bit of luck. I'd asked about red duiker, the Harvey red duiker found only in Tanzania. Michel acknowledged they were present, but I gathered there wasn't much chance of seeing one. We were passing through a bit of forest when I saw a small red antelope standing in a small opening. I let the vehicle drive on past, and then, as quietly as I could, I got Michel to stop. We went back a few yards, and the animal was still there. I had the rifle on him, but I could see no horns, nor could anyone else. Just as he turned to go, Michel saw the stubby horns and said, "It's a male. Take him if you can."

My second rifle was a Ruger M77 in .375 Ruger, a lot of gun for a duiker, but I'd remembered to load a solid and the big bullet passed through with little damage. In six years it was the third Harvey duiker taken in the area. Just maybe our luck was going to change.

Late in the morning of the seventeenth day, as we drove along a sand river, Sengi spotted a kudu bull standing in shade at the next bend. Michel took one look and said without hesitation, "He's a shooter."

The bull had already seen us and was really too far away to shoot. We tried a stalk, but when we emerged from cover within range, the bull was gone. Sengi wasn't in the least concerned. He led us to where the bull had stood, and we found his tracks and followed up into the *miombo* forest. It was very hot, and the animal shouldn't go far. We waited a few minutes and then Sengi led us up out of the riverbed and, fifty yards later, pointed out the kudu, just a hint of gray hide in a thick cluster of trees.

I got on the sticks and found the spot of gray, but he started to go just as I got on him. He came out to the left in a clear spot, running hard, quartering away. Perhaps I should have thought about the kudu I'd messed up on just a couple of months earlier, but that was that kudu and this was this kudu and I knew this .375. I took the quartering shot, knocked him down, and then he was back up, running in brush. Abandoning the sticks, I moved a few yards right to get clear, swung with him, and this time he stayed down.

Eighteen years earlier Michel and I had taken a wonderful kudu up in Masailand, where kudu are truly scarce. Kudu are not scarce on the Ruvuma, and this was a much better kudu, a beautiful bull with deep curls and heavy horns. It doesn't bother me in the least that Jimmy Crawford shot an even better bull two days later. The way he was working, he deserved that success!

We did our photos and caped the kudu quickly, then moved on to the Lukwika, where Michel had sent his second tracking team. One of his men awaited at the rendezvous, and, yes, they had found two groups of bull elephant and one was feeding nearby. We moved quickly and soon saw gray backs looming above green foliage. There were nine bulls, and from a distance it looked like one had long, beautiful ivory. As we started to close, a stray eddy of moving air caught us. The bulls bunched and rushed off, but it was just a small whiff, and they didn't go far. Ash bags puffing, we moved in again and soon had them in good, open ground, every one offering a shot. But there was nothing to shoot: Two were barely legal and none had long, beautiful tusks. We counted again, and now there were seven. Two bulls, probably the oldest and wisest, had taken that one little puff of breeze and left the youngsters to fend for themselves.

We cast around for the tracks of two bulls, but even Sengi couldn't pick them up. Little more than an hour of light remained, and we figured we had just enough time to take a look at that other group of bulls. According to our scouts, it held as many as fifteen bulls, but they hadn't gone close enough to see the ivory. Walking hard, we got to them just as they started moving out, probably on their way to raid a cashew crop. We hit the middle of the group, with the main mass to the left, fairly close, and a half-dozen bulls two hundred yards to the right, walking away through open forest.

I merely glanced at those more distant bulls and through a gap in the trees saw a flash of incredibly long ivory. Sengi saw it at the same time, and we both grabbed Michel and pointed. I will always believe this was the same bull that had so easily and cleverly eluded us in the first group, but who knows? The ivory wasn't heavy, but it was that long, beautiful East African ivory we sought. I'm not sure Michel was decided, but I was.

The bulls were lined out and walking slowly along an elephant trail, led by the big bull. The wind was perfect, just off our left shoulders. Sengi took us on a parallel trail, maybe twenty-five yards to the right, and we walked fast, passing one elephant and then another. With the big bull just ahead, Michel took the lead, and as he found a converging gap, I stepped in front.

The bull was crossing now, not much more than twenty yards away. Everybody wants the brain shot, but dark was coming fast and the bull was moving. I didn't consider it. I raised the double, found the shoulder and the deep crease behind it, and, as he stepped forward with the on-foreleg, I fired the first barrel, then the second. He turned back, already unsteady, and I have no idea where the other elephant went. I ran left, reloading, and heard Michel's .450 Dakota crash to my right. Now I had the left side clear, and I fired both barrels again. The bull stumbled forward a few more steps and was down. Up close he was magnificent, big-bodied, with long ivory showing beyond the lip. When drawn, his tusks were six and a half feet of perfectly matched ivory.

That night they carried me from the car on a chair, and we had dancing and singing. In the morning there would be much work. After skinning and butchering, Michel has a unique ritual that he calls "sanitizing." It is known that elephant mourn their dead, and he wants no evidence of an elephant's passing to remind other elephant. After the meat and skin and tusks are recovered, his crew gathers a huge pile of dry wood, and the skeleton and the earth for yards around are burned. So the final act in a Miombo Safaris elephant hunt is a massive funeral pyre. I don't know what effect it has, but at Lukwika he has been dramatically successful for six years, and the bulls he sees and passes are often seen again. They're at home, and apparently feel they are safe.

We had time remaining but were unable to make anything happen. I had shot a bushbuck, and Donna shot a nice impala. Those and the kudu provided baits for both leopard and lion, and although we had tracks of big male leopard, only females came to feed. The sable, of course, also refused to cooperate. During this period I wanted desperately for Donna to get a leopard or a sable or something good. But wanting something to happen doesn't make it so.

I was in even more of a panic for Jim Crawford. After all, I got him into this. Throughout, he kept his mind on the game, passing up everything else and thinking only of the elephant for which he had come. Every night I could see the fatigue increasing, and his resolve increasing with it. I was surprised—and pleased—when he came back with a monstrous kudu, but he wasn't looking for a consolation prize, as I had so many times in my African career. He was focused on elephant, and Bernard was focused right along with him.

They kept at it, and on the twentieth day, just at dark, he shot a beautiful bull, the kind he had been looking for all this time. His ivory was heavier than mine, and my tusks were longer than his. Take your pick. It was a tough hunt, from start to finish. Neither of us went home with the trappings of the typical Tanzania safari: no cats, no buffalo, no great selection of plains game. Tammy went home with nothing, and Donna went home with perhaps the most expensive impala ever shot in the history of African hunting. But that's elephant hunting, in Tanzania and everywhere else. Jim and I both got what we'd come for, those oily-smooth, gently curved, glistening tusks of ivory. I was wrong to hope for anything more, let alone to expect it. Jim, with so much less African experience than I, had it right all along. We didn't get much icing, but we got really good cake, our beautiful elephant. And what more could we want? That fine bull in late afternoon along the Lukwika made a perfect ending to my third decade of African hunting. After thirty years I'm still learning, and there's still so much to learn.